"I remember when there was a false air-raid alarm in New England and we were listening to the radio. My mother was in tears; my aunt, shivering under the dining room table, said: 'I hope if it hits, it hits us direct.'"

It was a time of air raids and ration coupons, of huddling around the radio for news of "our boys" in Europe and the Pacific. From Pearl Harbor to Hiroshima, Americans watched the war unfold before their eyes—and felt it change their lives. From Maine to Texas to California, they came together in spirit—doing their part for victory and sharing a turning point in our history. Now, experience that unforgettable time—by reading the stories of those who lived through it. . . .

AMERICANS REMEMBER THE HOME FRONT

AMERICANS
Remember
THE
HOME
FRONT

AN ORAL NARRATIVE
OF THE WORLD WAR II
YEARS IN AMERICA

ROY ★ HOOPES

Abridged Edition

BERKLEY BOOKS, NEW YORK

Grateful acknowledgment is made to the following for permission to
reprint previously published material:

Harcourt Brace Jovanovich, Inc.: For excerpts from *Navigating the
Rapids 1918–1971: From the Papers of Adolf A. Berle*, edited by
Beatrice Bishop Berle and Travis Beal Jacobs. Copyright
© 1973 by Beatrice Berle. Reprinted by permission of
Harcourt Brace Jovanovich, Inc.

Harper & Row Publishers, Inc.: For excerpts from *Roosevelt and
Hopkins: An Intimate History*, by Robert Sherwood. Copyright © 1948
by Robert Sherwood. Reprinted by permission of Harper & Row
Publishers, Inc.

This Berkley book contains the abridged text of the original hardcover
edition. It has been completely reset in a typeface designed for easy
reading, and was printed from new film.

AMERICANS REMEMBER THE HOME FRONT

A Berkley Book / published by arrangement with
the author

PRINTING HISTORY
Hawthorn Books edition published 1977
Berkley abridged edition / September 1992

ISBN: 0-425-13402-4

A BERKLEY BOOK® TM 757,375
Berkley Books are published by The Berkley Publishing Group,
200 Madison Avenue, New York, New York 10016.
The name "BERKLEY" and the "B" logo
are trademarks belonging to Berkley Publishing Corporation.

PRINTED IN THE UNITED STATES OF AMERICA

10 9 8 7 6 5 4 3 2 1

TO THE 132 MILLION AMERICANS
WHO MADE THIS BOOK POSSIBLE

CONTENTS

11 Aftermath

ACKNOWLEDGMENTS

This was a huge undertaking, and I must stress that it would not have been possible without considerable assistance from a lot of people; first and foremost, my editor Carolyn Trager, whose original idea it was, and the nearly two hundred Americans who were kind enough to grant me the time for an interview and permission to publish the results of their conversation in this book. And special thanks should go to Leo and Mary Emma Hershfield, of Bradenton, Florida, who were extremely helpful to me in the early stages of the book; to my brother David Hoopes, who conducted several of the interviews for me; and, of course, to my agent Charles Neighbors. Along the way, many, many friends and acquaintances were most helpful in suggesting and contacting interviewees and providing counsel and often a place to stay overnight for a weary, traveling interviewer. These include Jack Altshul, Rheidun Atkinson, Donald Baldwin, Mary Betz, Dick Bothwell, Barry Broadfoot, Kent Chetlain, Paul Christensen, Herbert Collins, Mary Jo Deering, Clayton Fritchey, Jim Gallery, A. E. Hoehling, Kay Hoopes, Lydia Hoopes, Grace Powers Hudson, Vernon Jarrett, Tom Kell, Howard Merriman, Amy Bess and Lawrence Miller, Margo Miller, Johnny Moore, Jean and Thomas Page, Tina and Richard Powers, Margaret Rafner, Phil Robbins, Patricia and Thomas Schroth, Hugh Sidey, Carl Spitzer, William Tague, Studs Terkel, Linda and Robert Tracy, James Wright, and Alice and Robert Yoakum.

Of course, the production, under the pressure of a deadline, of such a formidable manuscript could not have been achieved without the help, over and above the call of duty, from transcribers Rhoda Durkan, Pat Faucett, Sallie Hoopes, Margaret and Maxwell Merriman, Linda Texiera, and Beverly Unsworth.

And, finally, the project could never have been completed, especially within the prescribed deadline, without its managing editor—my wife, Cora.

INTRODUCTION

It was fifty years ago last December that America entered World War II on the side of England, France, and Russia against Germany, Italy, and Japan, which brought America into the war with its surprise attack on our Pacific Naval Base, Pearl Harbor. It was a momentous event not only for America but in world history, and one American, Marquis Childs, told me that he remembered telling friends at the time: "Nothing will ever be the same."

Americans have endured several momentous events in the fifty years since the end of World War II—the Cold War, Korea, tragic assassinations, trips to the moon, Vietnam, and Desert Storm. But for those Americans who lived through World War II, it was perhaps their most vivid experience. And as the people I talked to for this book revealed, the memories of those years were carried with them the rest of their lives.

During the Desert Storm operation in the Middle East last year, Americans appeared to be as united in their intent to stop Iraq's Saddam Hussein as they had been to stop Hitler, Mussolini, and Hirohito. In fact, many commentators compared the period from August 1990 to the spring of 1991 to the early 1940s in America. But it was of too short a duration and not enough men and women were involved to compare it to World War II. And, of course, "the home front" as we knew it from 1942 to 1945, hardly had a chance to emerge in 1991.

On December 6, 1941, the United States was a nation of approximately 132 million people. It had an armed forced totaling 1.4 million men, primarily the result of the Selective Service Act, which had been signed on September 16, 1940. A major war had been under way in Europe since September of 1939, and to those Americans who followed events outside their daily lives it seemed more and more inevitable that America would eventually be drawn into the war on the side of England, France, and Russia—against Germany and Italy.

Then, on December 7, 1941, the Japanese attacked Pearl Harbor, which brought America out of its isolation and settled conclusively the debate as to whether or not America should enter the fighting. On December 8, President Franklin D. Roosevelt declared war on Japan, and a few days later Germany and Italy declared war on the United States.

Thus, abruptly, America was involved in a world at war, and in the dark days of 1942 it became more and more apparent that the outcome would probably be determined by whether or not the American people had the strength and endurance to stay to the finish. For most Americans who lived through that period there was never any doubt about the outcome. In four tumultuous years, from 1942 through 1945, the country put more than 16 million men and women in uniform, and the other 116 million rolled up their sleeves to become, in the phrase that is now a cliché for America during the war, the arsenal of democracy.

The overwhelming majority of Americans agreed it was a war that had to be fought—and the relatively few who disagreed usually kept it to themselves. It was a time when, as Bill Gold puts it, "You just felt that the stranger sitting next to you in a restaurant, or someplace, felt the same way you did about the basic issues."

Economically, it was the time when the United States finally pulled out of the Great Depression, which, in 1940, was still lingering in many parts of the country. And, if the Depression has come to be known as "hard times," it would be fair to describe the war years as "boom times." Anyone who wanted to work and was not in the armed forces could find a job, and the pay was good. There were not too many things to spend your money on, but that was not important, because ostentatious living was out, at least "for the duration," as the saying went.

As a result, the booming war years were exhilarating, and many people I talked to look back on them as the most exciting years in their lives. This presents an odd contrast to the hard, grim times of the Depression years. During the Depression there was genuine human suffering in the country but little tragedy. Few people actually died from starvation or exposure. On the other hand, despite the fact that there were plenty of jobs and good money for everyone at home during the war—and no suffering from enemy military action, as there was in England, France, and Russia—there was the continuing concern for loved ones overseas. Americans were always putting a son or a husband or a father or a brother or a lover or a friend on a train, with the realization that possibly they would never see him again—at least not in one piece or in good health. Thousands of men never did return; over 400,000 Americans were killed during the war and nearly 700,000 were wounded. Although this is a relatively small figure for a nation of 132 million people, if you were the one who received that dreaded telegram, the statistics were meaningless.

The purpose of this project has been to record, on the printed page, conversations with Americans who were living in this country during the years 1941 to 1945. I have tried to talk with as many people as I could, to hear a variety of viewpoints and recollections of personal experiences. In planning the book, the first problem was to determine who would be included. The home front, at one time or another, of course, included every American. Some were in uniform, most were not; some were civilians for a while and in uniform for a while. Others who were in uniform spent all of their time on the home front, and some spent part of their time on the home front before going overseas. I finally decided to exclude anyone who was in uniform during the war. In some cases, I did interview people about their home front experience before they eventually went into the service.

Many people I interviewed were reluctant at first, but finally consented after some persuasion. Others were eager to talk about their war years, which they remembered vividly. Most people seemed to enjoy the interviews, which usually took place in their homes—but not always.

Such projects as this have come to be known as oral histories. But I prefer, in this case, the descriptive title, *oral narrative,* primarily because (1) it is not a history in the academic sense, and (2) once portions of the conversations have been extracted for certain chapters and the rest woven together in the way I have done here, they do tell a story with a beginning, a middle, and an end—a narrative. And although it is perhaps unreal to suggest that the nearly 200 Americans I talked to can tell the story of 116 million people who served on the home front during World War II, it is also unreal to contemplate talking to all 116 million of them. If you want to hear individual people talk about a national experience, you have to start somewhere. And maybe, with a little poetic license, a hundred people can speak for a hundred million. I know that, as I neared the end of an intensive period of editing this book, I would wake up in the night sure I heard America speaking—and remembering.

To help them remember, I began the interview with a series of prepared questions, the first one of which was, "Do you remember where you were and what you were doing when you first heard the news of Pearl Harbor?" (Those of you who were alive on December 7, 1941, how would you answer that question? I suspect you remember precisely where you were and what you were doing.) Soon the best interviews would become conversational, with people recalling long-forgotten incidents, as one thing reminded them of another.

A project such as this could not have been done without a tape recorder. I find it impossible to carry on a conversation while taking notes, and even the best journalists and writers cannot capture the pace and flavor of a conversation with another person as faithfully as a tape recorder does. Most people soon forgot the recorder was present, with the result that I was able to have uninterrupted conversations with approximately 200 Americans about one of the most unifying events in American history.

It was a rich and rewarding experience, made all the more so by the fact that World War II was something I had lived through myself. Until I went into the Navy in 1943, I was on the home front as a college student, and I personally remember many of the events and situations discussed here.

A good number of the people I interviewed were mature men and women during World War II, so quite naturally many of them have died since I first began interviewing for this project in 1976. But many are still alive, and the ones I have recently talked to agree that it is still the most memorable and significant era in their lives. Winston Churchill called this period the British people's ''finest hour,'' and I would have to say that for most Americans that is not a bad description of World War II.

Roy Hoopes
Bethesda, Maryland
September 1992

AMERICANS Remember THE HOME FRONT

1

"A Date Which Will Live In Infamy . . ."

On December 7, 1941, Americans were divided as to whether the United States should enter the fighting in Europe. Germany and Italy were at war with England, France, and Russia, and things were not going well for the Allies. Many Americans—including President Franklin D. Roosevelt—wanted the country to enter the war against Adolf Hitler, who most Americans had by then conceded was an enemy of civilization. But many others were reluctant to get involved. Japan was active in the Pacific and Indochina, but most Americans did not take the Japanese threat seriously. Hitler was the enemy.

By the end of November 1941 it was becoming apparent that the Japanese were getting ready to make a move in the Pacific, most likely to attack British or Dutch possessions—or both. The Japanese had sent to Washington, D.C., two men, whose last names have since become immortalized in American history—Nomura and Kurusu—ostensibly to negotiate a peace in the Pacific. In that this book is an attempt to tell the story of the war years in America in the words of the people involved, I will continue the narrative in the written words of two men who have since died but who were members of the Roosevelt administration at that time.

1

First, A. A. Berle, who was assistant secretary of state at the time of Pearl Harbor (the secretary was Cordell Hull; Sumner Welles was under secretary). Two entries in Berle's diary read:

"Saturday, December 6, 1941:

"I am not clear whether Saturday will go down in history as the day when [daughters] Alice and Beatrice went to see *The Student Prince* or the day when, in practice, the war really started. At all events, we were working on the proposed message which the secretary was getting up for the President to send to the Congress. It anticipated that the Japanese would break off conversations. The state of the record was that on November 26 we had handed to the Japanese a rather general plan for peace in the Pacific, that thereafter we had inquired of the Japanese what in the devil they were doing moving their troops around in Indochina, and that the delay in that reply had made it pretty clear that the demarche on November 26 would not be successful. At half past one, or thereabouts, we left the secretary's office; we then thought that we could get in some intensive work on Monday. I went to join the children at the Hay Adams House, where Freddy Lyon [assistant chief, International Conferences] (acting in my name, place, and stead) was feeding them eight dollars' worth of lunch; after which we went to the matinee of *The Student Prince*. At quarter of five we came back to the State Department . . . .

"I took the children home and had a snack, returning to the department about seven. Around seven-thirty, the Army Intelligence reported that they had intercepted the text of the reply which Japan was to make. It was not only a flat turndown, but a coarse and gratuitous and insulting message as well. Bad as this was, the accompanying message, likewise intercepted, was worse. The Japanese envoys were to keep this message locked up in their safe and present it only on the receipt of a signal; and during this time the final dispositions were to be completed. In other words, they were to hold up delivering the answer until certain military dispositions were completed.

"We worked up the text of a message; and I turned in to bed about 1:00 A.M., feeling very uneasy. The waltzes of *The Student Prince* seemed like a dirge of something that may have existed once, but certainly had very little relation to anything one knew today."

"Sunday, December 7:

"Sunday morning, and to the department. The secretary was closeted with Stimson and Knox. We fussed a little more with the message and took a few simple precautions; and when the three cabinet ministers adjourned, we went into the secretary's office. We were discussing the lines of the presentation of affairs to Congress, when the Japanese ambassador requested an immediate appointment with the secretary. He asked for it at 1:00—which happens to be 8:00 A.M. Honolulu time. The secretary fixed the time for 1:45. Sumner Welles and I stayed with the secretary until 1:45 and then left, just as the Japanese were coming in. We had lunch at the Mayflower and came back about quarter of three. The Japanese had already gone. The news had come in that the Japanese fleet and air force had attacked Pearl Harbor, Manila (this appears to be wrong . . .). A little later it seemed that one of the Japanese expeditions was headed for a British base in northern Burma. . . . At Pearl Harbor it seems that there had been a great deal of damage. The attempt was made to bomb the army airfield, and I gather they got two hangars and perhaps 350 men (this is not yet confirmed), and did a very considerable amount of damage to the shipping. The *Oklahoma* seems to have been hit and put out of action. We have as yet no knowledge of the Philippines.

"It was a bad day all around; and if there is anyone I would not like to be, it is chief of Naval Intelligence."

Before he went to bed on the night of December 7, Harry Hopkins, President Roosevelt's closest advisor, wrote down the events of that day, as recorded by his biographer, Robert Sherwood:

"I lunched with the President today at his desk in the Oval Room. We were talking about things far removed from war when at about 1:40 Secretary Knox called and said that they had picked up a radio from Honolulu from the Commander-in-Chief of our forces there advising all our stations that an air raid attack was on and that it was 'No drill.'

"I expressed the belief that there must be some mistake and that surely Japan would not attack in Honolulu.

"The President discussed at some length his efforts to keep the country out of war and his earnest desire to complete his administration without war, but that if this action of Japan's were true it would take the matter entirely out of his own hands, because the Japanese had made the decision for him.

"The President thought the report was probably true and thought it was just the kind of unexpected thing the Japanese would do, and that at the very time they were discussing peace in the Pacific they were plotting to overthrow it.

"At five minutes after two he called Hull and told Hull of the report and advised Hull to receive Nomura and Kurusu, who had an appointment with him, and not to mention that he, Hull, had the news but to receive their reply formally and coolly and bow them out.

"I heard Hull later report to the President about the interview and I gather he used some pretty strong Tennessee mountain language to the two Japanese emissaries. The burden of his remarks being that he didn't believe a word in the reply to his note and that it was false from beginning to end.

"At 2:28 Admiral Stark called the President and confirmed the attack, stating that it was a very severe attack and that some damage had already been done to the fleet and that there was some loss of life.

"At 2:30 the President called press secretary Steve Early and dictated a news release which Steve was to release at once to the press."

The press release confirmed what the wire services had already carried. The word rapidly spreading out like prairie fire through the government and Washington and across the nation. The first Americans to get the word were in Honolulu, the government, Washington, and the newspaper and radio businesses.

Cornelia MacEwen Hurd, from West Farmington, Ohio, had lived in Honolulu eight years. She was a teacher at the Punahou School, a missionary school that was founded in 1840 for the sons and daughters of Hawaiian chiefs and the children of missionaries. She was an exchange teacher from a New

*Jersey school who liked Honolulu so much that she decided
to stay. Cornelia Hurd describes the scene on that Sunday
morning, December 7, 1941, from her patio:*

It was 7:55 A.M. I was sitting on the veranda of our house,
about eight hundred feet above the ocean, and it commanded
a view all the way from Diamond Head to Pearl Harbor. I saw
the attack, I saw the bombs that were dropped in the ocean
very, very vividly. In fact, as I first saw them before I knew
about the actual attack, I still thought that it must be the Army
Air Force. Then I saw that they almost hit the Royal Hawaiian
Hotel, and I said to myself, that was awfully close! The
splashes were like plumes, going way up into the air, going
splash, splash, one after the other. Then, when I heard over
the radio that Hawaii was under attack, I ran up the side of
my property that had a slight elevation, and there I saw the
most dreadful thing I ever saw in my life. The fire, the blasting
of the ships, just one after the other, in flames! I had a good
view, and I knew it so well, having been there so many years,
the almost enclosed lagoon harbor. And the fire and the blaze
and the noise was absolutely something I'll never forget. A
Japanese plane passed right in front of my yard, not more than
forty feet from where I was sitting on the veranda. It was so
vivid I could see the face, the profile, and the rising sun on
the plane. By noon, we got our breath, the worst was over.

After the attack on Pearl Harbor, Ms. MacEwen cabled her
family three words: "WELL, SAFE, UNAFRAID." She decided to stay in Honolulu during the war and teach school.
She met and married her husband there, a submarine captain,
Adm. Kenneth C. Hurd (ret.).

Sen. George Aiken (R-Vt.):

I was in Washington. That was Sunday afternoon, and I had
gone over to the office for some reason or other. On the ticker,
I saw that the Japanese had attacked Pearl Harbor, no extent
of the damage done. The next day, I recall, Senator Toby of
New Hampshire said to me, "The report is that they've destroyed a good share of our fleet over there." That was the
first we knew of it. Of course, Pearl Harbor made our part of

the war inevitable. I remember [Sen.] Bill LaFollette, who had opposed our entry into the war and aid to England. The day after the bombing, he came into my office with his uniform on, ready to go.

In later years, to hear people tell it, it seemed as if half of Washington was out at the Redskins football game on December 7, 1941, in a stadium that would only hold twenty-five thousand people.

Melville Grosvenor, then assistant editor of the National Geographic *magazine, distinctly remembers being there.*

I was out at Griffith Stadium watching Washington get trounced [they beat the Eagles 20–14]. I think it was by the Giants. Anyway, it was an awful day. I was watching this game sorrowfully, and a whisper came around the stands. Everybody was shocked. It got to me, and they said: "Pearl Harbor has been attacked!" I couldn't believe it. The Japanese! I thought it was just talk. Then more reports came, and you began to see important people get up and go out. Then the public-address system sounded: "So and so, secretary of the navy, will you please come to the telephone?" and "So-so, would you please come to the manager's office immediately?" All the bigwigs went. And, of course, everybody was there at the football game, so you knew something hot was going on. And it was an awful feeling. You'd sort of known something like that was coming. And when it did, you said, "I hope they're ready, I hope they're ready!"

On the Friday before, I had had lunch with one of our editors. Ted Vosburgh. He was a violent isolationist. For lunch, we went down to the National Press Club, walking down Sixteenth Street, and he said, "Well, they just captured Singapore, or Malaya, and Japs are coming down there attacking the British, China. If we go to war, it will be the most terrible thing to pull old England's chestnuts out of the fire, we're always doing that," he says. "It would be a terrible thing. I certainly hope they won't do it." He was the most peace-minded person I think I've ever known. Well, Sunday came, and Monday came, and do you know, Ted was rabid that morning. He told me, "That was the most despicable thing, to attack like that." And he went right down and signed up in the Air Force. The last person you'd ever think. And he became an intelligence officer with the Air Force, and was assigned to Patton.

Nelson Poynter, editor of the St. Petersburg *(Fla.)* Times *was on leave, working in Washington for the coordinator of information, Wild Bill Donovan, who was later to become head of the OSS (Office of Strategic Services).*

We had offices in both New York and Washington and were operating twenty-four-hours a day, seven days a week, and we were in operation that afternoon, when we first learned about Pearl Harbor. I was at home, they called me, and I went right over to the office, and it was in full swing. It's amazing to me, to this day, that so many people were surprised at Pearl Harbor. Of course, it was learned afterward that our navy had broken the Japanese code. They knew, and we knew. It was not such a secret that the Japanese fleet had left its home base and was somewhere in the Pacific. I thought it would hit Manila or Hong Kong, and I think that's part of the reason why our own navy personnel was surprised. It was almost incomprehensible to them that they would strike for Pearl Harbor. I was surprised that they had picked Pearl Harbor, but I was not stunned. My associates in that office, some of the best newsmen you could find, felt the same way. They took it in their stride.

One man, Ed Stanley, who was working for our office had been a key man in the Associated Press. He had helped put the AP into the Wirephoto business in the early thirties. I said to him, "Pearl Harbor is in the Western hemisphere. Could you urge the Associated Press in sending out a Wirephoto picture to get that fact into the picture?" I thought it was terribly important, as far as the American people's public opinion was concerned, that we had been hit in our own Western hemisphere.

Bryson Rash was working for the NBC Washington office in the old Trans-Lux office building at Fourteenth and New York Avenue, two blocks from the White House.

I just happened to be at work that afternoon because I did a program on Sunday. After the program I was doing some other chores, when I heard running down the hallway. It was the news editor, who had a piece of teletype copy paper in his hand. I said: "What's the matter?" He said: "The Japs just bombed Pearl Harbor."

I ran into the newsroom, and he ran into the studio to get the bulletin on the air. All the printers in the place were going crazy. In those days there was a bell system, where five bells rang if it was a bulletin and ten bells if it was a flash, and the bells were ringing constantly. While I was in the newsroom, the phone rang, and I picked it up. It was the White House. The voice said, "Mr. [Steve] Early will have a statement." It just happened that I was the only person in the building at the moment who had a White House pass, so I ran over to get the Early statement. There was no statement. Early wasn't there, in the West Wing. This was minutes after the news broke.

Actually, at that time, Japanese envoys Nomura and Kurusu were meeting with Secretary of State Cordell Hull in his office across the street in what is now the Executive Office Building. So most of the people were interested in that story and were at the State Department, and there was nobody in sight at the White House except a policeman. I asked the policeman where Mr. Early was, and he said, "Mr. Early doesn't come in on Sunday usually." I said, "Where is the statement?" He said, "What statement?" So I said, "Don't you know what happened? Pearl Harbor has been bombed!" At that he nearly fainted.

Frank Waldrop was the managing editor of the Washington Times Herald. *He says: "You're damned right I remember Pearl Harbor."*

I was at my office attending to business. I had gone down there, as I customarily did, about ten o'clock on Sunday morning. By noon, or a little after, I had finished going through my stuff, and I went back in the wire room just to look at what the hell was going on, and I saw a dispatch from Reuters that said that two Japanese battleships had been sighted going south in the Gulf of Siam, so I thought, "What the hell. Things are right at the flash point. I believe I'll stick around a while." So I went back to work.

A fellow named Tom Stephens was on the city desk doing the dog watch, and I guess about two o'clock he came belting into my office, his face ashen, and said, "The police radio says that the Japanese have bombed Pearl Harbor!" So I said: "Call the White House and see if you can get a confirmation." I began to put the telephone operators to work finding out where everybody was. Fortunately all of our circulation people were out at the Redskins football game. They had some junket that the kids had wanted to attend, so there was a big crowd of them out there. I called the Redskins office and told them to put on their loudspeaker "All *Times Herald* people report to their office on the double."

I wrote the lead couple of paragraphs, and then after that I was too damned busy to fool with it. But people just filled in as it came along and built the story. I went to the composing room with the foreman of the typographical end of the paper, Irving Belt, and the *Times Herald* was on the street four hours ahead of any newspaper, I think, in the country. We were sure as hell the first newspaper in Washington. We were off and balling right smack out with it, and what I love, as I look back on it, was when those guys came in there, you didn't have to tell them anything. They knew right where they belonged, and they hit this damn thing, and the circulation department was up, and when the pressman pressed that button, those damned papers went out of there like scared dogs. I think there's a copy of it on the wall over at the Press Club: "Pearl Harbor Bombed." I had a double line on it; we just set type as big as we could get it. What the hell! Your country doesn't get attacked every day in the week.

Merlo Pusey was chief editorial writer for the Washington Post.

I was on duty and running the editorial page that day. The first word we heard came when a copyboy, who was a rather obstreperous youngster, dashed into the office screaming that the Japanese had attacked Pearl Harbor. We didn't believe him, because he was kind of a practical joker, and we thought he was pulling one on us. I didn't believe him because it seemed to me that the Japanese would be insane to attack Pearl Harbor. It was such a crazy thing, because there was nothing in the world they could do that would arouse this sleeping giant more effectively than an attack on Pearl Harbor. Once they launched that, their doom was sealed, and I had that feeling about it at the moment. But of course we checked immediately and found it was true and began frantic operations to prepare for it the next day. I didn't write the editorial. Herbert Elliston [editor], who was then writing most of our foreign-affairs editorials, dashed into the office and wrote it.

Dean Elmer Louis Kayser, George Washington University, in Washington, D.C.:

I had gotten up very late and was shaving when the news came in on the radio. I was then doing foreign-news commentary for radio station WWDC, and I called my wife and told her to call the station and tell them I'd stop shaving and dress and come in immediately and go on the air. I had to go past the Japanese Embassy, of course, so I stopped to see what I could see. They hadn't thrown a military guard around the place yet, just local police, but they were keeping people out of the embassy's compound. Here were the Japanese, working like bees, bringing out files, and they built quite a bonfire in the side yard. Then I went down and went on the air almost immediately, giving a picture of what I had seen at the embassy.

The next day, Monday morning, Cloyd Heck Marvin, president of George Washington University, called the whole faculty together. He had called me earlier and said, "I want you, Dean, to address this meeting, dedicating the faculty and the university to the cause of the nation in this war which is about to be declared." And so, in no time at all, I was stuck up on the platform to deliver a speech to rally the university. I wish I had a tape of it, because I have been told that it was good.

To set the temperature, I took that magnificent occasion where, at the time of the Nika revolt in Constantinople, when the forces opposed to Justinian could have swept him off the throne in the sudden cataclysm of violence which he couldn't meet, when the Empress Theodora said, "As for me, the purple is the only burial shroud of a princess." She would not run. That's what I took to cite the passion of resistance which would have to be aroused. Curious I'd still remember that.

Edward Stuntz worked for the Associated Press in Washington.

I was sitting there, drinking beer and getting ready for my afternoon nap. Connie [his wife] was making lunch, and this news came on the radio. The thing that brought me out of my daze was somebody on the radio who said something like: "Whatever may be said about this treacherous attack on Pearl Harbor"—I guess I was thinking it must be an Orson Welles type of thing—"the fact remains that the Japanese will have committed national suicide."

That brought me up, and I turned the radio up louder and yelled at Connie to come in, and we listened to what details they had. I ran up the stairs to get some office clothes on and yelled on my way up, "It's war, Connie. It's going to be war." My daughter, Ann, burst into tears. Connie drove me to the office—I was covering the Latin American diplomatic run— and I stayed there practically twenty-four hours. I called up all the various embassies and was getting some reaction stories, and before I got through that night, we got a message from our AP man in Costa Rica that Costa Rica had declared war and rounded up all the Japanese farmers—Costa Rica was full of them, you know. I was still making my calls when my dear old friend Alvareo Concheso, the Cuban ambassador, who was working then for Batista, called me up and said, "Mr. Stuntz, why is it that the Associated Press lets Costa Rica declare war before we do, the Cubans?"

And I said to him, "But, Mr. Ambassador, AP didn't have anything to do with it. We just got a story, which you have read, that the president of Costa Rica announced that a state of war with Japan existed so that he could go out and arrest all these Japanese who might be subversives."

The exact chronology of this escapes me, but after Concheso learned that Costa Rica had declared war and the United States had not, he was boiling and furious at the AP and at me for putting the story out. He thought I had done it. He said, "What am I going to tell Colonel Batista?"

I said, "Tell him that Mr. Roosevelt is said to be preparing a message to Congress for tomorrow." And he said, "But you let Costa Rica declare war. Don't you know that Cuba is always the first to declare war after the United States?''

They took great pride in that. Right after World War I, Mario Menolal, the Cuban president, had his message to his Congress all prepared before President Wilson went to our Congress, but he waited until Wilson made his declaration.

Twenty-year-old Mercedes Fritzching, a Venezuelan citizen born of German parents, was working at the German Embassy in Washington. She says Pearl Harbor meant that her world was "coming to an end"—and it did.

It was a Sunday afternoon, and I was on my way to Constitution Hall for a concert. I was just backing out of the driveway, when my father opened the window and called down and told me that Pearl Harbor had been attacked. I picked up several friends on the way to the concert and told them the news, and we simply couldn't believe it. The concert started, and it didn't seem like anything was unusual until intermission, and then we noticed that people were being called up, and after intermission the hall was only half full—important people had been called up. Then we began to feel the significance of the event.

At that time I was working at the German Embassy as a social secretary to the naval attaché, so going to work on Monday was, of course, quite dramatic, too, because we felt sure it was only a matter of days before war would be declared between Germany and the United States. So that meant that all the files had to be burned—everything, even such ridiculous things as table settings. As social secretary, I just had guest lists and invitations, but we burned everything. And then, of course, the war between the United States and Germany came the following Thursday. I was living at home with my parents. My father was a German diplomat, and we were told that we were just supposed to keep a low profile and stay in our homes, and the time would come when we would be exchanged for the American diplomats in Germany. So we started packing, thinking we would have an indefinite period to do this because they would have to find some ship to take us back to Germany. The State Department said, "Take it easy and just stay home." But apparently the secret service made other arrangements. By the sixteenth of December, we were given the order: All of the German officials had to spend that night in the German Embassy, and the families had to report in front of the embassy the next morning, so we really just had that one night to get our hand luggage packed and walk out of our homes as they were and report to the embassy. We were interned at White Sulphur Springs, in the Greenbriar Hotel, leaving everything behind. We stayed there for five months.

I thought Pearl Harbor was horrible, horrible! It felt like our world was coming to an end. In a sense, it did.

Leverett Saltonstall, a Republican, was governor of Massachusetts at the time of Pearl Harbor, having served in the State House since 1940.

I heard about Pearl Harbor over the car radio when we were riding from our farm to our home in Chestnut Hill. When I reached home, I called the adjutant general, and we agreed to call out the whole State Guard that night to guard the various railroad and highway crossings until we knew what the story was.

The first problems we had concerned the railroads and the various utilities—not to have those services broken down. There were no actual attempts to sabotage, or rumors, at that time; that came somewhat later. When Pearl Harbor broke, the army had the responsibility up to the high water, the Coast Guard took over from the high water to a certain depth, and then the navy took over. There was also the problem of how the state fitted in with them. Gradually, that was worked out, so that one phone call would do everything. Remember, we had submarines off our coast.

Kay Halle was working in Cleveland, where she was on assignment for radio station WGAR. A few months earlier, she had interviewed Barbara Ward as part of a series on what the roles of women might be if the United States were drawn into the war.

It was a very dramatic and memorable moment. I was attending the annual meeting of the Institute of Pacific Relations, being held that year at the Country Club in Cleveland, Ohio. Naturally, the subject of the conference was the crisis in the Far East. I was sitting at the end of one long conference table next to my friend Count Carlo Sforza. I had also interviewed him on his passionate opposition to Mussolini. Next to him was Ohio Congresswoman Frances Bolton.

The group's director, Edward Carter, had divided the delegates into two groups, who were to go into conference and reassemble after lunch with their assessments of whether and when the Japanese might take some military action against the United States. The two groups returned at around two o'clock, each with the same "educated" conclusion that the Japanese would not take any action for a year or more. While the conference proceeded to analyze their conclusions, I felt a tug at my elbow. It was Clayton Fritchey of the *Cleveland Press*. He handed me a slip of paper which he asked me to take up to the institute's director. It was the announcement just released by Steve Early, President Roosevelt's press secretary, that the Japanese had bombed Pearl Harbor. After Mr. Carter had read the news, my first thought was, where could I be most useful? I went to Washington, and at a cocktail party I met Sam Scrivener, who was an executive at the newly formed Office of Strategic Services—the OSS. He was on the alert for recruits, and, fortunately, I became one.

Jack Altshul was working on the Long Beach Life, *a Long Island weekly newspaper. He was covering a pro football game.*

I was up in the press box, and one of the other newspapermen said something was coming up over the radio that he just "couldn't understand." We listened very carefully, and what we got out of it was that the Japanese were attacking Pearl Harbor. None of us knew where Pearl Harbor was. We didn't even know it was in the Hawaiian Islands. The game was about to start, when somebody made the announcement on the public-address system, and we could see a little stirring, but it didn't seem to sink in. People stayed right through the football game, but by the time the game was over, everybody was talking about it.

I got a sense of it that night. Everybody seemed to feel:

Well, this is it, this is the war. And, of course, the next morning, Roosevelt declared war.

In Hopewell, Virginia, Gus Robbins, editor of the local paper, recalls, "It was a beautiful December day."

We got home maybe five-thirty, six o'clock, and I turned the radio on and heard it, and of course I was dumbfounded. Nobody had expected that. I belonged to a public-affairs club that had a dinner meeting once a month, and in early November, just a month before Pearl Harbor, we had Captain Lovett, the head navy PR man, down to speak to us. He talked for an hour about how wonderful the U.S. Navy was and if there was a war, we'd wipe the Japanese navy out in five days. The next week he was transferred to Pearl Harbor in command of a flotilla of six destroyers. Three of his destroyers were in dry dock, and all three were destroyed. He survived because it was Sunday and he was at home. But that is an indication of what was wrong with the United States government.

Bill Gold was the news director for radio station WCPO in Cincinnati, Ohio.

We were incredulous when the news came over the ticker. It was beyond immediate comprehension. It dawned on us, as the day wore on and as additional information became available, that it really had happened.

My first reaction was that I ought to go down and enlist right away. But at that point I had been married a dozen years, had a young child, and, you know, your immediate reaction and what you think after you've talked to your wife about it are two different things.

Ann Hoskins and her husband, Stewart, were running the Lakeville Journal, *a weekly newspaper in Lakeville, Connecticut.*

My parents were up for the weekend, and we'd been listening to a symphony concert. It was interrupted in the middle with the words that Pearl Harbor had been bombed. At first, we didn't understand exactly what it meant, and then suddenly we thought, "My God, we're in it!"

Our first reaction was, "Well, that's settled; at least now we know what we are going to do." It was a terrific feeling of relief that at last there was a solution. We had a very strong America First group here who were pamphletizing and talking against going in. Stewart, in his editorial, said: "Let's wait until we are armed. We can't go in with wooden muskets, for goodness' sake. Let's do it when we're ready, but not now." There was great tension and feelings between people not to intervene. But the minute Pearl Harbor happened, there was utter unity, absolutely. I remember that Monday morning after Pearl Harbor, I went down to the bank, and a woman standing outside said, "Do you suppose they will bomb us right away?" She was sure it would come.

Marquis Childs was a correspondent in the Washington Bureau of the St. Louis Post-Dispatch.

I wasn't at a football game as almost everybody else was. I remember hearing it first over the radio. And then driving out to some friends' house in Virginia, people I had known very well, and all of us saying, "Nothing will ever be the same again." And it never was the same. It never will be.

Robert Bender, a young man just out of college, was working for NBC in New York. Although not at the office that day, he had a special reason for remembering Pearl Harbor.

I was in Chatham, New Jersey, living with my folks, and I was stunned. But what is interesting is that a year before, perhaps to that exact date, I was studying journalism at Rutgers University, and I faked an Associated Press story saying that the Japs had attacked Pearl Harbor. I had been in Hawaii and in Australia with my dad, so I knew the area and the names of the fields. I described the Japanese coming over and the damage they did. All hell broke loose at the college! Then they realized it was a fake, and I almost got thrown out. Of course, I apologized profusely, and I remained in Rutgers. And at the time of the actual bombing I immediately thought of my story, and I thought if only there had been some way of showing people that this could happen so we should be better prepared.

Rep. John W. McCormack (R-Mass.) was the majority leader in the House of Representatives. On Sunday, December 7, 1941, he was back in Boston, and he got the news from a very reliable source.

The telephone rang. I answered it, and it was the White House calling me. FDR came on the phone, and he told me about Pearl Harbor. I hadn't heard about it. He also said he wanted me to be back in Washington by the next day. I told him that I came home to address a luncheon meeting of the Boston Chamber of Commerce on Monday, and he told me he needed me in Washington. I said: "That's all, Mr. President, I'll be there." So Mrs. McCormack and I went back.

Studs Terkel in Chicago:

I was lying on the divan when I heard the news, and I thought: "What's going to happen tomorrow?" The next day was Monday. I was a gangster in a soap opera, it may have been "Ma Perkins." But it was canceled.

Celeste Kavanaugh was a senior at the Florida State College for Women in Tallahassee.

I was on a house party with a group of friends, and we had gone to a movie that Sunday afternoon and returned to my friend's home, where we were met with the news. One of my best friends, Admiral Angus's daughter, was with me that day, and I remember she burst into tears. I think she realized the impact a little more than the rest of us, but we were all thoroughly shocked.

ViCurtis Hinton was a student at Howard University in Washington, D.C.

I'll never forget. I was at Camp Lee, below Richmond, visiting some friends. We were getting ready to come back to Washington when we heard about Pearl Harbor. All I could think about was getting home, as if something might happen at home. I was in school in Howard University. I was just scared to death of the war, I didn't know what it meant and didn't know what would happen about my brother. He was not in the service at that time, but he was old enough to be drafted. My father had been in World War I. I didn't know what was going to happen. I didn't know whether they were going to bomb Washington. It was a really funny feeling.

Coralee Redmond, her husband, and her boys, had gone up into the hills around Beach, North Dakota, to cut a Christmas tree.

When I came home and we drove back into the yard, the girls came running out—my girls were high school students at that time—and they said, "Mom, where's Uncle Ben?" And I said "He's in Pearl Harbor," and they said "Pearl Harbor has just been bombed!"

A promising young actress named Evelyn Keyes was in Hollywood, where she had just signed a contract with Columbia Pictures.

It was a Sunday. I was at Charles Vidor's house. He was later my husband; he wasn't then. It was quiet. I remember the sunshine, of all things, because it seemed incongruous that the sun was shining when we heard this news. Someone telephoned. They said: "Did you hear? The Japanese have attacked Pearl Harbor!" We immediately turned on the radio—that was before television—and we didn't ever stop listening. Of course, I thought it was the end of the world. Shock! Horror! We were on the West Coast, and we thought surely they would be along here.

Joseph Clement was married, had a baby boy, and was living in Milwaukee, Wisconsin, working for the Nesco Company, which made pots and pans.

That's one of those times when you remember everything. It was a Sunday morning, and we were at home having breakfast. We got the news over the radio that Pearl Harbor had been bombed, and like everybody else, we didn't know what the score was. I went back to the plant the next day, and it took a little time for everybody to get their bearings. But it wasn't long before they realized that they would have to shut our department down because we were making consumer goods. So I started making plans to get another job. I had a kind of interest in aviation. I had built my own glider, so I thought I might be useful in that area. I went home to see my folks and stopped at Curtiss-Wright Company in Saint Louis, and they definitely were interested.

Newton Tolman had a farm going in Nelson, New Hampshire, where he was living with his wife, Janet, and a young son.

I was down in the cornfield, and when I came up, Janet told me. I don't remember whether she had heard it on the radio or somebody had called her up. It could have been both, because everybody was calling everybody. I was never too happy about the war. In the Civil War, my grandfather, at eighteen, was hired by his brother, who was twenty-four and much richer, to go into the service. It ruined his health, and the old farm fell down. I had to eventually rebuild it. War was not for me. I didn't really believe in it much. On the other hand, I was young, and my wife was the founder of the Young Republicans Club in New York, with Tom Dewey and all those flag-wavers. But now we were attacked. The Japs bombed Honolulu, where my aunt had taught at the Punahou Academy, since the 1930s, and we had various relatives out there and Hawaiian friends. So, by God, they might as well have been knocking at our doorstep. I think I must have been bombed in my mind. I went off then and signed up with the navy.

But I got out of it; God was on my side. I never knew why I got out of it, except that when I was interviewed for the navy, they said: "What have you done for more than six months to make a living?" And I had twenty-eight sheets of paper to honestly answer the question, and I think the psychiatrist thought he was dealing with a lunatic. I didn't dare tell my wife until twenty-five years afterward that I was pretty relieved that I didn't get into that.

Clifford Eunice, a construction engineer, was about to take a job building an ordnance factory.

Yes, sir, I was on a Greyhound bus. It was almost within the city limits of Little Rock, Arkansas. I was working for Dupont and on my way to Pryor, Oklahoma, where we built the Oklahoma Ordnance Works. Dupont had already constructed the powder works on the Mississippi River north of Memphis, known as the Tennessee Powder Works. It was constructed for the British government. We hadn't declared war yet, so the U.S. built a powder works for the British. The bus was loaded. A gentleman on the bus had a small radio, and it was playing real low; then, all at once, he turned it up loud, and the announcer said: "I repeat, we have just received word that the Japs have bombed Pearl Harbor!" You could have heard, sir, a pin hit the floor. Nobody breathed hardly, so they could be sure to hear this newsman. He said: "The damage is not known yet, but we have just received this message that we have definitely been heavily bombed, and we won't have any report on damages until later." The reaction of the people on the bus was a form of paralysis.

Alice Newcomer was a student at George Washington University in Washington, D.C.

A very good friend who lived across the hall in the dormitory rushed over, and said, "They've bombed Pearl Harbor! I just heard it on the radio." I said, "Is it bad?" And she said, "It couldn't be worse." So I said, "What do you mean?" She said, "It's going to ruin my senior thesis on our neutrality in Latin America!"

W. P. Laws owned a grocery store in Ocean City, Maryland.

I was in here listening to the radio, and they came on the air about two o'clock in the afternoon on Sunday. Dr. Townsend was sitting across the street out front about half asleep, and the flies were kind of buzzing around him. But I went over there and woke him up and told him what had happened. I said, "I believe we're in war." Dr. Townsend came over here and he listened and he said, "Yeah, that's Roosevelt for you," or something like that. He was a Republican and he never liked Roosevelt, or made out he didn't.

John Rettaliata and André Hubbard were helping to open a new plant for the Grumman Corporation in Bethpage, Long Island. Grumman builds fighter planes.

RETTALIATA: Plant 2 was then by far the largest plant that we had ever built. It was specifically built to produce the TBF-Avenger, which was the navy's front-line torpedo bomber. We had an open house to show the plant to all our employees and their families, on the actual day—December 7, Sunday. We were there when the announcement came over the loudspeakers. I guess shock was the best way you could express my reaction. I don't think the word was passed on, but I think they got rid of most of the people. I can remember that.

HUBBARD: They thought they had better clear the plant immediately. There could have been sabotage. I remember them taking away the food. We gave orders to remove that. People started to take the hint.

A young boy, Tony Taylor, was doing what most people in Washington were doing.

I was listening to the Redskins football game. I was twelve or thirteen years old. I didn't pay too much mind. I was into the football game. But every time the news came on about it, I knew it was something kind of mean. Even a twelve-year-old kid knew it had to be pretty bad.

I was a youngster, and it didn't hit me like it would somebody a lot older. I felt this through my father and my mother. They were pretty upset, and naturally I was upset because they were concerned. If I was, say, eighteen or nineteen, I would have been thinking about going to school or college or a job. At that age, man, I was a youngster; I could only react through my folks about something like that. I remember them talking about tightening their belts. There was a lot to fear about who was going into the service and what that meant and who would be coming back.

Mabel Wiggins was in Saint Paul, Minnesota, where her husband was managing editor of the St. Paul Pioneer Press and Dispatch.

I was sitting in the living room listening to opera. Russ was upstairs, and I called, and he instantly went to the office. I thought: "Here we go, everybody is going to go to war. And I'll stay home." My older son had just graduated from high school, and I knew he'd go. I thought the younger one probably wouldn't. I thought: "There they go."

Charles Keller was a professor of History at Williams College in Williamstown, Massachusetts.

I was sitting at my desk, here in this house, reading the proof of a book that was about to appear. We didn't have the radio on. At four o'clock, two young men rang the bell. They were coming for tea. They were both students, seniors at Williams College. One was named Fred Rudolph, and one was named Bob Griggs. And they told us what had happened. At that point we turned on the radio, and that was it.

I have to admit, I was one of those who said, though I didn't teach that way, "This is our war, and we should have been in it before." And I had approved everything that Roosevelt had done. I remember the evening of December 6; we were at the faculty club, and the History department's Arthur Buffington, who died shortly after, said, "Don't be surprised if the Japanese attack." So we weren't surprised. I suspect my original reaction was, "It's about time."

Dr. Benjamin Spock:

I was at home working in New York City, where I had been practicing pediatrics since 1933. I remember my wife and my oldest son went to see *Dumbo*, the Disney film. They urged me to come, but I said I had too much desk work to do, so off they went. I had the music station playing, which soothes me when I have to do desk work. The music was interrupted to tell this horrible news, and I had difficulty continuing my work after that. After a while Jane and my son came back from the movies, and my wife said, "Oh, you should have gone, it was wonderful." And I said, "Do you know what has happened? Since you've been away the Japanese have bombed Pearl Harbor." And she said, "You really should have come."

John Holton, at that time the director of quality control for the Carrier Corporation plant in Syracuse, New York, heard the news while he was driving his car.

First, there was disbelief. Then I recognized that something of great importance had happened, I guess is the best way to put it. I began to try to figure what effect it might have on us. The Carrier Corporation had been manufacturing primarily air conditioners and refrigeration and some heating equipment. We knew, of course, from the activities prior to the war, that we were very apt to get into it and were concerned about the future of air conditioning. We'd felt that while it had a lot of industrial uses, it was primarily a luxury rather than a necessity and began to wonder what effect the war would have on the business. As it turned out, it was more of a necessity than we realized.

Democratic Congressman Norman Mineta (D-Cal.) was ten years old, a Japanese Nisei living in San Jose, California.

We were at home when the news came in. I think we had just come back from church. It was sort of a very quiet situation around the house and then a lot of phone calls coming to the house and people wondering. My dad was a leader in the Japanese community in San Jose, and people would seek him out for advice and for a number of reasons. So when the initial reports started coming in, people would call in, wondering what this means to us.

I've only seen him cry three times, and one was on Pearl Harbor Day. He could not understand why they had attacked Pearl Harbor. He was sitting in his office, which was in the house, wondering why they had done that, crying.

Also, on that day, the FBI started picking up a number of Japanese as suspects. My father was trying to prevent the FBI from arresting a lot of these people. They had done nothing; the only thing that they had done was to be born of Japanese ancestry.

The building next door belonged to the Japanese Association; it was a sort of a community building. The executive director of the association lived in the back of that building with his family, and the FBI came and arrested him on the spot and took him away. Their daughter, who was about my age, came running over, climbing under the hedge, coming into our yard yelling that they were taking her father away and crying as she ran. So my dad went next door to see what was going on, but by that time, in less than fifteen minutes, they had picked him up, and boom! he was taken away.

I really didn't know what was going on. But I remember my dad saying at mealtime that night: "They may take me, they may take Mom, but remember you are American citizens. They can't do these things to you, and whatever happens to any of us, this is our family home."

Thomas Page, in his last year at Harvard Law School, was at the Agawam Hunt Club in Providence, Rhode Island, with a friend who was skeet shooting.

I was sitting in a car listening to the New York Symphony when I heard it. For some odd reason, it did not really surprise me. The fact of Pearl Harbor, I think, surprised me, but I had decided about two weeks before, there was a very strong likelihood of war. There was an English couple, a guy named Tom Harris and his wife, who did a thing called mass observation. They would observe what people were eating, reading, and the way of advertisements to determine what people really were doing. His theory was that it isn't what people told you they were doing, but what they really were doing. And I looked at the *New York Times Sunday Magazine,* maybe a week or two before Pearl Harbor. It was filled with semiwarlike copy and ads. And I thought, my God, this is really an illustration of this guy Harris's theory of mass observation—the country has almost accepted the inevitability of some kind of military action and is all geared up for it mentally. And they were bellicose. I remember very clearly saying to myself: "If that guy is right, we're on the verge of war."

Ten-year-old Ray Hartman in Chicago remembers that day vividly.

I was at the Bear's professional football game in Chicago, Illinois, that Sunday, and they stopped the game and announced that Pearl Harbor had been attacked by the Japs. There was complete silence really—shock, I think, at first—and then there was a great disbelief. People really couldn't understand the impact of it at the moment. At my age it seemed a little glamorous, because I had an older brother that was anxious to enlist and I just idolized him for thinking that way and wanted to do the same thing he did.

At Leon Sylvester's gas station near Sedgwick, Maine, a gathering of Down Easters remember Pearl Harbor—Sylvester, Forrest Eaton, James Saunders, and later they were joined by Ronald Gray.

EATON: I was lobstering. I got the news when I got home. I don't remember how I heard it, but I heard it. I thought it was an awful thing, was what I thought.

SAUNDERS: I was working on a dairy farm in North Blue Hill. Yep. The first I got the news was from the *Bangor Daily News*. It must have been the next day. I don't remember my reaction. But that was 1941, and in 1942 I went to work for the South Portland Shipyard. All my friends were going to work there at the same time. I thought it would help out quite a lot more than it would to stay on the farm. And it commanded better wages—much better.

SYLVESTER: I was in Stonington, Maine. I'd just been to a wedding, and the fellow that was married was called out at midnight; they had to get him out of the camp; he had to go back into the service. My reaction to Pearl Harbor and the war was that there was nothing I could do—just pay attention and mind my own business.

GRAY: Pearl Harbor didn't change my life much. I kept right on lobstering.

Peggy Blassingame was eleven years old and lived on an island in the Gulf of Mexico, off Bradenton, Florida.

I was sitting in the living room at home in Anna Maria, Florida, and my mother was very, very pregnant. She was listening to the news; I am sure I was not—I would have had no interest in the news—and she started to cry, "Oh, my God! Oh, my God! The Japanese have bombed us. It's war! It's war!" I had my girl friend with me, Polly Moore. My father was down on the beach shooting shells with a friend with a BB gun, and at that time there were no other people on the beach. Polly and I just took off out of the house; war sounded pretty terrifying. We ran down to the beach, and when I saw my father, I started yelling that the Japanese had bombed Pearl Harbor. They didn't believe me, and we kept yelling, and finally they started running as fast as they could. The rest of the day is very blurred, but I do remember my initial reaction to my mother's reaction to the news, and I was scared.

Mary Moore Lacey was married to her first husband, a naval aviator assigned to a torpedo squadron on the U.S.S. York-town. *She was in Norfolk, Virginia.*

The *Yorktown* had been out in Pearl, and in the fall of '41 it came around to the East Coast, and we wives had met the ship up in Portland, Maine. They were in the northern Atlantic for a while, and then in November we went to Norfolk and lived in a hotel down on Virginia Beach. There was a whole crowd of wives down there in temporary quarters.

Pearl Harbor kind of stunned us. But, at the same time, we weren't really awfully surprised, because there had been a lot of rumors around Hawaii when we had been there the summer before. People in Hawaii in those days talked about moving up into the hills and finding a cave and putting food away in the hills, to get ready for the Japanese attacks. It was something that was going to come. It was a strange atmosphere. Still, there was immediate traumatic reaction. I felt as though I had been hit in the solar plexus. Then, if you tried to think about it for a minute, you'd rationalize that they were naval officers and military flyers; that was their profession. As navy wives, we had a role to play too. So we all had a stiff upper lip, and that's what we had to do.

Peter Scaglione was working in the front bar at the Columbia Restaurant in Tampa, Florida.

Everybody was so excited—and later they heard the president say that the war was on. Everybody was so mad. Some boys who were friends of mine said, ''I'm going to the war right now. I'm going against those Japs.'' They joined up right away.

Young Hugh Sidey in Greenfield, Iowa:

I had just gotten back from attending Sunday school and church, which we always did every Sunday and then had Sunday dinner. I can't remember whether we had had dinner or were preparing to have dinner, but I was up in my bedroom changing clothes. You always changed into your play clothes after church; and we always had the radio on during Sunday dinner—the Longine Symphonette, which we played as a kind of background music for our Sunday dinner. Suddenly I heard my mother exclaim and then call up the stairs: ''The Japanese have attacked us.''

Anna Mae Lindberg was living in a suburb of Pittsburgh, where her husband worked in a U.S. Steel mill.

I remember like it was yesterday. I was sitting at the sewing machine making something, and I had the radio on. My husband was working in the mill. We were in a two-family house; and I remember running down the stairs and telling the people downstairs to turn on their radio, that something big had happened. I don't know whether I was naive, but it was just a complete shock to me, and I remember not being able to absorb it. My husband and I were just the age. We had brothers and sisters who were all going to be involved. We thought, this is not the radioman's war; this is our war. My first instinct was for survival—how to keep my people out of it. There wasn't any great thing: ''This is my country, we are going to have to make do and go save everybody!'' That's not true. I wouldn't have said this before Vietnam.

Judson Phillips, a free-lance writer—mostly of detective novels:

I was sitting in the kitchen in a farmhouse in Vermont listening to the New York Giants football team play somebody or other; and I guess eight million other people were, too, because it happened on a Sunday afternoon during pro football time. I didn't know where Pearl Harbor was. But every ten minutes after that, there was more on it. So it wasn't very long before we realized it wasn't just a little bombing somewhere. I was thirty-eight years old, married, and I thought, "Jesus, I might have to go to war at this late date."

John R. Shepley, an eighty-one-year-old Saint Louis banker, has lived through more than one war.

I was driving home on the Ladue Road in Saint Louis County, and I was actually crossing the terminal railroad tracks, and I had my radio on, and the news of Pearl Harbor came over the radio—and I said: "Here we go again."

Mary Devereux Crist's husband was in the marines, stationed at the navy yard in Philadelphia.

I had come from Philadelphia down to my mother's house in Chevy Chase, Maryland, bringing my six-week-old baby on the day coach. My mother was just cutting her seventieth birthday cake when we got a telephone call from a friend saying that the Japanese—I'll say *Japanese*, I usually say *Japs*; I can't get over how I feel about them; anyway—that the Japanese had bombed Pearl Harbor; and there was a great to-do about how I'd get back to Philadelphia, where my husband and two boys were. I didn't believe it was the whole Japanese Empire. I thought some isolated group of dissidents under the Japanese admirals had strayed away from orders that had been given them.

We were told not to go to the railroad stations, so I had to figure out some kind of formula to give my baby. And the next day my husband was immediately ordered to put on his uniform and stand by in his quarters for further orders.

One ten-year-old boy living in Corpusville, Indiana, never quite got over the excitement of Pearl Harbor and the war. Twenty-nine years later Richard Lingeman published a best-

selling book, Don't You Know There's a War On? The American Home Front—1941–1945

I have a fairly clear memory that I was listening to the radio, I guess to a football game. I don't remember exactly hearing the words announcing it but just that I had heard the words. But I remember going out, seeking a friend who lived next door who was my age, as if I had a need to see somebody. Something that was kind of vast and beyond comprehension had happened. It was certainly exciting, though not exactly fear, but a kind of vague anxiety too. I can remember the next day at school the teachers talking about it and a lot of rumors going around. I remember one of the teachers said, "They've got Wake . . ."

In Mount Pleasant, Michigan, Betty Bryce was having company.

We just finished dinner when the news came over the radio. I was stunned, because we knew things were going on but never expected anything like that. My son, at that time, was about fifteen, and, of course, I thought the war would be over before he ever gets there.

Richard Spitzer and his wife were living in Shortsville, New York, thirty miles south of Rochester.

That's a date my wife and I remember very easily because our first child was born on December 9, and my wife went to the hospital in Rochester for that birth, and the hospital was blacked our under emergency conditions.

Pauline Christensen, a widow with two young sons in Evansville, Illinois:

It was Sunday, and we were sitting at home, and the housekeeper came tearing in to tell us what she had just heard on the radio; I thought it was catastrophic! It just seemed unbelievable. I was in the education publishing business, and I had two sons—one in grammar school and one in junior high school. They were too young for the service, and this was one reason, I think, I felt that I had to get involved and make a contribution to the war effort. So I joined the Red Cross Motor Corps as a driver.

Patricia Pavlic was a navy wife, living in Annapolis, Maryland.

My husband was on duty at the Naval Academy. We were having a cocktail with friends—and, of course, nobody believed it. It was a shock! But immediately the men called in and were ordered back to the academy. There was no waiting. They reported back to see what was to be done. Very shortly after that, on the seventeenth of December, my second child was born, early by a month or so, I'm sure because of the shock.

David Soergal was an engineering student at the University of Wisconsin in Madison.

I was in my room doing some homework, and I remember the news coming over a small radio that my roommate and I had. I turned back to my studies and continued. No comment from my roommate. We were nearing the period of final exams for the first semester, and people were more concerned about getting good grades than about a war starting. It was almost a subconscious awareness that the engineering people and the scientific people were not going to get involved.

Helen Wilson, in Mount Pleasant, Michigan:

I was a high school student. It was one of those traumatic times when you felt something important was going on. I had an older brother, and the thought immediately was that he would have to go. There was no women's lib then, and you thought in terms of "This will affect my brother."

Sally Lucke was a little girl living in Columbus, Ohio, where her father worked for the Galena Shale and Tile Company.

It was a really beautiful day, and my dad was out working in the yard right next to the window, and I was in the living room playing the piano. The radio was on in the background, and they came in with the news of the bombing of Pearl Harbor. I had no sense of fear, it was just like total amazement at first, and then I ran out into the yard and told my father what had happened. His reaction was anger!

I was not very aware at that age of people going off to war. I was just mainly afraid that my father would be going off to war, and I can remember being afraid we'd be bombed.

Kent Chetlain was in his first year of high school in Winnetka, Illinois.

My father, who is still practicing law in Chicago and almost eighty years old, had foreseen the approach of World War II and felt that we should buy a farm so that we would be assured plenty of food in case of scarcities, which ultimately developed. So we were in the process of looking at farms. It was a cold, wintry day, and we had blankets on our legs because our heater didn't work in our car. We were en route from Glencoe to Woodstock, Illinois.

Like everybody else, we were astounded. I guess our reaction was no different than millions of other people.

Mary Dandouveris lived in Racine, Wisconsin. She was in high school at the time, the oldest of six children.

We were all sitting around home listening to one of our favorite radio programs when they interrupted to tell us, and we couldn't believe it. As teenagers we tended to romanticize. I was a great buff of the Civil and Revolutionary wars and I remember thinking: "Oh, what a thrilling experience this is going to be to live through a war!" It took a couple of years before maturation set in so that I began to fully appreciate the horrors of the war. But I'll never forget that first instant of thinking what a glamorous, romantic period this was going to be.

Smith Johnson owned a small rubber plant in Middlefield, Ohio.

We had just driven back from Warren, Ohio, and when we got to Middlefield about five-thirty, we turned the radio on, and that's where we got the news. Of course, I was shocked like everyone else, and I knew we were in the war, and it flashed through my mind, "What's going to happen to me? What's going to happen to the family? What's going to happen to the business?" We had a business there with five hundred people, and I was president of it.

We were manufacturing rubber products for civilian use. We didn't have a single job for the government. I realized immediately that the rubber business was probably going to be affected, and, boy, was it ever! The next week I laid off three hundred of our employees and kept more or less of a skeleton crew.

The President began his speech:

"Yesterday, December 7, 1941, a date which will live in infamy, the United States of America was suddenly and deliberately attacked by naval and air forces of the Empire of Japan . . ."

2

Washington at War

The impact of the attack on Pearl Harbor was almost as dramatic on Washington as it was on Honolulu. As Bryson Rash says of the nation's capital: On December 6, "you seldom, if ever, saw a uniform on the street. By the evening of December 7, there were uniforms all over the place."

President Franklin D. Roosevelt, the man who had put the nation on the road to economic recovery in 1939, quickly became the nation's wartime leader, our commander-in-chief. And with FDR providing the words and inspiration, almost overnight Washington was transformed from a sleepy little southern town, as more than one person I talked to described it, into the capital of a free world. With Paris burning, London under siege, and Moscow threatened with a Nazi invasion, the people of the Allied nations instinctively looked to Washington—invulnerable from land, sea, and air attacks—as the center of Allied resistance.

For Americans, Washington became the focal point of everything that went on in the nation. Washington regulated prices; allocated scarce commodities; rationed gasoline, tires, sugar, shoes, meat; organized a nationwide system of civil defense and blackouts; awarded defense contracts; told the farmers what they could and could not plant and industry what it could and could not produce. And the War Department, soon to be housed in its huge pentagon-shaped headquarters across the Potomac in Virginia, recruited the nation's young men and women, and drafted as many additional men as it needed to build an army, navy, and air force that would turn back the enemy in Europe and the Pacific. At the same time, Washington became the communications center of the nation. The Office of War Information, assisted by the nation's newspapers, magazines, and radio networks, kept the nation informed of the latest war news as well as of the stream of regulations and orders pouring out of Washington.

To arouse this great sleeping giant of America, and transform it into the most devastating war machine in the world, Washington needed people—and they came to town by the thousands. One of them, Smith Johnson, who had to close his small rubber plant in Ohio immediately after Pearl Harbor, tells how he decided to come to Washington: "I went out to lunch with a fellow in Cleveland—this was about December 20th—and he said, 'Let's have our tea leaves read.' I said I never thought that tea leaves were anything to go by but that I would. The lady came over and looked in the cup and said to me, 'Well, you're going to make a big change.' I said, 'What's that?' and she said, 'You're going away and work at another job. You're going to work in Washington.' I said, 'Who, me? In Washington? When's all this going to happen?' She said, 'On the 13th of January.'

"I didn't really think of going to Washington, but after a while I began to think, well, why not? So on the twelfth day of January—which was no preconceived plan, I didn't even think about it until quite a while afterwards—I packed my grip, got on the train, and went to Washington, knowing nothing about it at all. I had heard there was a rubber office there, so I went up there that morning and told them my name was Johnson and that I was president of Johnson Rubber Company in Middlefield, Ohio. This fellow said, 'What do you want?' 'Well, nothing,' I said. 'I just came down to help you win the war.' He said, 'Who sent for you?' I said, 'Nobody. I just came down. I know you're going to need help.' He said, 'Wait a minute.' He went back and talked with the boss and they came out and we had a talk and, would you believe it, twenty minutes later I was on the payroll.''

In different ways, thousands of Americans shared Mr. Johnson's experience, and in the following pages a few of them recall what it was like to work in Washington during World War II.

Stephen Ailes came up from Martinsburg, West Virginia, to work for the Office of Price Administration. He still lives in Washington today—as president of the American Railroad Association.

The city then was full of a lot of people running around not sure what they were doing. Although a lifelong Democrat, I had been quite disillusioned with FDR's ability to run anything, and I was terribly concerned about how the government was going to get organized to fight the war. However, when I went to work in OPA, I was overcome by the enthusiasm, the dedication, of everybody in that place. Working in a war agency was a hell of an experience. You just routinely worked till midnight; you worked Saturdays. You always had in mind the fact that all these guys were in foxholes someplace or sitting out on some cold deck somewhere. All of us had relatives and pals doing that, and the result was that the amount of effort you put out to do a good job in these war agencies was incredible. I was in OPA for four and a half years, and I remember thinking, I'll never again work in a situation quite like this where there's so damn much enthusiasm and so much cooperation, so little rivalry. Everybody just had to get the job done.

I suppose I was as well educated as most people around, but the word *inflation* was literally not in my vocabulary. The idea that you could have a spiral up and a spiral down was something that was lost on me. But early on, you began to understand what the hell was going on there and that OPA did a hell of a job. But you know, at OPA we were trying to hold the line, and we thought a point-one increase in prices was a disaster. You take a look at the four or five years that OPA control remained in effect: I bet the total increase in the cost-of-living index isn't over 2 or 3 percent. A remarkable job. It had a lot of concomitant bad results, you understand.

I was in the end of the business where we were writing the

regulations. OPA was also in the rationing business, and then we had an enforcement department. We had industry people working with us, and they fell into two categories. There were people who understood what the hell this was all about and believed very strongly that it would be bad if the price level went way up in the country; there were a lot of guys overseas whose families were going to be in great hardship because of the nature of the allotment. Don't forget, that soldier, in '42, made something like thirty-one dollars a month. A lot of people understood that. But you still had a lot of boneheads who said: "I've got a right to raise my price. One of the rights of the private enterprise system is to set the prices on your product. The government shouldn't be interfering with that." You have to tell people like that that they just don't get the point.

You also ran into some chiselers but not a great many. Interestingly enough, if you have an enforcement department which will go after the chiselers, the remaining 95 percent of the people will comply. The one thing that loses compliance altogether is the notion that you're making a sucker out of a guy, that he's complying but the guy down the street is not. But if you say, "You have an obligation to comply, and we're enforcing that obligation," then the guy will do it, and you get damn good compliance.

I'd say that one of the startling things for me was that it was the first time I'd ever worked with blacks. When you came here in '42, there were black secretaries. And I'll never forget, a fellow called me up—a lawyer—and asked me if I'd come up and explain to him some part of one of our regulations. I went up, opened the door, and walked in his office, and I'm sure I must have looked just as startled as I could be to find a black sitting behind the table. I never even thought about there being a black lawyer. This fellow was a professor at Howard, extremely able. This was just a totally new experience.

Al Sweeney was from Cleveland, Ohio. He served in the navy three months in 1941, until he contracted pneumonia and was discharged.

I had graduated from Wilberforce University in Ohio—they call it Central State University now—before I went into the service. Right after I got discharged, I was given a TR, or whatever they called it, for a Pullman back to Cleveland, on the old C&O Railroad. When I got down there, they wouldn't give me a Pullman. So I got angry, tore that TR up, and caught a Greyhound bus to Washington. In those days, you know, there was discrimination. I always wanted to come to the nation's capital, so I came to Washington.

I got a room at the Twelfth Street YMCA in Washington, where I stayed for several years. And the first job I had was as a building guard at the Department of Commerce. Then, after about two or three weeks, I got a job with the General Accounting Office as a clerk. In those days they called a civil service grade CAF; I guess I was CAF-2, made about $1,440 a year. I stayed there about a year and went over to the Office of Price Administration, first as a clerk, and then got involved with several of the black employees who felt they were being underutilized. They were college graduates too. At that time, the OPA, under Leon Henderson, was a pretty progressive agency, probably way ahead of its time, as far as equal or fair employment practices were concerned. Finally they hired me as a junior economist. In those days they called it P-1 grade.

As I recall, it was the first time blacks in government got really top jobs. The head of sugar rationing was a fellow by the name of Charles Quick, a lawyer. Robert Ming became the interstate-commerce commissioner. He was a big attorney in the Office of Price Administration. It was probably the most liberal agency that came along to this day.

Several of us blacks made a breakthrough because of OPA. We got professional experience there. I remember a fellow named Louis Welters, in personnel, who later became personnel officer in one of the large agencies. But he would not have gotten that experience without the opportunities at OPA. Right after the war they sent me over to the International Monetary Fund. That was about the only place we could go, but they wouldn't hire me.

For Tom Page, a young man in his mid-twenties, working in Washington during the war was a heady experience.

I went to work shortly after I was married, which was on December 8, 1942, for an agency called the Board of Economic Warfare—partly because I liked the guy I was going to work for, W. Park Armstrong. Then I discovered the guy I liked so much had gone somewhere else! A typical government story. So for a couple of years I was engaged in a lot of things, like collecting information about enemy countries to be used as target information. For example, where in the German aircraft production line do you bomb to achieve a certain effect? Would you bomb airframe factories or would you bomb the people who made the motors or would you bomb the aluminum plants? At that time, we were mainly after things like aluminum plants. In later years we turned to things like ball bearings. I remember seeing a document of our British counterpart in our files. It laid out basically the whole bombing programs of the British government for the next year and a half. I was amazed that you could find this while wandering around in somebody's files. Almost anyone could see the damned thing; we all had security clearance, but it didn't mean much.

During the war years our interests were identical with those of the Soviet Union. And our agency had a whole apartment building at 2501 Q Street loaded with refugees, interesting people—a Babel of languages, a wealth of information, and a lot of them had come out of very liberal backgrounds. When the war in Europe was drawing to its close, the interests of the Soviet Union started to go in different directions. I had an idea that the industrialization of Japan had been done by three nations, the U.S., England, and Germany, which had built most of the major factories in Japan. This information was very useful for the purpose of bombing targets, and my idea was to get hold of what had been done in Germany to round out our picture. So we put together a whole team of people, and we ran around the United States and England asking everybody who had worked in Japan where to go in Germany to find what we wanted to know about Japan. We would go to people and say, "Who are your German counterparts? Who represented German engineering firms in Japan? Who represented Krupp for gun manufacture, steel companies? All of the companies, where were they? Who were the people?"

By 1944 the war had moved into occupational phases—they were landing and driving tanks through the valleys—and economic warfare faded out in significance.

I was going to go back to California, but a friend who lived here said, "Oh, don't do that. I know a guy who would love to have you. He worked for a thing called Office of War Mobilization and Reconversion for a general named Lucius Clay, and Justice James Byrnes." I asked someone who Clay was, and he came back a day later and said he was probably the most powerful man in Washington.

Planning for blackouts was a fascinating exercise. I think General Clay or somebody felt that the United States was sitting up singing and dancing all night. Goddamn it, they ought to get next to the war effort. No more of this fancy civilian living. So we would have blackouts. This would curb the Sodom and Gomorrah aspects while everybody was being frozen to death in Europe. Everything was supposed to close—places of entertainment and public assembly—at midnight, every night, effective almost immediately! ... The thing was comic. There were two old ladies who had chili parlors in Washington with an all-night trade, and they refused to close. Byrnes wrote them a letter on White House stationery saying that the national war effort required that they comply with the law and close. And the old ladies wrote back in their scribble that they didn't use much power and they made very good chili and they weren't going to close. It all got in the paper, but we never could get it to the lawyers.

The whole country started questioning the point of this blackout. Arbitrary bureaucracy! It became a helluva hot potato.

And then suddenly Mayor LaGuardia, under pressure from New York nightlife industry, announced that nightlife was a special part of the economic life of New York, and they were going to stay open until three o'clock, or whatever.

Overnight this stream of fire hoses that the press had played on us just swung and played on New York. The rest of the United States then said: "New York may be unpatriotic, but we're not. We're going to do our part for the boys overseas. It's disgraceful that New York cannot see its way to do the same."

Meanwhile, we all were trying to figure out how the hell to get out of the blackout mess. This took the heat off for the moment, and then spring may have come, or something happened in a matter of weeks, and we said, "The coal shortage is now ended, and we are happy to announce we can eliminate the blackout.''

Life in Washington was kind of interesting during the war. Generals were big out in the country. One star—a brigadier general—was a big man. But in Washington I remember riding in a bus, hanging on a strap, right next to a guy with one star. They were nothing much. You needed at least two or three stars to make an impression. Lot of brass.

I think you always felt sort of guilty being out of uniform. I had a theory that everybody overseas really would like to be back in the United States living it up. And everybody in the United States felt guilty about being in the United States and thought they ought to be overseas. So nobody, in that sense, was happy.

Alice Newcomer found herself immersed in the war effort immediately after graduating from George Washington University.

I graduated in 1943 and went to work for the Lend-Lease Program as an economic analyst. It was a very small organization, only four or five hundred employees, and yet they handled billions of dollars worth of war materials. It really was the agency which established the orderly economic way of supplying war materials to our allies. The atmosphere at Lend-Lease was great because you felt you were doing something that was worth doing. It was pretty heady for someone who was twenty-one years old.

I worked in a section called Reverse Lend-Lease. We were responsible for encouraging assistance to the United States from our allies to the extent that this could be given without involving foreign currency. The problem was not what they could do; the problem, especially for the British, was how many dollars they had. For example, if bases were built for the Americans in Britain, and British workmen were used to construct the base, the British paid the workmen and the cost was entered as reverse lend-lease, a war contribution from Britain to the United States. Obviously, it couldn't even out financially, but that was not the idea. It was to even out with "equality of sacrifice."

There was never any question of our supplying planes, ammunition, all those materials. That obviously was sent as lend-lease. But when we got into things we called "essential civilian supplies"—foodstuffs and related materials—to what extent should we supply these to the British population on lend-lease, and where do we draw the line? I remember there were endless memoranda about toilet paper, whether it was an essential civilian supply which the government should finance or whether the British should pay for the toilet paper that we sent. I don't remember how that one came out. But those things just went on endlessly.

Sherman Briscoe was working in the Department of Agriculture as the only black out of more than 490 information specialists.

When I went to work for the Department of Agriculture in 1941, they brought in five or six of us at that time. In the civil service regulations then there were very strict requirements for coming in. For example, in the newspaper field, one who came in as an information specialist would have to have written in a specialized field for at least a year. This doesn't mean sports or society or something; this means writing in the field of agricultural production or economic affairs or some specialized field like financing or finances. Well, you don't have this on black newspapers. So no one would ever have qualified to come in under this rule. They relaxed the rule for about a year, and then they were going to go back to the old system and make it very difficult for anyone to come in without these qualifications. The Roosevelt administration had been convinced that it ought to bring in some blacks, so all of us came in at the same time, in June 1941, because the law would be changed on July 1.

I was hired specifically to serve black newspapers, to get them the kind of information they could use about the programs and activities of the Department of Agriculture. I worked there twenty-seven years. I could have been promoted out of this job and into programs serving everybody, working across the board, as they called it. But I refused to do that because there was something like 490 working in information in the department, and there was just one serving the black press. And I didn't want to move out of there.

The black press deals in personalities rather than subject matter. It deals with a black person in relation to the subject matter. In order to bring the program of the Department of Agriculture to life, I would visit farm families all across the South and Michigan and Ohio, and I would interview these farmers to find out what help they had been able to get from the Department of Agriculture and how they had utilized this help. We'd take pictures of the people, prepare a story, and send it out to the black press. They were very widely used. They had never had anything like this before.

Ray Madden [D-Ind.] came to Washington in 1943 and served in the Congress for thirty-three years.

When I came to Washington, there was far more activity than there was in Gary or Indianapolis or any other Indiana town, although we had three major steel plants in Gary and they were humming to provide steel for the war effort. I was on the Naval Affairs Committee. Carl Vinson was the chairman; Lyndon Johnson was a hillbilly rookie from Texas and nobody paid much attention to him. Carl Vinson put me on a subcommittee to go to Honolulu to hold hearings on defense housing in March of 1945. He said there were thousands of mechanics, engineers and electricians, and bricklayers, carpenters, over at Pearl Harbor preparing those ships and they couldn't get any place to live. So we went over and held hearings for about two weeks, and found out that the Chamber of Commerce, the fruit people, the pineapple people, and the army and the navy were all feuding with one another about where they were going to build defense housing and that was what was holding it up. So we went out and designated the land and wired back that we had gotten a location and everything was all set to go. And two months after we got back around 250 defense houses were built for families to move into.

In 1941, "the media" usually meant radio. One of NBC's, and later ABC's, men in Washington was Bryson Rash.

There was only voluntary censorship, and immediately after Pearl Harbor we became very conscious of what we were doing—too much so, perhaps, because we had no firm guide-lines yet. But they were quickly set up for voluntary censor-ship, and there were few breaches of this procedure—only two or three incidents throughout the entire war when the media breached the voluntary censorship. Of course, the biggest one was the report of the breaking of the Japanese code after the Battle of Midway. After guidelines were set up, it was a simple operation. We felt little constraint—we didn't report troop movements or ship movements, and we didn't do weather fore-casts on the air, which was interesting. Had there been an enemy attack planned or executed, one of the vital things would be the weather.

What I did, and others in the other networks did, was to help act as liaison between the networks and the government. The government could go to an individual in a network and say, "We need this"—things like recruiting, information on food rationing, scrap metal, and all the other programs that existed during wartime.

I did the broadcasts out of the White House when the pres-ident went on the air, or when the secretary of state went on the air, which was rare. Most of the traveling I did was under government auspices with the president. We always left here in secret with the president. We'd be told by the White House, say in the morning, that the president would leave that evening. Frequently, you wouldn't be told where he was going, and you didn't know how to pack, whether for cold or warm. Usually it was someplace like Hyde Park or Warm Springs. They'd tell you you were going to leave town at six o'clock and to be at home at five, packed. The phone would ring, and they'd say, "We'll meet you at such and such a place." Sometimes it was the White House garage on M Street; sometimes it was the Bureau of Printing and Engraving; odd, obscure kinds of places, not necessarily the White House. Then the army would come along with the secret service and take all your luggage, and you'd get into automobiles or a bus and go to a railroad train. It would be parked out on the line somewhere, not nec-essarily a station. All the shades were drawn, of course, and you'd start moving. Then you'd get someplace else, and you'd stop, and the president's car, with him aboard, would be put on, and you would take off.

On trips to Hyde Park, I don't know what the routing was,

but it was a circuitous one so you wouldn't get too near a coastline. You also had an engine running ahead of you and an engine behind you so that if you had a problem, the engine and maybe a car running ahead of the president would take the flak, if there was any.

Many times we took our vacation at home. Traveling was crowded and hard to get. Air travel was not very easy in those days. Practically all the aircraft manufacturing facilities were devoted to the war effort. You didn't have an airlines transportation system like you have now, and the military had priority. As a matter of fact, where the Pentagon is now was the airport for Washington before the war. The old Hoover Airport was the darndest thing you've ever seen, because it had a major highway running through the middle of it. They had a big traffic light, and when a plane was going to take off or land, they'd turn on the red lights to stop the traffic.

Hilda O'Brien, just out of Columbia University Graduate School, came down to work in the war effort.

I was first hired by the Justice Department in a section that really had to do with foreign agents who were registered in the States . . . . Right after that I received a call from the Office of Censorship and went there to be interviewed by Colonel Shaw, who was head of the special section they were just setting up. He sold me on the glamour of this work and how they really felt that my background was just what they wanted. So I went to work there. I felt very much involved in the war, because our little section was really a counterespionage section. We did basic research on any suspected espionage that might show up through the watch on the mail. This mail was picked up in offices all over the country, and anything suspicious would come into Washington for further analysis. There were some cases that developed out of finding a microdot on a piece of mail. It was a tiny little bit of film, no bigger than a period on an envelope or on a letter. And stuck onto the period would be this tiny little dot of film, which, when blown up, would reveal some code or something of that sort.

Another very interesting thing was the use of open code, which is extremely hard to find and requires people who have a keen knowledge of the idiom in a language. For instance, in our section we had people who knew French very well and Spanish and other foreign languages and would be able to recognize in the letter where the language was strained. It would be recognized that "Aunt Louise had pneumonia last week" would mean something else. The language would be forced a little bit to get across the message. Open code is difficult to detect because it's not like a cryptogram, which is mathematically set up and can be analyzed much more easily.

One of the things I did in Washington was to volunteer in a service center near Union Station. I worked every Sunday morning from eight to twelve. There, of course, we were right in the heart of the problem of servicemen going in and out, and their wives and children—particularly the wounded men coming out of Walter Reed or Bethesda who had been very badly injured, amputees. Many times this would be their first weekend out or first night or day out from the hospital. That brought us very close to the war. We got to know them well.

Frank Waldrop was managing editor of the Washington Times Herald, *owned by Cissie Patterson, daughter of Robert McCormack, who owned the* Chicago Tribune *and was a bitter opponent of Franklin Roosevelt and the New Deal. The* Times Herald *and Patterson also opposed Roosevelt.*

I don't think I actually expected an attack on the city of Washington by a military force, but in those days, anybody who didn't expect the Germans to do anything they could to make life difficult for us was an idiot. There used to be a great deal of sardonic wit about which city was the more important target. Birmingham was pretty sure that Hitler had it number one on the list because it was a steel-making town, and since steel is the base of war, naturally Birmingham was more important than any other city in the country, and it was going to be bombed first. Atlanta's position was "What the hell are you hicks talking about? Atlanta is a great rail transportation crossroads of the Southeast, and if you take out Atlanta, no trains can run." So obviously they were going to take out Atlanta.

But when you'd look out the window, you'd see that the only rail link on the East Coast crosses the Potomac River from Alexandria right into southeast Washington. Now, where in the hell are you going to run a train from all the troop-training stations—all through, Southeast? The army was all stationed south of the Potomac, and there's that damned one bridge to come over. Alexandria figured it was going to get it first, but the troops were hung on that bridge, just like blackbirds. It was under twenty-four-hour guard. Not only did they have that under guard, but they had a standby—an engineer's pontoon bridge downstream. So Washington was quite visibly prepared for the possibility of genuine military assault of some kind.

It was difficult getting out the paper. And we had an extra problem. We had to maintain protection from the sabotage of patriots. There were guys who were certain that Hitler was running the paper and that Tojo was downstairs setting type. We weren't supporting the war, we were supporting the country. We didn't believe that the United States should have been put in the position we were in—of being confronted with a war on two fronts—and we never hesitated to say so. But that's a far cry from attacking the troops, you see, and attacking the whole war effort, whatever that means. We had to win the war. We never had any difficulty on that front.

We had the same problems as everyone else as far as the loss of people to the military. But we also had the problems of people on the paper who had been uncomfortable—even before the war started—because our policy was not sympathetic to Roosevelt and his program. There were people who had scruples of all kinds about the war, and they were perfectly legitimate, and it was natural that there would be such things. They took it very hard that we were not properly worshipful toward the administration, even in peacetime. It would reach a point from time to time that they couldn't stand it any longer, and they'd leave.

Cornelius Pitts was an eighteen-year-old boy, from a family of eleven children, living in New Orleans when the war began. He came to Washington to work in the government during the war.

My first job was as clerk-typist in the quartermaster general's office out at the Army War College. I was there roughly about a year and then transferred to the Pentagon in 1943, to the Ordnance Department.

I felt I was making a contribution to the war effort and was very glad to be a civilian. I didn't have any philosophical reason for not wanting to go in the army, but I felt it was rather risky and dangerous. I also wanted to be around to help my parents. I had two brothers in the navy and one in the army, so I felt that three out of my immediate family was sufficient. They didn't have to take the whole family.

I made quite a name for myself in the Mail and Records Section of the Ordnance Department. I was considered a speed demon on the typewriter—over one hundred words a minute—so they decided they'd give me a little better job. I was soon transferred to the Charts Section, doing statistical typing.

At the Pentagon most of the blacks were assigned to the mail and records sections. Seemed like in almost all the agencies the blacks were concentrated in those sections, and they had low-paid black supervisors who would really drive the workers all day long. That's why I enjoyed the transfer to the Charts Section, because I moved into a white section, and of course it was entirely different. Nobody pushed you, nobody rushed you. You just did your work. I knew I was a good worker, and I think they really respected me for my ability. I stayed there through the war. My highest pay was $1,620 a year.

I was so anxious to avoid going into service that I talked to some fellows in New Orleans while I was classified 1-A here. I was getting ready to be called for my examination, and the fellows told me that in New Orleans they were turning down blacks for the least of things. So I went back home for a little while, just so I could get called by the New Orleans draft board. The examination officer asked me if I had any physical defects that I knew of. I said, "Well, my feet are always giving me trouble, these fallen arches I have, I just can't stand on them." He just took my word; he looked at my feet and rejected me on the basis of what I told him. In the South, in New Orleans, the whites thought it was a big honor to serve the country, all that sort of thing. They didn't feel that the blacks really had a stake in it. So if they had any reason to turn you down, they'd turn you down.

R. W. Danischefsky spent the first year and a half of the war working in Detroit for the Reconstruction Finance Corpora-

tion, then was transferred back to wartime Washington, which was an exhausting, but exhilarating, experience. He is an industrial engineer.

I moved into Washington as regional engineer, and then after about another year I became what they called the principal engineer, in charge of all field operations. You see, just before the war and immediately after the outbreak of the war Detroit had the bulk of the defense-plant program. A lot of the procedures and methods that we started in Detroit later became standard, and so my being transferred to Washington was primarily an effort to unify the operations all over the country.

At that time Washington was very interesting. There seemed to be a universal feeling of doing something for the government—much different from what we ran into in the Vietnam situation. It was amazing to me the spirit and the willingness of everybody to do something—work odd hours, work nights, change their schedules, or work overtime. From the day that the hostilities broke out until Labor Day of 1945 I didn't take a day off, including weekends. It wasn't unusual—seven-day weeks. We had to; we were so far behind in purchase orders. The rest of it was in travel, and no one bothered about overtime. I think the shortest day I put in in all that time was probably twelve hours.

Mostly what I did in Washington was apply some of the Detroit know-how that we had developed out there into the other outlying regions. In the Ford setup, which probably had more subcontractors than anybody, a machine tool would be bought and delivered to, say, the River Rouge plant in Detroit. It would be there for a couple of months, and then that machine tool might be sent to a plant in Tulsa, Oklahoma. A machine tool of a special nature might move around four or five times. It was extremely difficult to maintain records of both the location and condition of that tool, so it became necessary to set up what we called asset property records for these leased tools.

Ultimately we realized that this equipment would become surplus, and we'd have to sell it or store it or do something with it, so we had to know what we had and where it was. It was amazing to me how many of the industries after the war adopted the program that we had established for maintaining records of the machine tools.

Kay Halle, a young radio broadcaster from Cleveland, worked for General Wild Bill Donovan at the Office of Strategic Services.

One's training period at OSS was like the best telescoped college education. General Donovan had assembled so many top experts in so many fields and he was smart enough first to learn the rudiments of intelligence gathering from the British. I was assigned to a branch called Morale Operations—MO—whose chief concern was to destroy the enemy's will to fight.

Most of the operations still remain secret. I did exact a note from General Donovan before I left the agency, as we called it, which he signed, giving me the authority to refuse for publication any interviews revealing specific MO wartime activities.

Everyone I saw and worked with at headquarters felt a strong sense of mission—a fire in the belly—and enjoyed working at concert pitch.

There was fun, too. I became known in our branch of Morale Operations as Mata Halle, after one of our graphic artists surreptitiously transposed the letters of my name on my wooden desk marker. For days I was puzzled at the smiles it inspired because I had not faced that side of my desk. Then one day a grinning Douglas Fairbanks, Jr., who had come in for a briefing, picked up the marker and turned it around for me to see.

Washington was then a quiet southern town. It was within human proportions then. But the war was a transition period for Washington. In the bringing together of our allies during the war, whose leaders worked here and came to know our city better, Washington seemed to grow from a bureaucratic conglomerate to the powerful world capital it is today.

Connie and Ed Stuntz were living in Wellington Villa, a "suburban commune," as Stuntz calls it, halfway between Washington and Mount Vernon, Virginia. Connie worked for the Red Cross and the United Nations Information Office. He had been a reporter for the Associated Press, and although he was not in good physical shape, he knew he had to get in the war effort somehow.

ED: I had tried to enlist before Pearl Harbor. As I told a friend of mine on AP, "We're either going to become the biggest military force in the world or we're not going to survive. I want to get in and get a commission. I don't want to have to be a foot soldier or anything." I was too old, even then, to be drafted, and this was just before the draft.

In June 1942, I went into the State Department—in [Nelson] Rockefeller's Office of Inter-American Affairs, the forerunner of the Office of War Information. Among other things, we put out a radio news report to Latin American radio stations.

I was put on as the day news editor, to sort of tailor the report that went out and check with the Spanish translators. I had a policy laid down for me not to cover up our losses, to let them know the truth. We had a lot of eager beavers in there, and I had to watch several people very carefully for fear they might minimize the Russian losses and overplay the German atrocities. I knew perfectly well that if we started talking about the German atrocities, we wouldn't get anywhere with the Latin Americans, because they knew damned well that we were committing just as many atrocities as the Germans. I mean, you can't put men in war out there without there being atrocities.

They wanted to minimize our losses in the Pacific, but my theory was that you'd never get any sympathy from Latin America by claiming victory all the time, or supremacy, because they didn't like our supremacy anyhow.

In Washington they ran the gamut from complete lethargy to what you might call a silly acceptance of the necessity of war. Then you had the flag wavers and the chest thumpers, who said, "We'll go over there with a division or two, we'll clean them up like we did in World War I," which we didn't.

We shipped our children off to Cuba because it had gotten to be impossible to find a place to live in Washington with four children. They had two sets of grandparents in Cuba, and we figured they'd be just as safe there as in Washington and a lot more comfortable. Washington was getting to the point where you had to queue up maybe a block or two before you got to the drugstore to buy a pack of cigarettes.

CONNIE: We were able to get along very nicely with our rations, but there was a lot of black market. I remember the wife of one of the AP correspondents who was very proud of herself because she had what she considered prominent friends. When he came home, she gave a big dinner for his return. Everybody at the table had a beautiful Delmonico steak—there were about twelve of us—and he said to his wife over the table, "Good heavens! You must have given up all the ration points we have for a month of Sundays." She said, "I got it on the black market," and he said, "If you got it on the black market, I am not going to eat it." And he picked up and left. Several of the guests got up and left too.

In April of 1942 I walked into the Red Cross and told them that translation was my forte, Spanish, Italian, and French— and I went to work right away on the search for lost people.

I remember once having a call from a senator's secretary who said that the senator wanted to get in touch with somebody they thought was in Saint Thomas, the big concentration camp in the Philippines. I said that we had no lists. And she said, "Well, what are you doing over there? Why don't you have any lists?" I said, "Lady, we are losing this war, or don't you know that? They have two hundred thousand of our people, and we don't have eighteen of theirs." The attitude in Washington was they just couldn't believe we were losing the war.

I had been with the Red Cross for ten days when they put twenty-five thousand messages from all over Europe on my desk and said to sort them out according to languages. I told them that I spoke Spanish, Italian, and French, and none of those messages were in those languages. They said, "Well, make a try at it." So I sat down and called every legation and consular service in town and said. "What is the outstanding characteristic of your language?" I remember the Bulgarians said that if it looked like French and wasn't, it's ours. The Hungarians said that if every third word ends in *unk*, it's Hungarian. I distributed those messages by the rules they had given me.

ED: The spirit in Washington after 1943 was beginning to be "Well, all we have to do is to just keep in there." One of the great sayings of the time was "Don't forget there's a war on." If you went out to dinner with some friends, someone would say, "Well, I can't stay long, you know, there's a war on"—that sort of thing. Nobody challenged that; those who weren't doing much and didn't feel very close to it were seeking ways to get involved.

During the war I was very restive about being kept in Washington, what I called the Battle of the Potomac. In our office whenever one of our younger people would go and sign up in the marines or the infantry or the air corps, we'd say. "Coward. You can't take it here." Because we were working fourteen, sixteen, eighteen hours a day and on call most of the time, never knowing when everything might collapse around us, and these guys went off and had good company command—we envied them very much.

Then there was the flak you would get for not being in uniform—not from the servicemen but from civilians, girls. "There goes a 4-F. Look at him, he's young enough to be in uniform." The servicemen did not do that. I think there were some occasions when they would see a civilian living it up and say, "Well, buddy, you're having a hell of a good war, aren't you?" and that sort of thing. But not too much in Washington, because the servicemen either came back from duty or were about to go out on duty and were all scared to death anyhow, and they realized that if you weren't in the war, you probably had a pretty good reason.

Merlo Pusey was an editorial writer for the Washington Post, *later a biographer of Charles Evans Hughes and* Post *publisher Eugene Meyer, as well as author of, appropriately,* The Way We Go to War.

The *Post* was in the forefront of the campaign to get us quickly into the war mood. And the four years during the war was the most interesting period since I've been in journalism. My recollection is that we worked a six-day week; in those days, I usually worked on Sundays and had a day off during the week—when I usually went home and worked on my book.

Herbert Elliston was the editor, and Alexander Casey Jones was the managing editor, a very dynamic character. We supported Roosevelt most of the time during the war. The most interesting interview I attended during this period was immediately after Pearl Harbor. Within a day or two after Pearl Harbor, Churchill popped over here by air and suddenly turned up. Not a word was said about it, but it was whispered about that Churchill was in town, and surmising that he would probably be at the press conference, I made a special point of being at the White House press conference the next day. Sure enough, he was there, and after a few preliminary questions to FDR, he turned the forum over to Churchill for questions. Everybody wanted to know everything that Churchill could tell us about the war and how it was going. He was a short man, and as soon as he started to speak, the people in the back cried out, "We can't see him. We can't see him." So he got up on a chair and answered questions from there, and he was a marvelous character. I've never met a man who had quite the sparkle and vigor, and the profound flow of information that came out of that man was amazing. It was just a marvelous experience to listen to him.

Eugene Meyer, who was the publisher of the *Post* in those days, was a great admirer of Henry Kaiser, who had turned to mass production of ships as soon as we got into war, realizing that the war was likely going to be won or lost by shipping. So when Meyer heard Kaiser was coming to Washington, he invited him over to the *Post* for lunch. Kaiser came in, and after the pleasantries were exchanged, Meyer said, "Well, what brings you to Washington, Mr Kaiser?" He said, "Well, I have an idea. I'm trying to sell the government on the construction of some baby aircraft carriers because it takes two or three years to build a big carrier, and these things can be produced in a matter of months. While they don't have big armor and all that, they're small ships, and we can turn them out in relatively fast order, and the ship I have in mind would carry fifty planes, and it could ferry planes to any part of the world where they're needed, very fast, and I think it would be a great aid in continuing the war and winning it."

Meyer asked him what he'd done about it, and he said he had an appointment that afternoon with a navy committee. But he called Meyer within an hour after lunch and said he'd already been over to the Navy Department and they'd given him eighteen minutes and turned him down. Meyer was distressed, and Kaiser was terribly upset. Meyer said, "Well, stick around for a couple of days." Kaiser had said, "I'm licked. I'm going home. I'm catching the afternoon train to California." Meyer said, "Oh, stick around for a couple of days, and let's see what can be done." So Meyer got ahold of Wayne Coy, who was a White House aide at the time, told Coy about it and then he pulled some other strings, and Kaiser got busy and pulled some strings and got an appointment at the White House. He laid the idea before the president, and before Kaiser left, he had an order for building fifty of those carriers, and then he began turning them out about one a week.

Meyer did a lot of things at that time of that sort, in which we all were involved in a way. He put on a show called "Back the Attack," which was a tremendous display of armament on the Monument Grounds. He got the army to put this on—it was in connection with one of the bond drives. His idea was to let the country know what the country is turning out to support our boys abroad, and they put on a magnificent show, which got a big press.

There was one very important contribution that the *Post* made, and I was only incidentally involved in it. Near the end of the war the government had developed this unconditional-surrender formula, and they were going to smash the enemy governments completely, as they did with the government in Germany. But after the collapse in Germany, unconditional surrender became an awfully big hurdle to get over in Japan, because the Japanese interpreted this as meaning that they'd sweep out the emperor and he'd never be permitted to come back again. And since the emperor was tied in with their religion and national feeling and Shintoism, they were not willing to surrender. There were a good many estimates that it was going to take so many hundred thousand lives to force unconditional surrender on the Japanese and that we would have to invade the islands directly at a tremendous cost in American lives. This bothered us, and we spent a lot of time worrying about it over at the *Post* and thinking about it and what could be done and began to write a series of editorials questioning the unconditional formula. We thought the government ought to spell out precisely what Japan would have to do, and if we spelled it out precisely, not necessarily sacrificing their emperor, we'd make much more progress and end the war that much sooner with less loss of life. There were a lot of editorials to that effect, largely written by Elliston. At the same time, Admiral Zacharias was quietly working in the navy to the same end, trying to convince the Japanese that unconditional surrender didn't mean what it seemed to mean. We didn't think that that was enough; we thought the government ought to spell out what they had to do precisely. Truman finally did that at Potsdam, and we were delighted to have him do that, and then the Japanese did come along and surrender. No invasion of the mainland was necessary, and obviously a tremendous saving of life resulted. Of course, the bomb played a big part. But after the war the navy gave us credit for helping to convince the Japanese that they could get by without giving up their emperor system and finally inducing the president to do the spelling out he did at Potsdam.

Marquis Childs, syndicated columnist:

I was a Washington correspondent for the *St. Louis Post-Dispatch*. The change in wartime Washington occurred so rapidly. It was a change of pace and mood, above everything else—an acceleration. As usual, Roosevelt was right at the center of it. There was the famous time when he presented the Iron Cross to *New York Daily News* correspondent John O'Donnell—I don't remember the date, but it was after the war had begun, I think—for his continuing isolationist, anti-Roosevelt activity. I don't know whether you could go so far as to say pro-Nazi, because he probably was not, but he was very isolationist and anti-Roosevelt and faulted our military people for having allowed Pearl Harbor to happen. That group had a powerful appeal to a helluva lot of Americans, who believed that Roosevelt was bent on an intrigue to get us into the war.

Lindbergh came back from that trip to Germany and talked about how the German air force was invincible. You remember the outcry, and perhaps the thing that fed this very feeling was Roosevelt's statement that we could produce fifty thousand airplanes a year. And, of course, soon after Pearl Harbor we started out to do just that.

I wouldn't say Washington was exhilarating. It was a time, in the first place, when most newspapermen wanted to get overseas. The ones who were really smart got into the liaison field—got into China, into Chungking. But a lot of us were in

Europe, in and out. I was in South America for a while, but that was not in the heart of it. When my draft number came up, I was too old. I suppose I could have had a commission, but I didn't have any great urge. I guess I felt I was contributing to the war effort. I don't know that it was true. It was sort of a rationale.

Smith Johnson, a rubber manufacturer from Ohio, could not wait to get involved in the war effort, and by January 13, 1942, he was working for the Rubber Division of the War Production Board.

In a very few days I discovered that there were seventy people in the Rubber Division and not one rubber man. There were nickel, steel, leather men, and no wonder they were glad to see me. I was first put on an allocation board with five fellows, and none of them knew anything about rubber—their job was to decide who could use reclaimed rubber for articles—so they more or less left it up to me to decide whether the thing was necessary or not. We had everything you could think of. I remember one request for rubber pads for rams out in Wyoming, so they wouldn't kill each other when they were fighting.

Later I was put in charge of rehabilitation, the conversion of the industry to war. I was coordinator. They moved me into another office; I was in fifteen different offices before I got through the year and a half. One day my assistant brought in a pile of requests. I leafed through them, knowing the rubber business. Here was a rubber factory requested by a man whose company was owned by the deputy director of the WPB. He was the guy who was supposed to be enforcing the law, and he was breaking it completely, because on a factory you had to put in a facilities request, and he was putting through machinery requests to build a whole factory. My assistant said, "What'll we do about this?" And I said we shouldn't sign it because that's absolutely illegal, and he said, "But the deputy director is asking you. If I don't sign it, what am I going to do? I've got a wife and two children." He said he was going to lose his job if he didn't sign it. Finally I said, "Oh. I'll sign it. Give them the plant." So he got the plant, but it was completely illegal.

There was also one company that wanted to get rubber for tire patches, and, boy, they wined and dined me. They sent me a case of champagne and took us to Atlantic City—we spent a weekend there, and they footed all the expenses. But I didn't give them any extra rubber. There were so many times that people would give us cocktail parties, and we went and didn't even know why we were invited. I don't drink much of anything, but there was a lot of this going on. Nobody offered a cash bribe—just gifts, like a dozen pair of silk stockings when nobody could get them.

Most people were patriotic, except for these big companies. It appeared in Washington as though every company in the country was saying, "How much can we make out of this war and how little do we have to give for it?" The rubber companies, the steel companies—all of them—they were so selfish, it seemed to me.

Eventually Mr. Johnson left Washington and spent the rest of the war in Ohio making rubber for the war effort.

3

Industry at War

Except for Washington, the war had the greatest impact on the nation's industries. And they performed what has since been described as a "miracle of production." In 1942, American industry built 48,000 military aircraft; in 1943, 86,000, and more than 96,000 in 1944. During the war it also built 5,200 ships, and by the end of the war it was able to build a Liberty ship from stem to stern in forty-two days. In 1944 it produced 50 percent more munitions than the enemy nations and 45 percent of all the munitions produced by all the nations at war. Industry also increased its labor force 36 percent between 1940 and 1944 and the average work week from 37.7 to 46.6 hours.

Smith Johnson's small rubber company in Middlefield, Ohio, had made washing-machine and refrigerator gaskets, and he was ordered to cease all civilian production work. While working in Washington, he was lucky enough to land a war contract for his plant back in Ohio:

I didn't go to Washington to attempt to get business; I was honestly going to help them win the war. But it just happened that I met a fellow one day at a cocktail party—his name was

Burns. He was an engineer, a very nice elderly fellow. I told him about being in the rubber business and making certain things and thought no more of it. A month later I got a call from him asking me to come over to his office. He said, "I talked with you at that party, and you interested me because of your rubber experience and what you were doing in your plant. I'm putting ten ammunition companies in business making boxes for holding ammunition—.30 and .60 caliber. Every one of them is going to need a gasket. Can your company make it?" I told him I didn't know. But I phoned my uncle, who was looking after the business, and asked him if he could make this gasket. He said, "Well, sure. Try anything. We're not doing anything here." I told him to come down to Washington and we'd work it out. In about a month we were in production, and the business continued through the entire war. We made sixteen hundred dollars' worth of gaskets every day, which was pretty good for a little company. In fact it saved our existence, I guess, because it took time to get into these other things. We also had a molding company, and we got to making gaskets for B-29 bombers and shell gaskets and all sorts of things. Our employment went from nothing up to 850 in about a year and a half. But it got going from the fact that I was in Washington—no other reason. If I hadn't gone down there, I would never have got the business.

While I was in Washington, we had a fire in the plant, and I went home.

The fire didn't destroy the part that made the ammunition-box gaskets, but the other part was gone, the part making gaskets for B-29s. We decided to build a building because we wanted to continue to make these gaskets for the B-29s. We were one of three suppliers to the government.

So I made up plans for this facility and had to send it to Cleveland for the War Production Board, and from there it went to Washington. Remember, this was a 100-percent war plant—very essential. So one day the manager of the WPB in Cleveland came up, and I talked our plans over with him, and I thought we got along fine. Two days later I got a call from a friend of mine in Washington who said, "You know your plans for that building got turned down by the facility board in Cleveland." He said that I had better get the hell down there.

So I got on the train and went to see him. He said, "I don't know where your request is, but it's probably over at the Facility Bureau. Why don't you go over there and see?" So I walked in cold turkey, not thinking I knew anybody at all, but who was sitting at that desk but one of my former receptionists. She said, "Boy, have I got something for you." I said, "Did they turn it down?"

"Well," she said, "it might be turned down. We got a letter from Cleveland yesterday, and it was denied; but look here." On her desk was the Johnson Rubber Company request for my gaskets. I asked her what happens now. She said, "You know, mail gets lost down in Washington, you never know when a letter is going to get anywhere. I'm about to take this in and have it signed right now." She took it in, and the fellow, not knowing it was denied, signed it and sent it out to Johnson Rubber Company. I never heard one word from the guy in Cleveland. We built the building in about six months and continued the rest of the war making gaskets for the B-29s.

R. W. Danischefsky, an industrial engineer with the Reconstruction Finance Corporation in Detroit before he went to Washington:

At the time of Pearl Harbor we had five projects in Michigan. By the end of December we had forty-two projects. Our plants included the Packard Motor Corporation, making engines for the British, and Continental Motors, making tank engines. All of this was under what was then called the Lend-Lease Program—the Reconstruction Finance Corporation was a lending agency. The purpose of having the RFC in these operations was to avoid the necessity of the military services going through the routine of getting appropriations through Congress to finance these things. The total program ran to almost $10 billion, and this was to provide machinery and equipment in existing plants, the building of entirely new facilities such as the Willow Run Bomber Plant, magnesium plants, aluminum plants, and all sorts of industrial facilities to provide materiel for war. The plants were owned by the government and subsequently were declared excess. They all became surplus at the close of the war.

The operator of a plant became an agent of the government,

and the plant was completely supervised by supervising engineers. Here's an example of the way it worked. Chrysler Corporation became a subcontractor for building the nose and the center section of the Martin-bomber fuselage. They arranged to utilize the old Graham Page automobile plant in Detroit, which took money to pay the rent and equip the plant. They provided an estimate of their requirements, a complete, itemized list of all the machine tools and equipment they would need. They submitted that to the air force. Most of the contracts at that time were fixed-fee contracts. Assume that, for the sake of simplification, you could make x item for a million dollars. It was determined that probably a normal profit on a million-dollar contract should be, say, 10 percent, so the government would provide you with all the machine tools and everything that you needed, taking into consideration your cost figures, and when the contract was finished, you would get $100,000 profit, the government paying all the expenses of manufacturing, with certain controls. The air force would come to RFC and say, ''We've got a contractor in Detroit that needs $90 million to equip a plant to build something that the services need.'' They would approve it, and it would go ahead. It wasn't a direct negotiation with defense plants. It was all what we called sponsorship by one of the services.

You hear a lot about the miracle of production. It was America! It was unbelievable to me. One of my first experiences was with Chrysler, where we were faced with the question of clearing their plant and moving a bunch of machine tools. We sat and discussed this for maybe an hour, then one of the men, sitting over there with a pencil and pad, said, ''Now this is what it's going to cost to clear this equipment out and bring in the new equipment.'' I said, ''What did you do, just reach up in a hat someplace and get a number?'' He said, ''No, this number will stand up.'' I subsequently found out that these people had knowledge of that type of thing because of their model changes every year. They just take the number of machine tools, and regardless of whether it's a small tool or a big tool, they have an average figure of so much, and that covers it. I finally got to where I'd go out to these outlying places and become a genius, simply because I'd figured out that the average machine tool cost roughly one dollar a pound to move out. You could apply it across the board. That's what it cost to bring it in, set it down, move it out, process it for storage.

At the time of Pearl Harbor, Capt. Fred Kirkham was on the Destroyer Lang *up in Reykjavik, Iceland. After being discharged from the navy because of an ulcer he developed spending thirty-four days on a raft, he was returning to Quincy, Massachusetts, on a train when . . .*

. . . a fellow sat down beside me. I was reading, and of course I was in uniform at that time, and he started asking me a lot of questions. He asked me where I was going. He wanted to know what vessels I had been on, what I knew about the submarines that had been sinking some of the vessels off the coast. I said it was none of his business. Well, to make a long story short, he thanked me and said I gave all the right answers. Then he identified himself as an FBI man. He wanted to know what I was going to do. I told him at this point I hadn't made up my mind. He said:"Do you still feel that you want to do something?" And I said, "Why not?" He said, "All right, we've got a job for you down at Hingham. We built a shipyard down there, making LCIs, DEs, and LSTs. We're hiring men, and we want you to go down there to be in charge of the installation of the radios." But he said I was strictly on my own. "I'll check with you every once in a while, or someone will," he said, and they did all the time I was there.

They wanted me to make sure every man did his job. In other words they were afraid of sabotage, and I think not without reason, because some of our cables were sabotaged. But it was never found who did it.

I turned in two different fellows who were sort of drifters. They had hooked up some of the wires in the electronic equipment wrong. I asked them why, and they answered: "Oh, golly, I don't know." Once, you could understand, but when it happened two or three times, then you checked them out. I just couldn't take a chance that they might have been saboteurs. After you help pick up fellows at sea, you just don't take a chance. Also if they hook it up wrong, I'd want them out of there anyway, because I couldn't get paid for the job until it was accepted by the navy inspectors. After I turned them in, I asked the FBI fellows about it, and they said not to worry, that they were in the army now—drafted.

We had a bit of bribery. In fact, I got a lot of that myself because I was the one that promoted the men. First I had gas coupons offered to me and then meat coupons. I would lie if I didn't say I had a little piece of meat once in a while. You got so damned little meat.

We also had "Rosie the Riveter." A lot of gals did welding work. As a whole, I'd say they did a pretty good job. Of course, some of the Rosies were conducting a little business on the side. The oldest profession. Some were doing it for promotion and some for actual dollars.

I did have some uncomfortable experiences being in civilian clothes. But then, of course, I wore my "ruptured duck"— remember the ruptured ducks? There was a mistake and they had rated me a 4-F when I was supposed to have been a 2-B—anybody that come out of the service. When I got the ruptured duck, I always wore it, and everybody knew what it was and that helped a lot.

Patricia Megargee was just out of high school when the war began, and her parents wanted her to go on to college. But she felt the times were out of joint, and she wanted to get involved.

Gradually everyone started going off. All the boys who had been going to Lawrenceville and Choate and the various schools were graduating and instead of going on to college were taken into the army. I had a brother, two years younger; later on, he was in the navy. He was on a ship that went to Anzio; he was very uncommunicative, like kids are today. He didn't finish high school, ran off and joined the navy before the proper age. My parents were very upset about that. They were also upset about the fact that I didn't go on to college.

It was a strange time; there didn't seem to be any point in going to college. Everything was out of kilter. We went to visit a very good friend of my mother's up in Connecticut. Her husband was an officer in the navy, and she had gone to stay on a farm. She had just decided to leave her apartment in New York and sort of hole up there for a couple of years. It was strange. People were going into things like that. I went up to stay with her. I wasn't getting along too well with my stepfather. He wanted me to go to Finch and be finished. I thought that was a complete waste of time, so I stayed with this friend of Mom's and heard that they were looking for help at Pratt & Whitney, in East Hartford. We were in a little town called Winsted, Connecticut. I drove in one day with some neighbors and was interviewed. I was either just eighteen or not quite eighteen. Anyway, they said, "Fine."

They were desperate for people to work. They put me into a training program for about two months, every day, eight hours or whatever. Oh, I was so pleased with myself. Mother was furious. I just kept telling her it was for the war effort. I got this certified machinist certificate, and I remember I was so proud. They put you through this thing about how to run these machines, how to read calipers and micrometers and various testing devices. We were in a separate building for the training. Then we went into this big factory; it covered miles. You'd check in, and then you'd walk and walk and walk and walk until you got to your own little niche. It was very exciting. As a matter of fact, I really wouldn't mind doing it again.

I ran a Norton OD grinder, OD being "outside diameter." We would put parts under this thing and then grind various portions of the flanges and what have you. These were parts that would go into the Pratt & Whitney engines. Pratt & Whitney made the engine, and I think Republic made the airplane itself. I was in the engine section, and Hamilton Propeller was right adjacent to it.

It was nifty! Great fun—if you were eighteen, anything was fun. In my particular area there were mostly men working, but it was so vast, it's hard to explain. There were trucks that drove right down the aisles where people would walk. Small, sort of Jeeplike things. Or if there was a fire, a sort of mini-firetruck would come. It was so vast that you couldn't see from one end to the other. It was like a small town all under this one roof.

I was very unsophisticated at the time, but I'd get into the thing and geared up for it and I'd just keep plugging away, measuring and grinding, measuring and grinding, and they'd say, "Hey, kid, take it easy." They'd been doing it for fifteen or twenty years, and they didn't want me approaching what they had done at the end of the day because then they didn't look good, and of course they could do it with one hand tied behind their backs.

I got into the night shift because it paid more money and it worked out better as far as my getting a ride in the car pool. You paid so much a week to drive with these guys, nice country-type of guys, who had been doing this kind of thing all their lives and were either too old or for some reason or another didn't go in the service. The ones I rode with were kind of paternalistic about the whole thing. They thought it was funny that I would want to do that rather than go into the hairdressing business or something. We'd work from midnight to seven, only seven hours instead of eight hours. You got the benefit of the extra hour because you were on the night shift.

Finally enough pressure was brought to bear that I said, "All right, I'll come back home." At that point Mother was in Bay Head, New Jersey. So I went down there for a couple of weeks for a vacation and then went to New York to look for a job, because I still wasn't going back to school. Because of the training I had had in Pratt & Whitney, I applied for a job at the Navy Department, at the Office of Inspector of Navy Materiel, and got a job as inspector of materiels the navy had ordered to be shipped to various places out of the New York area. I'd go to a different factory every day and inspect different types of gauges that go into aircraft. I even went to a nut and bolt factory in Purchase, New York, to inspect the bolts and nuts. It wasn't that involved. All you did was measure the bolts, take test samples, and make stress tests, mechanical tests.

Later, I started working for a modeling agency, and they told us very definitely that they would prefer that we go one or two afternoons or evenings a week to this Stage Door Canteen. The atmosphere there was sheer desperation. I mean, people coming in, and it wasn't just our own servicemen, people from Australia, Canada, anyone who happened to be passing through. They wanted someone to talk to, and there was a desperate kind of quality about the thing—like here you are, now sit down and be charming, sparkle—a very unnatural situation. I didn't like it at all; I wasn't good at it. I met some very nice Norwegian sailors, but we were not supposed to go out with them, which was great, because I didn't want to.

Some of the girls did violate the club rules and go out with them. Why not, if they felt like it?

James Majors, from Nashville, Tennessee, came up to Chicago in 1939, job hunting. "There was just no place you could get your hand on money at that particular time—especially the blacks. The way things were in the South, I said this is not for me, and as soon as I got big enough, I was going to cut out. So I dropped out of school. Everybody was crisscrossing the country, riding the rails, thumbing, hoboing, getting where they could, checking to see if they could find a job and moving on to someplace else if they couldn't." He ended up in Chicago because, he says: "I had noticed on packages, most every one I picked up said Made in Chicago. I figured I couldn't help but find a job there."

At the time of Pearl Harbor I was working as an elevator operator for VL & A, a sporting goods firm down on Wabash Street, one of those high-class places. I had no idea we would be involved in the war, because of the snow job we had had that we were going to stay out of this thing. Then they started taking guys, and guys were volunteering. First they took the unmarried guys, then married guys, then married guys with kids, then married guys up to age forty-four. I was working with the WPA when the draft was going. I had quit the job at the sporting goods company. As an elevator operator a guy had to pay half of his salary to stay groomed, so to speak. They demanded too much for the salary. This was a place where all the movie stars came. Wallace Beery—I met him there on the elevator—and Cary Grant, because we sold all that big safari-type sporting goods. So I just quit and went to work as a supervisor of a play lot for the Urban League.

But this was not what I wanted to do. So I got a job in a plant at 147 South Market Street. The Select Novelty Manufacturing Company. They were making boutonnieres out of walnuts and peanuts. And then they went into making boutonnieres out of war stamps. I became supervisor of a bunch of women there, and it was my job to go down and buy these war stamps in big sheets: fifteen hundred, two thousand, five thousand to a sheet. I remember I used to go up and down La Salle Street. They had booths out in front of the banks, and it used to be a real thrill to me, because I would walk up and say: "I want to buy some stamps." They would ask me how many I wanted, and I would say: "Oh, about two hundred." And they would say: "Two hundred stamps?" and I would say: "No, two hundred dollars' worth." They'd look at me as if to say: "What in the hell is this dude doing?" They didn't know whether I was a damned fool or patriotic or what.

After the boutonnieres were made, they would be delivered to five-and-ten-cent stores and other shops; we used to take them in big soup boxes. There would be dollar boutonnieres and fifty-cent ones, and the stamps were made in the shape of a flower. They were very beautiful things and very popular. They used to give them away as prizes. That company pioneered this thing.

At that time I had gotten married and had one kid. I wanted to get in a defense factory because I would hear of guys making forty-five dollars a week, and I said this is good money, plus a defense job. My goal was always to do as well as I possibly could. So I went to International Harvester and applied for a job. At that time, if a guy worked for the stockyards or McCormack or as a Pullman porter, he was considered upper middle class. Those were the best jobs for blacks at the time. I had a second child on the way, and on the seventeenth of February, 1943, I was hired at International Harvester.

They had a lot of black guys at Harvester, but they were in the foundry. They must have had about forty-five hundred to five thousand workers, but in the production work, where the machine work was done, they had approximately fifty blacks.

I started out pushing a broom. They put me on third shift—six nights, at forty dollars a week. I thought that was something, because I was working five and a half days as a supervisor for thirty dollars at Select Novelty. Here I was pushing a broom for about the same time at forty dollars a week. Then I went from broom pushing to a single-spindle drill. This was in one of the highly classified departments—Department 11. I thought, well, here I am on my way up, and I went from a single-spindle drill to a drilling machine. On the drill I was working on all sorts of things—drilling roller shafts for the tank treads to roll on and then the shaft that supports the roller. Then I moved up to a milling machine, and from that to a lathe operator. I would take the raw material, fit it into the lathe, trim it down, and measure it with a snap gauge with a ten-thousandths-of-an-inch tolerance in diameter. Then I went from the lathe to a grinder—on the finished product.

By that time, I was making seventy-five to eighty dollars a week. They had given me these six-month deferments—three of them—because I was a father and worked in a defense plant, that sort of thing. So when they finally decided they were going to reach back and grab everything walking, I went down and took my physical. They grade you based on your ability, and I qualified for the marines all the way down to zip. While I was there, here come three guys into this room. And the marine standing up there was some kind of sharp, believe you me, in his marine blues, his white cap, the salad on his chest, and a little braid on his shoulder. I looked at him and said, ''Now, there's a guy.'' So I went into the Marine Corps.

David Soergal, just out of the University of Wisconsin, went to work for General Electric, in Schenectady, New York.

I went to GE headquarters with no sense of wartime emergency, working in test-engineering programs that were being carried out during the thirties, so nothing was different there. Then they had engineering-advancement programs that you had to qualify for, and I got wrapped up in them. The initial job I had was a war-related effort, but it was hard to distinguish. It was working on big electrical-system equipment that would process bauxite into aluminum. And, of course, the aluminum would go for airplanes, but the connection was pretty remote. GE made the processing equipment; we never handled the aluminum. There were a lot of navy, army people around, coming in and out of GE, but when you're a test engineer, you're not involved with them. The bosses handle them.

I guess I spent about six months, nine months, on that test job, and, incidentally, when you're a new employee, you work third shift, from midnight till eight o'clock in the morning. Actually, we worked longer hours, worked overtime too. So really it was just a lot of hard work; we were just doing a job. I was married during those days, married in 1944—and I don't think war was too good for marriages. The intensity of the work—sixty-hour weeks weren't unusual.

The first indication that there was a war on, about 1944, was my transfer to electronics engineering. I immediately got assigned to the Cape Cod–New London submarine area. GE had a contract, competitive with RCA, to test underwater sound devices, and that was quite interesting. The vehicle we used to test underwater sound was a captured German cruiser. Actually, it was a luxury boat, not a cruiser. It was beautiful; must have been eight feet long. It was outfitted with electronic gear in the hull, and of course the navy operated it. They had a crew of about forty, and another fellow and I were the engineers working on the system. There were three of us, actually, and another ship on the receiving end. They talked to us and we talked to them by transmission underwater. And that's where I used another captured German device—a wire recorder. It probably came along with the luxury boat. It was a bad design, because the wire would snare up, like a fishing line. Half the time we sat there winding the wire.

We'd spend these wonderful days going out to sea on the German ship, one-day trips. When there was clear sailing weather, we'd go down to the docks about seven o'clock in the morning, go up there and get breakfast, beautiful silverware, the whole thing. I guess that came along with the capture, too.

We paid fifty cents for a meal and, man, ate like a king. They had navy chefs, black fellows, coming out and serving and waiting on you. Conversation was great, lots of wine at lunch. For them, it was a boring assignment. All they'd do was cart us GE guys out in the ocean and bring us back.

Frank Platt was working for an elevator company in Louisville, Kentucky, when the war started. It immediately went out of business, so he went to work for the American Air Filter Company, which was building carburetor filters for aircraft.

Building carburetor filters suddenly became a booming business, particularly after we got involved in desert areas, where aircraft just didn't last any time because of the sand and the grit. There was a big demand for filters. The major problem in our plant was the manpower—or lack of manpower. As a result, in my plant we converted about 90 percent to women. That did create some problems, because the plant wasn't designed to cope with it facility-wise, and certainly the men working there were not used to working with women. We ran a twenty-four-hour, seven-day-a-week operation, and as superintendent, I would try to cover at least a part of all three shifts and would spend a good many Saturday nights bailing somebody out of jail. We took a lot of young fellows in there who were just below the draft age, and a lot of them came out of the hills of Kentucky, had never been in a big city before. As a result, they kind of went wild. They made money that they had never had, and they were on the loose. From time to time we had some troubles in the plant, too, with the girls, but nothing of a real serious nature.

It was a completely new experience for me; I had never been involved in anything like that, and it was interesting. The reason, I guess, I avoided being in the war was that, one, I had two youngsters when the war started, and a third one came along; plus, two, I was plant superintendent for a vital defense industry.

It was not a pleasant period. I certainly wouldn't want to go through it again or see anybody else go through it, even though we didn't suffer directly by deaths or being injured ourselves.

During summer vacations at the University of Wisconsin, Mary Dandouveris worked in a war plant.

I was able to get a job during the summertime in the J. I. Case Company in Racine, Wisconsin. They had a contract for building whatever was the biggest troop-transport airplane there was—a huge, enormous thing. I worked on the swing shift as a riveter, and I didn't like the shift—3:00 P.M. to 11:00 P.M.—it was cutting into my social life too much, so I asked to be transferred to a later shift, and then I did filing. It was on the graveyard shift, eleven to seven. We were filing the metal for the leading and the trailing edge, which is the outside edge of the plane. You only had one-one-thousandth-of-an-inch error, and there were gauges and inspectors who came around to make sure that you didn't go beyond that. Women were particularly careful, you see, and light fingered enough so that, working the files, you didn't make heavy dents or go beyond this minimum tolerance. It was intricate work that women are particularly good for.

It was interesting how fast these plants converted to an almost all-female crew, except for the older men and the 4-F
types who were still around and a few of the older supervisors.
These were our schoolteachers in high school and young college people and women that they had recruited from all over
town, and they were manning the factory. That first summer
of 1943 that I worked at the plant it was almost like a picnic.
People were working both on the graveyard and the swing
shift. People knew each other; there was a lot of conversation
and lots of camaraderie. Most people had relatives and boyfriends in the service, and the discussion was where and what
they'd heard and exchanging news and trying to dope out what
was going on. They were pretty nice to us college kids. I never
encountered any kind of problem. The second summer I did a
different kind of work. By that time, the full-time people had
taken over working on the plane parts. Then I was trucking—
I was the supply girl on those little trucks that you move parts
around on. I would supply the riveters with their parts, and
there were some marvelous old men; I can remember that we'd
have good conversations, philosophical conversations. There
were a couple of rough types.

*Luther Cashdollar was a metallurgist and department head
with the Union Electric Company in Pittsburgh.*

The first thing that happened after Pearl Harbor was the
army ordnance personnel visited our plant to view our operations and to place us in some war production. They quickly
decided we were ideally situated to produce fairly large cannons, and we got into production reasonably soon.

I was married and had one child at the time. My age, however, fitted the 4-F category. I suppose that my performance
here was more productive than I would have been as a foot
soldier or as a technician somewhere.

The morale in the plant was great. The attitude was totally
cooperative and all-out. I can't recall a major problem between
union and management during that time. Everyone worked a
little bit harder, expanded their efforts somewhat, both on the
workers' side and the management's side.

We had women workers there but not in production. We
had women on the lathes who would cut and test pieces, be-

cause a lot of testing had to be done on the cannon from both the breech and the muzzle end. I had two women in the metallurgical machine shop, and all the personnel in the laboratory that worked on the testing machines were girls. In two cases, I think, they were wives of servicemen.

From management's side, we would do what had been our normal work at our desks, and then some of us would go into the shop, and function as foremen. I remember being a foreman in the melt shop, a chemist in the laboratory, and doing metallurgical work, all at one time, that is, in the same eight hours, or, I should say, in the same twelve hours. There were times, rare, when we were here as long as thirty-six hours. It didn't affect my family life adversely, because my wife was understanding.

The war was not productive for our company financially. We had no regrets, certainly, but we used our equipment much more rapidly than we would have ordinarily in our regular production. The maintenance became high. When it was all over, we were renegotiated out of any profit we had made. I've heard some bitterness, but I'm not certain whether we actually lost money. I would say if one considered the abuse of the equipment, we probably lost some money. We did get recognition from the government—but extremely tardily, I would say. We were one of the last to get the navy "E," and we felt rather badly about this because we had been definitely instrumental in creating a new alloy that minimized the use of nickel and released nickel for other areas that required it. But a lot of us gained valuable experience in a short time that we might not have had at all. I know that I did.

John Nies had a master plan for avoiding the draft. Before it broke down, he spent some time in defense plants, working first at the Ford plant in Dearborn, Michigan, later at Willow Run.

I was on some kind of engineering system—a euphemism for a guy who doesn't know what the hell he's doing but has some formal education. I was doing the preliminary work on the manufacturing of the B-24. B-24s at the time were being made in San Diego by Consolidated Vultee, and they shifted all the drawings over to the Ford Motor Company. They were basic drawings of the airplane to be converted to the famous Ford mass-production line. That is what I was involved in, first at the plant in Dearborn, then, in early '42, I moved to Willow Run. I stayed there until the draft board got me.

What I remember most about Willow Run is chaos—total chaos. We had lots of big promises, with no one able to produce. We had a new plant manager every two or three weeks. It was filled with draft dodgers, draft evaders, relatives of plant managers. It was a haven from the war. It was filled with people who viewed it as that and not as a place to build bombers. That's part of the thing that made it not too difficult to leave. A totally unsavory atmosphere.

The B-24 that we had there was a mock-up, assembled and disassembled thousands of times, hundreds of times at least, into subassemblies, which the Ford people thought they could make like Model Ts or Model As. At the end of about the first year of operation at Willow Run they had to have something come off the production line; so they put that thing together for the final time and towed it out to the hangar doors for the newspapers. There were big stories saying, "The B-24 Rolls Off the Assembly Line at Ford." There was absolutely nothing behind it at all. They were still months away from the first production.

The other thing I remember about Willow Run is Mr. [Charles] Lindbergh. At that time he was being excoriated by official Washington and President Roosevelt and by the American people. He tried, as far as I could tell, to help out the war effort. And there was only one place where he was accepted. It was the personal decision of Henry Ford to bring him in there as a consultant test pilot. And that is the only thing I can recall in the way of creative thinking in the factory. The workers were against it, but Henry Ford still had total personal control of the organization, and if he wanted Lindbergh in there, Lindbergh was in. That was a cause of tension. The Detroit newspapers said, "Ford Employs Nazi," and there were some overt demonstrations at the plant, but they were minor.

The draft finally caught up with me. I was registered in my hometown, which was in a small farm community in the western part of Michigan. The draft board there knew what was essential to the war effort, and it wasn't boys making money in the war plants, it was the farmer. And I wasn't a farmer. It was just that simple. I was in a nonessential industry, as far as they were concerned.

The mood in most homes was set by a wife's concern for her husband or a mother's concern for her son. In the Collins home in Bowling Green, Virginia, it was different. A young boy was concerned about his mother—as Herbert Collins recalls:

My father operated a store, and after the war began, business started to slow down. So my mother took a job up at Dahlgren at the old proving grounds. She worked for about three years there. They had a bus that went from Carolina County to Dahlgren every day, and we got up at three o'clock in the morning, and I studied at that time by lamplight from three o'clock until time to catch the school bus and go to school. That would have been about eight o'clock. Then she would come home on the bus at night, and I would prepare meals and have them ready when she got home. I learned to cook that way.

Her job was to write down numbers off the shells they had there. I made some lamps out of some empty shells that mother would bring home. She also brought the little round containers the shells were packed in, and I made a table from them, and I kept that thing until I sold it at an auction down there two years ago.

Each shell would have a number on it to identify it, and they were packed in cases. In shipping them to the different installations you had to record the numbers. Several times the fuses would begin to go off, and the commanding officer there would throw them out the window. Some of them exploded. There were casualties; in fact, one woman was killed. I worried very much about my mother.

When the company he was working for in Wisconsin, making pots and pans, went out of business, Joseph Clement went to work for Curtiss-Wright in St. Louis:

Curtiss-Wright was already making, I think, an aircraft they were selling to Russia. They had a plant in Buffalo and in St. Louis, and I came in under their training program to do production illustrations. I stayed there a year and a half or two years, until I got a letter from a friend with whom I had worked in Milwaukee. He had gone to a small bomb-making plant and felt that I could be of more use to him down there in developing target-identification bombs. It was called the Kilgore Manufacturing Company, in Westerville, Ohio. They used to make cap pistols. They were in gunpowder, so they were given contracts to make these identification bombs that would emit a light and color from a distance to be seen from high altitudes.

I had one close escape—it was a more dangerous job than I realized. I knew there were a lot of explosives around. You had to walk carefully, with no nails in your shoes, and you couldn't just walk around anyplace. I had a drawing board in a small cubbyhole and I had gone out into the machine shop. We were looking over some drawings out there, when we heard a tremendous roar—it just shook the entire place. The superintendent was there, and he said, "Oh, my God, I know what it is." We ran out, and my office, which was right across the courtyard from one of the bomb-loading areas, was completely ablaze. In my drawing board was embedded a huge piece of shrapnel right where my head would have been. They called the FBI in—it killed four people. They had no idea what caused it. It was thoroughly investigated and found that it could have been static electricity. It's highly uncontrollable.

Rudolph Spitzer, a high school teacher in Shortsville, New York:

There were two years when I worked in plants in Rochester, and I had real mixed feelings about it. I didn't like the idea of being associated with manufacturing 16-mm shells, because I have a great antipathy toward anything military.

One summer I worked a four-to-midnight shift—I guess that was in the same plant—and the job there was to grind castings. Nobody ever did explain what castings were. They came out of the molds. They were about as big around as I could span with my arms, maybe bigger, sort of cone-shaped things, with a burr that had to be ground off. You stood in front of a three-foot grinding wheel, and every night your clothes caught on fire several times from the sparks. Of course, we wore goggles, but by the time I got through with that job at the end of the summer, my own glasses were so pitted, I took them to the personnel department, and the fellow there looked at them and said, "Well, go order a new pair and send me the bill and we'll take care of it," which they did. There were no women in that job. It was in the foundary, hot as hell, and the noise, I have a recollection of the noise! And I encountered the most ignorant group of people I've ever known. We had a break, I suppose at eight o'clock, half hour to eat, and there was another fellow who never did say anything, and he sat on the running board of a car. There was never any communication. He'd take a sandwich out of his bag and devour it in exactly four bites. Just like an animal, snapping at it.

There were large, heavy boxes, wooden boxes, in which they crated these 16-mm shells. And this one guy would come in, carefully arrange an old coat or something, lie down, and go to sleep. I'd be standing there putting in my eight hours, getting absolutely furious that this son of a bitch was getting paid and sleeping. I remember one day I finally went over and woke him, and I said, "You son of a bitch, you're getting paid the same as the rest of us, get up and go to work." He was so startled, he didn't know who I was, and he was too dumb to reflect that I didn't have any right to tell him to get up. He only had to say to me, "Go to hell," but he was so startled, he got up and started working.

The sheer monotony of the thing, oh, it was ghastly. These shells would come along the assembly line, and the job consisted of taking the shell off, inserting this thing into the mouth of the shell, and pressing a pedal which spun the shell—that was the way you checked the threading for the cap. Then you reversed the pedal and unwound the shell, and it went on. I used to type out on five-by-three cards poetry I wanted to try to memorize, and I would lay the cards on the corner of the bench. Then as I lifted the shell off and put it back, I'd glance at them. The dumb strawboss was very upset with this. I'm sure he thought I was doing something subversive or unpatriotic. He would make an effort to see what this was. So one night I had cards I had typed of "Kubla Khan" and deliberately walked away from my bench and out of the corner of my eye watched him. He edged over and picked the card up, shook his head, and put it down.

John Rettaliata and André Hubbard worked for the Grumman Corporation in Bethpage, Long Island.

RETTALIATA: I was assistant amphibian production manager, which sounds like a big job. There were only two of us in that department, my boss and myself.

HUBBARD: I came under the engineering department that handled communications with the navy. Everything was coded.

RETTALIATA: The whole plant went from what you might call medium gear into high gear overnight. We were already in production on the F-4 Wildcat, which was fortunate because there were no other carrier-based fighters that were immediately available. We had problems with the draft, but I think on the whole the company probably was able to keep the people it wanted. We always have had outstanding management, especially in regard to the personnel situation. In those days Jake Swirbul was executive vice-president of the company. His name was Leon A. Swirbul. Andy, do you remember the time early in the war when Jake asked us to work through a weekend, and we kept the plant open for forty-eight hours?

HUBBARD: That was done to assemble an airplane—I think it was the F-6. We turned out twenty or thirty over a weekend.

RETTALIATA: I think it was early enough in the war to have been the Wildcat. They needed two squadrons' worth of airplanes immediately, so we all stayed here around the clock.

HUBBARD: In early 1940 we were building about fifty or fifty-five airplanes every year. By late 1940 we were already building fifty a month. So you can see, it was picking up.

RETTALIATA: The war meant fantastic training programs. We wound up with major training programs in every major high school, I think, in every town on Long Island. We were training women, lawyers, dentists, bakers, and just about every kind of person you could find.

People would drop their careers temporarily, often because they were motivated to do something to help out in the war effort. They were overaged or otherwise unsuitable for the armed services. They wanted to pitch in and help out. During the war I think you could walk down our production line and find any kind of skill that you wanted. A fine artist, a sculptor, dentist, musician, anything.

Thirty-some percent of the people were women, at the peak

of our war effort. We even had women test pilots. I think we were the only company that had three women test pilots.

HUBBARD: Women did a lot of electrical harness work and the detail and fine work.

RETTALIATA: The old-time fighters had miles of harness, that is, electrical wiring—very fine copper extended wire that winds up in a very complicated maze, because naturally everything you have to do in an airplane has got to be as light as possible. You don't have all the room you would like to have. You wind up with miles of wiring cramped into a space the size of a Hellcat or a Wildcat. Women were very good at that.

We set up what now you would call day-care centers. A mother could drop off her children on her way to work and pick them up on her way home. There were dozens of these around the Long Island area. We had what we called a little green truck service. If a woman came to work and remembered that she had forgotten to turn off an electric iron at home, she could call them and they would go home and take care of it.

Margaret Oakham started the war working in an airplane factory and ended it joining the Army Nurse Corps.

Shortly after Pearl Harbor I went to school and took a short course in electrical work at night and went to work at Glen L. Martin's in Baltimore. I worked my way up until finally I worked on the B-26s. At one time I could wire the whole center section. The soldering that you did was very important because some of it was connected with giving signals and things. Sometimes I worked with girls who were not as conscientious about the work, and I became very annoyed, because I remember saying what if some of their own family were on a ship and they had done inferior work and things did not work the way they should. A lot of people could be killed. I was infuriated, because I was very conscientious about my work. If it took me longer than it took somebody else, it didn't worry me, because it had to be right. There were no problems with the men—they just resented, like some men do today, a woman entering their field.

Stewart Hoskins was editor of the Lakeville Journal *and lived in the little western Connecticut town of Salisbury, but he spent part of the war working in the war effort, first in a defense plant in Torrington, later in Canaan, where they were processing magnesium.*

I was thirty-five years old, and they were taking many people older than I was. So I said to myself, "What the hell are you doing here?"—doing nothing, so to speak. I thought I would help a little bit doing something reasonably intelligent. So I went and applied for a job, and they took me right away, which was all right. I didn't mind it, because I was energetic and used to working long hours anyway, even without the war work. But the burden of the *Journal* fell on my wife, Ann.

Most of the people I worked with were dedicated. They were learning as they went, including me. But a few months after I started working, the unions started to get on the ball.

I was sort of an all-around guy around the office down there. I would take magnesium in and out, drive the truck down to the railroad station to pick up something. And all of a sudden one day, they said, "You can't do this, you aren't a member of the union." I was a semi-executive. I said, "The hell with you," and went on doing it. But they sort of frowned at everybody, and the top people said you'd better go along with this. They didn't, to my knowledge, attempt to slow down anything, but they did attempt to organize and got a little nasty.

The same thing happened in Torrington. There I did get in, because it was a union shop. I paid my dues. But I ran into another thing. I was in the grinding department, on a machine, part of the time—had to turn out so many thousand ball bearings, which were used in airplanes. They started putting people on piecework, simplifying everything so there was no lost motion, speeding it up for the sake of the war and because it was more efficient. I love efficiency anyway, so I devised my own method of working. I got so I could produce a fair percentage higher than other people because I just stuck with it. I didn't fool around. And then, all of a sudden, the people on that machine said, "You're wrecking things here because if you turn out more, all they will do is set standards higher for the same rate of pay, so you will get nowhere."

I said, "Look, there's a war on. They need these bearings." And I know some of the men working there had sons in the army and navy. But even with sons in the service, this was their attitude, at least a fair percentage of them.

Genevieve Lewis, in Clairton, Pennsylvania:

I went into the steel mill at Clairton. When you go into a mill, they tell you you are taking a man's job. But I just kept the mills clean. When the mills were shut down, we would sweep up the wet scale that would come off the steel. That was it. We swept the mills. It wasn't so hard a job. But they told us we were taking a man's job, because the boys were all going in the service. We had quite a few coloreds, but the whites had the best jobs, working in the office and things like that. I don't know how the morale in the plant was because I didn't work around much with the men in the plant. Down in our department we didn't have any racial problems, and we got along real well in our neighborhood during the war. I didn't follow the war too much, but when I would come home, my husband would be talking about it.

Horace Hubbard was an engineering manager in the General Electric plant in Pittsfield, Massachusetts. Most of his work at GE was related to the process for manufacturing the materials that went into the atom bomb.

We did a lot of top-secret work at GE, and the thing that amused me was some of the methods that intelligence used to find out who was who and what was what. They probably should have scrutinized the people properly, but sometimes there were minor things, some remark that someone had made, or something that was blown up, and sometimes it hurt people who were innocent. We all make cracks that we don't mean, or shouldn't. I don't think security had to be that tight. Up here in the country it's a little different, too. It's not as easy for people to infiltrate. Everybody knows everybody. They keep together pretty well.

We had a lot of women there. They did light construction and intricate wiring on the controls, switchboards, and control devices. The women were very adept at that, and we had some who could really outclass the men. I think the men respected them—they did their part, and I think it worked out very nice.

Women stayed on after the war, but of course the size of the force was reduced somewhat.

Jack Lynch was manager of the Commander Hotel in Ocean City, Maryland, and he decided to go up to Baltimore and work in the Glen L. Martin plant building bombers.

I learned a great lesson up there. I wondered how we won the war. I used to go home so mad from there so many, many times that I said, "Well, if we beat the Germans, it's going to be an accident." It was the attitude. Not everybody. Some people there actually worked themselves down to a nub. They had twice as much work. Then other people were in there who weren't trying to do anything for the war effort at all. I can't say that I saw this, but I heard many times that there were a lot of people who came out of the shipbuilding yards and would come in there on second shift, go in the bombers, and go to sleep, and sleep the whole night out. They'd get up the next morning, hit the time clock, and go on back to the shipyards. They hadn't turned a peg all night. I remember one instance where we had a part that we had a lot of trouble with. The part was 162B48172, I still remember that to this day. It was a bolt about yea long, and it had to go through three or four different processes before it could be shipped out. I guess it was a very important bolt. They would write us that they had to have some of those bolts or they would have to stop production on the bomb hoists. Trying to get the bolts out, I went to procure some of these little cardboard caps that you put on a bolt to keep from scarring the threads. And there was one man at the desk where there was supposed to be two. He said, "I can issue the caps, but the guy is not here to put them on." I said, "You just give me the caps and I'll put them on." He said, "Well, you're not supposed to do that," and I said, "I don't care whether I'm supposed to or not but I'll do it, if you'll just give me the caps. I'm not worrying about getting fired." Here they were going to stop production on this bomb hoist, and it was when we were getting the tar beat out of us. So I put the caps on and carried them back to the fellow I was working under, told him the story, and we shipped them on out.

They had a lot of women working there, and by my obser-

vation I would say they were good. I really marveled at the
way they could take it, the continuity. They'd take a piece of
metal that's maybe a triangular shape, one by four, and sit
down and work those things, not doing anything else but cutting those or drilling holes in those according to the pattern. I
used to pass them and wonder how in the world they could
just sit and do that one thing over and over a thousand times.

I don't think I was ever quite so mad as when I went to
work one morning and saw about two hundred placards for
people to go out on strike. Here people were dying everywhere
waiting for that equipment, and then to see somebody out on
the street with placards trying to stop you from going to work.
They weren't successful, but they were trying.

*While in Florida interviewing for this book, I happened to be
sitting with my friend Leo Hershfield early one evening, in the
bar of the Columbia Restaurant, in Ybor City, which is part
of Tampa, when I looked up and noticed a gentleman in his
mid-sixties, or early seventies, standing near our table; I asked
him to join us. It turned out he had not been in this restaurant
since he used to hang out here during World War II days, and
he had come back now in something of a nostalgic mood. This,
naturally, led to a couple of drinks and a somewhat rambling
conversation. Believe it or not, he worked on concrete ships
during the war. The gentleman's name is Clifford Eunice.*

During the period of time that I was here, this was our so-
called headquarters—not that we were heavy drinkers. We
were heavy eaters. We drank light and ate heavy, this being
one of the oldest and best established eating joints in America.

Mr. Hoopes, are you personally familiar with the origin or
the advent of concrete vessels?

Well, they had their beginning, as far as we know, in World
War I, when the British built the concrete barges used to ferry
troops across the channel, and they were very successful. The
government decided to build concrete vessels. McCloskey [and
Company] was the third contractor to be awarded a program
to develop them. They had a Scotch marine boiler and triple
expansion, three-cylinder engines. They were maritime vessels, meaning that they were both cargo and men of war.

There is a material here in the state of Florida which had

its origin possibly in Tennessee, Georgia, North Carolina—a form of red clay that was washed south and redeposited in the ocean. By taking this clay and burning it in a kiln, then running it through a ball mill and then out over a screen where it's powdered and droplets of water dropped on it, it forms a lightweight aggregate used to make concrete. So this concrete vessel was made from a very highly impervious aggregate in the first place, and the cement was manufactured in the state of Florida. Very few people realize the value of those ships.

Laddie Sadler worked in a shipyard in Tampa, Florida. He also helped build concrete ships, until he was finally drafted.

I was working for McCloskey and Company, located at Hooker's Point—it was called the Hooker's Point Shipyard. We built reinforced concrete steamships. Actually, the ships we were building were for the merchant marine; they were cargo ships. There was a lot of feeling among unknowledgeable people that these were skyscrapers afloat; we got razzed about building concrete ships. But I sailed on the trial runs, and they were pretty fair ships. They didn't handle too bad. Some of them are still in use, down along the South American coast.

Why a concrete ship? Actually, there was more steel in a concrete ship than there was in a steel ship, by volume. But it was bar steel, stuff that was just cold-rolled. And there was a big shortage of steel plate, which was necessary for building steel ships. One of the advantages of concrete was brought home by one of the first three ships that we sent out of there. On its maiden voyage to the Philippines, with a full cargo, it took a Japanese torpedo, right dead amidships. It happened that it hit in a wing ballast tank, which didn't carry cargo—they filled these tanks with water to keep the ships level. Of course, it blew a hole about six feet in diameter in the tank. On a steel ship, this would have just ripped steel in every direction, and it would have destroyed the ship. But on this thing it just punched a hole, and nothing went beyond the confines of this tank. So they simply leveled the other tank, trimmed the ship, and kept on going to deliver their cargo in the Philippines, made a beeline back to Tampa, put the ship in dry dock, put the steel men on it, and took airhammers and chipped away all the concrete that was damaged, cut out the reinforcing steel, welded in new steel, made forms for it, and poured new concrete in the thing. All in a matter of a week or two. And then they cured the concrete for three or four weeks, threw a coat of paint on it, and went back to sea again. But these ships were slow. They didn't do but about twelve knots, and they slowed the convoys down. The whole configuration of these ships underwater was quite similar to an LST, and the freighters up in the Great Lakes, the oar boats. It's just a great, long tube, rather narrow.

As far as social life was concerned, I was pretty well acquainted in Tampa, and there were groups among shipyard employees that you made friends with. While we were building a house, on Sundays, sometimes great numbers of these fellows would come out with their families, and the girls would cook up a batch of spaghetti, and we'd have a big outdoor dinner. These guys would all pitch in and help on the house. In turn, we reciprocated and helped others fix their cars and do things like that. A great deal of that sort of thing went on. It kinda went back to the pioneering days.

4

Keeping the Country Informed

The communications industry played a unique role in the war effort. In addition to providing the essential link between government and the people it was the source of what little information Americans had about the battlefronts where their loved ones were. And because of the nature of their jobs, reporters and editors often knew more about what was going on in their communities and in the country than anyone else.

After serving for about a year in the army in 1942–43, Studs Terkel was discharged when he tried to go overseas with the Red Cross. He has since obtained his army files, under the Freedom of Information Act, and is sure he was discharged because of the things Army G-2 had put in his files. He says he was kind of "leftish" then, and he also made some cracks about his colonel, "that sort of thing." So he went back to Chicago and started working in radio again.

After I got out of the army, I had a call, in maybe less than a week, from some gal in the Arthur Meyerhoff Agency representing the Wrigley account. One of the first things I did was to go out to Catalina Island, which Wrigley gave to the merchant marine during the war as a training center. I lived out there in California for several weeks writing scripts for the merchant marine to be played on CBS radio for a program called "We Deliver the Goods." It was about the heroism of the merchant marine—the North Atlantic, the Murmansk Run. The shows were based on actual experiences and played over nationwide radio for the home front. For morale—but also informational. I was not in uniform then. And I won't deny I had something of an uncomfortable feeling not being in uniform. I also went to Washington for a while and did a couple of things for a program called "First Line," about the navy and naval encounters.

I also did a news show about the war—heroism, pro–New Deal, pro-labor. For example, I did a show on Ernie Pyle. I also had a blue-collar news show—doing the human side of the news, from the other side.

Of course, everyone was conscious of the war. I was making speeches for the Office of Price Administration. And you were worried about the guys overseas, your friends. But there was an exhilaration, strangely enough, in contrast to the Vietnam War. You would follow the war and the argument about opening up of the second front and how they were doing at Anzio, the Battle of Leningrad, beachheads, Normandy. The war was always in the news and on our minds.

It was a very congenial time. Everybody was popping drinks for the soldiers in a bar. And sometimes the house would pop. Chicago was a great liberty town. And do you remember the Liberty girls? The little girls; they had a certain way of walking. They'd go arm-in-arm, three of them. And their feet wouldn't come off the pavement. They'd kind of shuffle like. Made them look a little sexier, more challenging. They were young—fifteen, sixteen, maybe—but they would chase after the boys, and the boys would chase after them.

If you want to know what it was like in a small town in New England during the war, the best person to ask, usually, is the editor of the local weekly paper. Stewart and Ann Hoskins owned and edited the Lakeville (Conn.) Journal. *When Stewart went to work in Torrington in a defense factory, Ann took over the paper.*

ANN: Our first reaction after Pearl Harbor was "What can we do?" Stewart had registered for the draft, but could not get in because of his bad hearing. So he said, "I will see if they need me in anything else," and he went over to Torrington to register for war work. As he left, he said, "I don't think they will take me for months." I was down tending the paper and the phone, and the first call was from him, saying, "Can you carry on ? I have to start today." So I did, although I had no real training in newspaper work at all.

Stewart would work at night and straighten out my mistakes, because I'm the world's worst bookkeeper. He also did a lot of the presswork; I got so I could make up the paper in a black apron and put the type together. Of course, it was all hot metal then. We had a linotype operator and a pressman, and then later we got an extra foreman, and we all worked together. I kept writing feverish letters up to the draft board saying they couldn't possibly draft my men, because we were communications and we were important and we had to keep them: and so we kept our men.

We sent the newspaper free to all the guys who were away in service. In the second year of the war we decided to do a special Christmas thing. This particular year we felt that the thing the ones who were away needed most was a picture of their hometown. So we asked the photographers in the six towns in the area if they would do the work for free. And we asked the Legion and other patriotic organizations if they would do the mailing. We did the editing and split it up into eight pages of pictures of people and places, casual pictures, funny pictures, candid-camera shots everywhere, and we got marvelous letters back. One boy wrote back, "I've taken down all my pinup girls and put up the *Journal*."

STEWART: People knew we were knocking ourselves out, and we felt that one of the things the paper should do would be to be a public service. We said, if you had any questions on anything, ask us and we'll find the answers. At one point one woman came in and said you're supposed to answer questions, what should I feed my dog when there's no meat? So I did a little research on the various kinds of dog foods and found one for her.

ANN: I would say, in a village like Lakeville the war was a waiting game—waiting for news of the men who were away and waiting for food. We were the last on the line practically, we were isolated, and the food trucks, when they came in, were half-empty. Very often, to get food, people would gather at four o'clock in the morning with their boxes and sit outside at the First National, which was then in town, and wait for the trucks. I decided I'd try it, and by the time I came in the line, I was able to get one-quarter of a pound of hamburger. So I thought, the heck with that! I'll do with Spam and things we can get, and make dishes out of that, casseroles. I never could understand why we ran out of such silly things. I was sure the army wasn't eating an enormous amount of onions, but I didn't see an onion for six months. Nobody had onions. You'd think that everybody would grow them or something, but they didn't. And butter, of course, was an absolute rarity. It was very funny, we'd be sitting in the office, working feverishly, and someone would come along the street and say, "Butter is in," and everybody, the pressman, the linotypeman, everybody in the office would shoot down to the market and buy the butter and work would stop at that point.

Of course, we had a little of that rumor kind of things where somebody would suspect somebody of having German leanings. There was a restaurant up in Canaan, the Blackbury River Inn, run by a German family. They were refugees, poor darlings, and I understand they had a really tough time. Everybody suspected them. And there was this woman who had been an expatriate for years and came back here to live because it got too hot over there. She wanted to get news from Europe, so she built this tremendous antenna to get foreign news, but everybody thought she was sending secret messages. And there was a long thing in the paper at one point; a professor and his wife from Columbia University had a house in Salisbury. They had some Nisei friends and wanted to bring them up, so they wrote a letter to the paper asking how the community would react to it. One of the officers of the American Legion, whose son was in the Pacific, said, "Sure get any Japanese you can around here so I can knock them down." That was his reaction. Then John McChesney, a great liberal, came out and said this is not what we are fighting the war for, this is exactly the kind of thinking that Hitler has. The fat was in the fire with everybody arguing about it back and forth, and the poor people who wanted to bring up their friends for the summer finally said to heck with it and brought them up anyway. And the people came and marketed and everything else, and nobody paid any attention to them.

Then, of course, there were the real concerns: The young men who were away. We would watch them saying good-bye to their girls in the little village restaurant at night, playing "The White Cliffs Of Dover" and "When the Lights Go On Again All Over The World," sitting earnestly over a cup of coffee or a beer. And you'd see them go off and wonder about them, and they'd come back in different ways. Some of them never came back.

Bill Gold began the war with radio station WCPO in Cincinnati, as its news director. But before long, he was in Washington working for the Washington Post's *radio station— WINX.*

In Cincinnati you had more of a sense of "Hey, aren't times good economically," whereas in Washington there was more of the patriotic vote, people who had dropped what they were doing at home to come to answer the call of the government, which needed lots of new talent. Washington was exhilarating for me because I was just a rube from the country. I had never associated with top national figures. In Cincinnati you covered the mayor, the city council, the state senator, and people of this kind. If one of Ohio's congressional delegations or the governor was your assignment for the day, that was big stuff. Here people at that level of importance were a dime a dozen.

I covered Roosevelt's news conferences regularly. There would be two a week—a morning and an afternoon, so the morning papers and the afternoon papers would have an equal shot at the latest news. The morning session was supposed to start at ten-thirty, and I don't recall it ever starting before eleven. When Mr. Truman became president, that was a big upset, because people had become accustomed to arriving at five minutes before eleven for the ten-thirty newscast—knew they'd wait anyhow. When they arrived at five minutes to eleven for Mr. Truman, it was over.

A small station had to use ingenuity. I remember one day we were waiting for V-E Day or V-J Day, or some big announcement, and I stationed Lew Aiken at a pay phone in the

White House. He was the biggest newscaster we had, big barrel-chested guy and a scrapper, tough.

I said to him, "As we go into the press conference, just tie up that phone, get on the phone and stay on it." This was right outside the pressroom, where there were perhaps some fifty direct-line telephones. I said, "As we bust out of there, there are going to be some people who are going to try to yank you off that phone. When they do, just puff out that big chest of yours and growl, and keep talking, I don't care what you say, and in a few seconds I'll be along."

I don't remember life being very difficult during the war. I heard people say there were shortages and inconveniences. I just thought it was such crap that I would rather not talk about it. The inconveniences we experienced at home were so minor compared to what other people were undergoing in the armed forces. It seemed to me then, and it seems to me now, utterly selfish to think it an inconvenience to line up for cigarettes. What a helluva hardship! Really!

Occasionally somebody would say, "What's the matter with you, you look healthy, why the hell are you not in uniform?" But usually this came from a man who was in uniform and had had a couple of beers, and how can you get mad at him? You just pay no attention to that. Yeah, I felt bad myself; it was just awkward that I was at that age. It was like in bingo, my number was still in there when everybody else was called.

The thing that sticks out in my mind about the war years is the tremendous thrill of having a sense of participation in these things. There was a tremendous social change at the time to admit blacks and females to full citizenship, to accept them in terms of their own abilities, or inabilities, instead of in terms of the stereotypes we were accustomed to. We had no choice except to take anything that was alive and warm and see if we could use it. We learned a great deal. This was our reserve. And we found we had one hell of a reserve we hadn't been using.

The security was so lax in Washington at the time. I remember one session in one of the navy buildings attended by Forrestal, Nimitz, and the head of Eisenhower's air force, and a couple of other people of this sort. The reporters who covered the meeting were not asked to show any credentials. All they had to do was sign a book; you could sign "Mahatma Gandhi" in the book. And the smiling girl sitting there would have said, "Thank you, Mr. Gandhi," and passed you on. It was just fantastic what access the public had to terribly important people. The Pentagon was one of the few places where there was any meaningful security. The rest of Washington was very casual—and God was on our side. We just never got into any difficulty.

And there was no question about the country's unity. You just felt that the stranger sitting next to you, in a restaurant or someplace, felt the same way you did about the basic issues.

Don Baldwin began the war on a small weekly in Idaho Falls—but soon was working for the Associated Press in San Francisco, where he spent the rest of the war.

I never really felt that we ever caught up with the war news. I always felt behind. and so many things were proscribed. For instance, when the Japanese were sending balloons over with incendiary bombs—not over California, but over Oregon—we knew and couldn't write about it. The censorship was voluntary. Anything that might telegraph something that was going to happen was taboo.

Early in the war, right after Pearl Harbor, there was some real fear of an actual invasion by the Japanese. Nobody knew how many Japanese ships were out there—there were all sorts of rumors. As a matter of fact, they would have had no great trouble landing. They would have had a great deal of trouble staying there, but no great trouble landing in the San Francisco area, or particularly south of there.

Late in the war, when you began to get the kamikaze pilots around Okinawa and that area—man, the ships that used to come into San Francisco were a terrible sight. They had been hit sometimes two and three times, and they were just coming in every day. Some were so badly damaged you wondered how they had gotten back. This made a city like San Francisco feel very close to the war.

To begin with, I didn't like the idea of the Nisei evacuation. In Idaho we had quite a few Japanese Americans. They ran truck farms, and I had been to school with some Japanese and liked them. I had had long talks with them, and the feeling around Santa Barbara was that the rich, white farmers were making a grab for the Japanese truck lands, and I think it's true.

But I think the general feeling in California was that it was necessary and a good thing. I think most people felt there was the potential for sabotage, telegraphing information about the movement of ships and troops. Fort Mason was there, ships were coming in and out all the time, so you had to get the Japanese out. This was a state of hysteria—in California more so than other states.

Mary McMurria worked for the Columbus (Ga.) Ledger.

Suddenly, from one day to the next, I was snatched out of the Women's Department and put in as city editor over this big newsroom. They had had trouble getting men to fill the post, and they had had a fellow, an unusual type, who wore purpley pink pants. When the editor told one of the newsmen that a new city editor was coming in, the newsman said, "I hope he doesn't wear pink pants." And the editor said, "Well, I don't think you'll be able to tell."

It was an experience for me. I was one of the first female city editors of that size paper, and it was exciting. I had to borrow a really snappy suit jacket from a woman—most of my reporters were women—to have my picture taken for *Time* magazine.

Henry, my husband, had arthritis, and it began to get worse about then, and we decided to go down to Homestead, Florida, which was almost as far south as we could go. So I quit the job in that first winter, and when I came back, I was a feature writer. The paper decided to sponsor tin-can and newspaper collections at the schools. Every week I'd have to visit the schools. We'd have the papers and the cans collected and keep a record of who had collected the most. There was a lot of excitement among the schoolchildren because about once a month our publisher, who was a colonel in the army reserve, would present a pennant to the school, which would be raised on the flagpole. I had to keep the excitement generated by writing features on this program.

Paul Kneeland was a reporter for the Medford *(Mass.)* Mercury. *But the war gave him an opportunity to move to the* Boston Globe.

From a personal point of view, Pearl Harbor didn't mean a thing to me. This sounds terribly callous, but I was 4-F. I had been classified October 16, 1940, because of a congenital defect in my left arm.

The editor of my paper was drafted, and I became editor of the paper. I had a small staff: one woman, and two men who were 4-F, for whatever reasons, I don't know. The woman was a middle-aged lady; she hardly was going to join the WACs. So the war didn't affect my working. As a matter of fact, when I became editor, I was given a fifteen dollar raise, plus the glory of it all.

At that time the *Medford Mercury* was a provincial newspaper—printed no news about what progress the war was making on the eastern and western fronts. This was a common thing for many small daily and weekly newspapers at that time. If Dunkirk was invaded, you'd never learn it from the *Medford Mercury*. You'd buy a Boston newspaper or listen to the radio. In November '42 advertising was dropped because food stores didn't advertise. There was no necessity for advertising that a pound of butter was 49¢, with people standing in line to buy it. So financially the *Medford Mercury* was in straits, and instead of getting $37.50 a week as the editor, I was getting $15 cash and an IOU. Well, after a pocketful of IOUs I went to the manager and said: "What about this?" He said: "Well, we're doing the best we can." I said: "That's not good enough for me." I said I'd take it to the state labor board, and I did. The week after, I was fired—for wanting to collect my just and due salary. But they paid me off, over $200, and that ended my career at the *Medford Mercury*. After that I shopped for a job in Boston and was taken on at the *Boston Globe*.

I know for sure that I wouldn't have gotten the job had it not been for vacancies caused by the war. My early assignments were general reporting. I knew this war was going to end, and I had to do my very, very best to work up some sort of specialty so the editors would consider me when the returnees came back.

In 1943 I covered OPA (the Office of Price Administration)

as a regular beat, five days a week. An OPA press conference was held every day at three-thirty with the codirectors of the information bureau, plus one of the men from enforcement, who might have a story on black markets, or one of the men in price, who might have an announcement to make about the fact that butter was no longer going to be two coupons but three coupons. It was nothing to walk out of that office and write a story which was guaranteed page one. Everybody wondered: Are they going to cut down on tire rationing? When are we going to get more nylons? After two or three months we all got to know the directors of each department. They would come down and be interviewed by the press. Well, the trick was not to wait for the press conference but to jump the press conference and talk to the directors the day before. So that's what we did. In all my years in this business I never saw such rivalry. Everybody was trying to get the scoop, an extremely old-fashioned word, which is no longer used, about the fact that nylons were going to cost two coupons instead of one beginning on a certain date.

Boston was an extremely happy city during the war. We had the Charlestown Navy Yard here, and we had sailors on the streets, going to the movie houses when they had stage shows, and you could hear Vaughn Monroe or Harry James. People—servicemen and nonservicemen—were out for fun. The Charlestown Navy Yard was working nightly on three shifts, around the clock, repairing vessels and making equipment for the navy.

It was a happy town in spite of the tragedies, because every family shared that tragedy. "I lost a son"; "My daughter lost her husband." This travels up and down the town. A lot of that conversation was common in ration lines, swapping stories: "Is your boy here?" "Is he there?" "He's in the hospital, I hope he lives." "He lost his leg, lost his arm."

Gus Robbins was the owner and editor of a small newspaper in Hopewell, Virginia.

At the beginning of the war I had planned to make it a daily. It was the biggest semiweekly newspaper in Virginia—the *Hopewell News.* Of course, the war came along, and I couldn't get newsprint, so I went daily immediately after the war.

We had a National Guard company, Company E, which I was sort of godfather of—I had promoted it. In February 1941 they were taken into federal service and sent to Fort Meade, and the day after Pearl Harbor they were sent to Washington to guard the government buildings.

When the company left Washington, they went down to Fort Bragg. Then they were broken up, and the two hundred boys scattered all over the world. I must have had a thousand letters from them, which I had to go back at night and type, because I published every single one of them.

There was a great deal of sorrow over all the boys leaving. In addition to Company E, the draft started taking the boys, and, of course, that hit a small city pretty hard. But the general attitude was one of the utmost support of the war.

When the first big scrap drive came along, the government did not run it or pay for it. I was president of the Virginia Press Association then, and I got five daily newspapers to put up the money to rent an office and get an executive director. We put on a statewide drive, and every single newspaper in Virginia, from the smallest weekly to the biggest daily ran every release that I wrote and mailed out to them about the scrap drive—every one of them.

The public responded beautifully. We had a very wide boulevard in front of one of our schools—and the city roped off one full block, and we had that street full, piled as high as you could get it. The scrap dealer went through it, separated it, baled it, and shipped it out by rail to where it was needed. That was the way it was handled, not only in Virginia but across the country. We were proud of that. I've got four or five National Guard commendations for this effort.

Jack Altshul began the war working on a Long Island weekly newspaper but soon transferred to Newsday.

A guy I knew, who was working on a small paper on Long Island, decided he was very draftable, so he ducked out to South America and let me have some of his clients. This meant I was stringing on Long Island for the *New York Times* and the *Herald Tribune*, until, all of a sudden, they had a newsprint problem and stopped it. So I found that my most profitable vehicle for breaking news was at the new newspaper *Newsday*.

After about six months they asked me to come work on the desk at night, in Hempstead, and six months after that, in January 1943, they asked me to become city editor.

I had this limited deferment because of my eye. The first impact of the war you felt was the boys going away. All of a sudden you had almost a full female staff, which in those days was a little innovative. My wife, Edna, for instance, was the first female photographer in the metropolitan area at the time. She walked in, a beautiful girl looking for a job. Hathway looked at her and said, "We're hiring her." And she came out a hell of a good photographer.

Even then, the Island was a fairly prosperous area. They didn't have any ghettos in those days. It was a commuting community, and most people had white-collar jobs until the start of the war. Then, all of a sudden, you had Grumman, Republic, and Sperry in our own midst advertising for women machinists, welders, and riveters. They must have hired 100,000 people.

That was the first big influx of that kind of industry on Long Island. A lot of women had husbands away at war. I think they would have worked at these defense factories whether or not they were paid for it in many cases. In those days most people were making fifty, sixty bucks a week. Today you consider that a pittance, but fifty or sixty bucks a week then was good bread. But you didn't have a feeling of boom times. Even if people had a helluva lot more money than they had before, what could they do with it? They couldn't buy new cars, they couldn't buy appliances, they couldn't get gas, fancy cuts of meat, butter, or any of the status-symbol commodities.

Ted Giddings was the city editor of the Berkshire Eagle *in Pittsfield, Massachusetts.*

I think the war affected our community the way it did most. It was rallying around the flag, so to speak. Civil defense and war gardens, a lot of volunteer activity, and that sort of thing. I started my own garden. Also I was involved in civil defense, an air-raid warden.

We went in pretty big for salvage drives. During the war, a reenactment of General Knox's march down from Fort Ticonderoga was staged, picking up some salvage material—old cannons. A lot of the towns donated cannons, scrap iron that had been in front of town halls and places like that for years, practically back to the Civil War. Those were all lugged off to Boston and shipped out to be used for scrap iron, to some ordnance factory somewhere. *Life* magazine sent a photographer up here on that occasion.

Frankly, I was more aware of food shortages in World War I, as a child, than in World War II. At the *Eagle* we did have a shortage of paper, and there were times when we had to run smaller papers because of it. Gasoline shortage created some problems in this rural area. With what they called an A-ration card, you really couldn't go anywhere outside of the community very much.

When the first servicemen began to come home, they had a dinner party for returnees, and they didn't have too much to say. But one of their associates who had stayed behind in our composing room gave a talk on the hardships that he endured trying to have a war garden. It cracked them up. He was a very amusing guy. He told of the hoes he broke and the trouble he had with seeds. He kind of stole the show.

Alison Arnold was society editor of the Boston Herald *as well as a mother with two children and her husband in the service.*

The war changed the pattern of social life in Boston, because all of the social affairs—the big events and parties, whenever there were any—were all to benefit some kind of war relief. The debutante parties were cut out. Everything was done for war relief.

Partly because the lighting was dim, people didn't go out much at night. The streetlights all had shields over them, and we had trial blackouts. You never knew when it was going to happen. You would hear this horrible siren blowing, and that meant you had to turn out all your lights and sit in the dark until the all clear blew.

Downtown I felt uncomfortable. Sometimes the servicemen sort of got out of hand in Scollay Square, which is now the government center. In those days it was pretty bad. Sailors would come there on leave and cause havoc, and they would have riots down there. Nothing major, but the police were always down there. Young ladies were more or less advised to keep away from Scollay Square. I had a daughter thirteen, and I think she was at the age where she was intrigued that there were so many soldiers and people in uniform. Like all the girls at that age, she thought it was quite thrilling to see all the boys in uniform, but she wasn't allowed to date any of them. There was a war, and people were going off to war. She thought it was quite romantic. She eventually got over it. All the glamor went out of uniforms and war as time went by.

Artist Leo Hershfield worked in New York for the newspaper PM *and later for the office of War Information in Washington.*

I recall doing many cartoons and caricatures of Nazis, Fascists, quislings. There was one cartoon which brought plenty of fan mail—it showed a toothy Japanese militarist with tank cannon pointing out of the page with the caption: ''Maybe Honorable U.S. wish return of scrap iron, yes?'' That was more than a year before Pearl Harbor. The U.S. had been a prime source of scrap metal for Japan for years. In fact the miles of track of New York's dismantled elevated had been shipped there.

A lot of folks couldn't get used to the idea of our being allies with the Russians, but we were. And there would not have been an Allied victory if they had not rallied from the Nazi push toward Moscow and with such battles as Stalingrad.

People, if they argued too strenuously for aid to Russia, were suspected of having Communist leanings or perhaps being card-carrying CPs, but I can't say truthfully who were or weren't. I never laid eyes on a red card. The Hearst press in particular baited *PM* as a Communist stronghold, and it was all a lot of hogwash.

I left *PM* in early '43 to join a group of good friends and former *PM* editors in Washington. My job at the imposing new Social Security Building on Independence Avenue, which the Office of War Information took over, was as art director/artist for the Domestic News Bureau, which meant helping put out a paper called *Victory Bulletin*—a sort of showcase for information and illustrations to be sent out to newspapers around the country, with drawings and charts to be mailed to the smaller dailies and weeklies in mat form.

I also had the job of urging editorial and gag cartoonists to contribute drawings, and they were most cooperative in wanting to help in the war effort. There was Ed Duffy, two-time Pulitzer Prize winner on the *Baltimore Sun*, and Dan Fitzpatrick of the *St. Louis Post-Dispatch*, to name a couple of the editorial artists. Among the gag cartoonists were Bill Steig, Garrett Price, Richard Decker, Chon Day, Sogolow—all *New Yorker* contributors—and many others.

PM liked the idea of having an artist-correspondent in Washington. I was given some assignments but dreamed up many for myself. One was a double-page feature of "A Day at Walter Reed Hospital." Heading for the designated operating room, I went in the wrong door. Looking down at an operation in company of doctors and nurses. I learned I was watching a hysterectomy. The military hospital also operated on wives of military personnel. In another operating room, properly gowned and masked, I sat and sketched while the surgeon sawed away at a resection of a leg stump. Blood all over the place. The young soldier, with a local anaesthetic, seemed quite unconcerned about the whole thing. In the manner of standard TV correspondents' queries nowadays, I asked, "How do you feel?" "Well," he said, "it's like sitting on a board and somebody sawing on it."

PM's Sunday editor, Bill McCleery, had me do a number of covers of generals and other notables. It's a long list. De Gaulle on the White House lawn; General Wainwright, after his ordeal at Corregidor and as prisoner, at the Pentagon; James Byrnes, director of war mobilization, in the East Wing of the White House—a shocking experience, that. Walking across the thick carpet to shake his hand, I built up enough static to light a bulb. Our hands crackled, and I jumped. He grinned and said something about his magnetic personality. Good guy to sketch. So was Dean Acheson.

Melville Grosvenor, later editor-in-chief of the National Geographic *and chairman emeritus of the board of the National Geographic Society, was assistant editor of the magazine during the war and a graduate of the Naval Academy in the 1920s.*

At the magazine, believe it or not, my Naval Academy training came in handy. One doesn't ordinarily think of Annapolis as a good preparation for editorial work, but, for me, it proved to be ideal in the circumstances of the war.

At the academy we had been taught to think globally; I was used to studying maps to the concepts of strategy; I knew of battles and their place in history. But we weren't so much interested in the battles; we wanted to describe the background of the islands and archipelagos involved, and we worked very closely with the government.

Take the case of Okinawa. G-2 came to the *Geographic* in 1943 and asked in confidence to see all the photographs, maps, and material we possessed on Okinawa. I made a mental note of this. Then I studied the map, and it seemed obvious that our forces would have to hit Okinawa before proceeding north to attack Japan itself. It was an excellent jumping-off place for this final attack. At the *Geographic* we had very little in the files on the island—just a few pictures. But we learned of a retired member of the State Department who'd been stationed on Okinawa for seventeen years and lived out in Virginia.

He had an excellent collection of pictures. He agreed to do an article for us on the island, and our article was published in May 1945—and delivered the very month that the U.S. Marines landed on Okinawa. One of the things the author had told us about were the deep, elaborate tombs employed by Okinawans. He maintained that they would be very effective in a military defense, and that's one of the things the Japanese did on the island. They employed the tombs as defensive installations. We often managed, throughout the war, to be a jump ahead of the action. We felt at that time that our mission was simply to present the facts so that people could understand where our forces were operating.

Throughout the war we felt that we were being helpful, not only to the American public but to the military as well. Soldiers and sailors would write letters telling us how they had *Geographic* maps everyplace they went. We printed them by the hundreds of thousands. We even had special printings of our regular maps, which were distributed all through the army, the navy, and the air force.

Just after the marines had landed on Guadalcanal, Adm. Chester Nimitz made an inspection tour to that island. He took off in an airplane from a New Hebrides base. The airplane, the only one available, was an army B-17 with a brand-new young pilot and a new crew just out from the States. They had never before flown in this area. All they had was a strip map showing the route up to Guadalcanal, with nothing appearing on the flanks before or behind. Well, after they'd been flying for several hours, Nimitz said, "Given this length of time and this air speed, we've obviously flown past the island and are now heading out into the Coral Sea." So he sent his aide up to ask the pilot where they were and when they would land. The pilot replied, "Quite frankly, I don't know; I'm lost. I'm off the track and I've not the slightest idea where we are." Nimitz said, "Does anybody here have any maps?" One of his aides said, "Yes, I've got a *Geographic* map of the Pacific in my suitcase." So they got it out, and the admiral plotted their course from the Hebrides. They discovered that they had probably gone right through some clouds and missed the island chain, and they were truly flying over the Coral Sea. So Nimitz plotted it out again and said, "We've got to make a 120-degree turn, and if we do, we're bound to hit the islands coming around like that. So he sent orders to the pilot saying, "Lieutenant, I'm taking command of the airplane now, and I order you to change to such-and-such course and fly that until we pick up the island chain." Well, they did that, and very shortly the islands were looming up on the horizon. From the map, they managed to identify the individual islands immediately. This enabled them to change course again, and they landed on Guadalcanal with only half an hour of fuel left. Nimitz told me after the war that the *Geographic* map had undoubtedly saved his life. This was no small thing, since he was commander-in-chief of the fleet at the time.

Before the onset of World War II, admirals and generals as a class had little use for air power. Even Pearl Harbor didn't shake them up much. I myself had always been enthusiastic about what a big fleet of carriers could do—particularly in the Pacific. My aviation friends said that if would be possible to take tankers, cover them up, and put flight decks on them, thus converting them into instant carriers. I wrote all of this in an article in the magazine. Not long before the war I was discussing this with Adolphus Andrews, who was chief of naval operations at that time, and he said, "Grosvenor, you've been out of the navy too long. You're out of touch with things. We only have these carriers to please the flyboys. They are very vulnerable, and when they fire their five-inch antiaircraft guns, the concussion damages the airplanes on deck.'' This, I repeat, was just a few months before the war. While I couldn't argue with him, given his position, I did go and write an article and got permission to publish it in the magazine. The lead of my story was about the German battleship *Bismarck* being discovered and disabled by carrier aircraft before battleships closed in for the kill. Then there was the sinking of *Repulse* and the *Prince of Wales* off Malaya. Then, before we went on press, the Battle of the Coral Sea was announced, which was a great naval victory, due largely to air power, and we put that in the story. We were on the press and down to the last few pages of the run when news came about the Battle of Midway. So I updated four or five times right straight along, just like a newspaper, changing the lead as the news broke. The article came out with the title ''Aircraft Carrier: New Queen on the Sea,'' and pictures accompanied it. When it was in proof, the admiral in command of the naval air arm asked for sixteen galleys, and he sent them all around the Navy Department saying, ''Look, the *National Geographic* is publishing this article, and they're a pretty conservative organization; there must be something to what they are saying.'' This was a time when the navy air arm was trying to put a bill through Congress to authorize one hundred new carriers. The admiral sent some galleys up to Capitol Hill, and President Roosevelt was told about it, and I think it actually helped to get the vote for these additional carriers. I'm very proud of that.

5

The War Effort—Almost
Everyone Was Involved

*John Lacey was a patent attorney for the firm of Lacey and
Lacey in Washington, D.C. He had also been doing part-time
work for the Carnegie Institution. When the war came along,
he decided to leave his law firm and to work first for Carnegie,
then for the Johns Hopkins University research program.*

The basic project I worked on during the war was the proximity fuse. It was a radio device put in the nose of a shell or
bomb which caused the shell or bomb to go off when it came
within an optimum distance from the target, such as an airplane or ship. They even used them in the Battle of the Bulge
in howitzers; the shells sprayed the ground with fragments and
killed people in the trenches and foxholes.

The proximity fuse was not invented in this country; it was
invented in England in its basic form, but the development
started at Carnegie in the fall of 1940, and then it was transferred to Hopkins in 1942.

The Germans and the Japanese were also trying to develop
it. The big problem was the little radio tube that was necessary—we didn't have transistors in those days. The problem

was to develop a tube which would withstand the shock of going off inside a gun. You have to remember that when a shell is fired, let's say a five-inch, 38-mm gun, the setback was on the order of twenty thousand g's or twenty thousand times gravity. There was also a problem with spin. To get a radio tube to stand up under that, it had to be very carefully designed. We started by dropping hearing-aid tubes—Western Electric and GE and a few others had already come on the market with them—from the top of a building over at Carnegie. Then they fired one from a smooth-bore cannon out in Virginia, and they finally got one to work.

The work was all top secret. This was down in Saint Mary's County at a place called Northern Neck. The fellows would load the station wagons in the morning and leave at the crack of dawn, go down to the proving grounds and be there all day. They had a draft board in Saint Mary's County, and one of these fellows was from that area, so our problem was to keep the draft board from drafting these men into the army, because they were highly specialized people. I remember going down with an attorney to try to convince those fellows that these men were necessary to the war effort. One farmer said to me: "Well, all I know is these fellows come down here, and they go in there in the morning and come out at night. I don't know what they're doing; they may play pinochle for all I know." But we did get most of them off.

The Reverend Harold Toliver was pastor of Grace Memorial Church in Pittsburgh. His wife, Elva, who taught Sunday school, joined us as we talked about the war years.

HAROLD: Being a minister, I realized it would not affect me personally, as far as going into the service was concerned. We had only one daughter, and she was very young. And Elva's brother was too young. Of course, war made us more aware of the rigid segregation in our armed forces. It became apparent that this was not going to be an easy problem to solve there, any more than it was in the national scene. So we listened to what the boys were saying and read what they were writing back. They were all loyal young men, as far as serving their country was concerned. They went where they were told, but they reported experiences that were very unpleasant. And it made us feel more and more that no matter what the outcome of the war was to be, we had to continue our efforts and our struggle toward recognition that blacks who served their country had a right to equality. This was one of the main issues we pursued all through the war and have been pursuing ever since. One thing that impressed me a great deal in the latter stage of the war, when General Eisenhower was in command, was that his attitude was not very favorable. It was President Truman—a Southerner, a Midwesterner—who took a stand and said, "Now, this thing has to change." I remember very well one speech he made somewhere in the South—I think it must have been a military group. He said very vigorously, in his typical style, that greater concern had to be shown for the black soldiers and that this rigid pattern of segregated units had to go. He was in the Deep South when he said it, and of course, it wasn't a very popular thing for him to say. But he didn't court popularity. And eventually the thing that he set in motion became a reality. He desegregated the army by executive order, and Eisenhower went along with that.

ELVA: One of the things that, I think, helped the relationships between the races during that time was the organization in communities to get people together in case there was a disaster in our own country. I remember even in Schenley Heights, there were people who came together, organized, and did community things of unity and fellowship. Women began taking jobs they'd never taken before. Some wanted to operate the streetcars. I really wanted to drive a taxi or something.

HAROLD: I didn't let her, not that I was making any money as the pastor of a small church.

ELVA: So we organized nursing classes, and there were also women who were involved in trying to relocate the Nisei. They were very much disturbed by the fact that these people, who were American-born citizens, were uprooted because they were of Japanese descent. One of the things our relocation committee did was try to find communities which would accept them, and that wasn't easy. People were afraid of them. They were prejudiced against anyone who doesn't look white.

One of the effects of the war among black people was the new job opportunities that opened up. There were openings that they'd never had before in some industries. They were making good money, and there were those who were happy to take advantage of that to buy homes they had been wanting to buy for a long time and send their children to college. There were many who didn't rejoice in the war but rejoiced in the opportunities that came. One thing that wars do is to cut down on discrimination.

HAROLD: For the time being. But then as soon as the pressure is off, things tend to go back just the same as they had been before. And those who had jobs are laid off.

ELVA: Another thing the war did, it brought interracial marriage very close to many of our people. Because sons, when they were sent all over the world, brought home brides. One of them brought home a German bride and another a Japanese. We had young men stationed in Hawaii, Africa, the Middle East, and in Germany, Japan, well, you name it.

But I was very impressed with what the young men who had been in my Sunday-school class and were sent to different parts of the world said in their letters. They didn't talk too much about the horrors of war, but they talked about the kind of things that brought them together in ways that they had never expected with other people. There were those who spoke of feeling that the only way that they could ever worship in a church was in a certain kind of building and how they learned that even in mud and rain they could pray and have a service. Or to have someone who was in Italy find that there would be people who would take them in, almost as a member of their families. And having a young man who was in the Middle East write back in descriptive words of places that he had only read about sometime in the Scriptures or sometimes in his geography book. And one young man who, during the eruption of the volcano Vesuvius, sent an envelope of ashes. I still have them in a little jar.

Margaret and Esther Dudley, sisters, lived together in Philadelphia at the time of Pearl Harbor. They were interviewed together at Leisure World in Silver Spring, Maryland.

ESTHER: I was a legal secretary in the office of chief counsel of the Internal Revenue Service—in the Philadelphia branch office.

MARGARET: I was a nurse in a dispensary for the treatment of tuberculosis. Having been turned down for the army's Nurse

Corps—it wasn't the Army Nurse Corps then; it was under the Red Cross—I didn't feel the war would make any difference in my way of living. I was turned down several times by the Selective Service people. One of the things I immediately did was to go and take a course in first-aid nursing. As the war progressed and as things settled down—no, not settled down, because everybody was upset—I thought I had to do something. So I joined the civil defense, and during a blackout I would have to go down to the fire station on Chestnut Street and report in. After work I'd go to the Red Cross Blood Bank, and if we had an alert, I would have to leave there to go to my station.

ESTHER: We were located on the twentieth floor of the Lincoln Liberty Building, at the corner of Broad and Chestnut. And on about the eighth floor, the interceptor command had been set up. After Pearl Harbor an emergency call went out to I don't know how many government agencies. We, being located in the same building, and every one of us having been cleared by the FBI earlier, were asked to report to interceptor command. My work was plotting. Of course, it was volunteer work. But while you were there, you were under the authority of the army, and there was no foolishness. Philadelphia was practically an arsenal, so it was very serious. You had the Frankfort Arsenal and a lot of heavy machinery plants making war equipment. Then you had the navy yard, and I think it was felt that Philadelphia would be a target of a suicide attack.

There was a big board in the center of a big room, and the plotters were around the board. Around the top was a balcony. The people there had earphones, and they were connected with people who watched outside, located all around the country. They would call in to the people on the balcony. Then these people would call down to the people on the board, and we would set up what represented airplanes and plot them across the board. Over on one side were the officers in command; they could look down and see the picture, and they would know what to tell the interceptor command, which was located somewhere outside of Philadelphia. The officer in charge could tell if it was a commercial plane or an army plane, and, of course, we were always on the lookout for unknown planes. One night it was very, very exciting. We don't know whether they were pulling an exercise on us to see if we were on our toes, or if it was the real thing. About fifty miles off the coast of Atlantic City a plane was coming. The navy was out there and started calling in. The plane was unknown. We didn't know whether it was a suicide squad. Major Quesada got his boys, and out they went in P-40s—you saw the P-40s going across the board moving out into the ocean; they chased the plane away. But whether or not it was the real thing, they didn't tell us.

MARGARET: What was very painful to me was the feeling I had as the war went on, you know, your country right or wrong. I felt very strongly that I should be doing more. Here I looked good, and the Red Cross kept sending me letters, even though they had turned me down. So, finally, I wrote to the Red Cross—they were just about to be put under the Army Nurse Corps—and I said, "Please! Either let me have an examination and see whether or not I can make it or just stop these letters." It was a trauma to me; it made me feel like I was a slacker every time I got one of those letters. Finally, they did let me go for a physical and said I was okay, and I got my orders in August of 1943 to go. Through a friend of mine, I met Nick, a British boy on the *H.M.S. Manchester*. The ship was in for repair. It had been hit in the middle. I dated Nick for about three months. It wasn't one of those terrific affairs—just fun. His interest was to get the war over with. He did think we were millionaires because we had a refrigerator. He couldn't believe it—the standard of living two women could have! I never saw him after the war. It was just sort of a wartime friendship. A lot of fun. He'd bring up liquor and cigarettes—you know, that was all rationed.

ESTHER: There were a lot of exciting times. It was a whole new way of life. I wouldn't say it was all sad or depressing. You would go through some very deeply emotional periods, either on a very high note or on a very low note, like the day my sister left to report to camp. You put someone on the train, say good-bye to them, and knew you might never see them again.

Dean Elmer Louis Kayser was a professor of European History at George Washington University in Washington, D.C.

As I look at it now, it's a wonder the university wasn't temporarily closed. Take my own department—History. I was about the only man that remained. And so I found myself teaching eighteen hours a week. At the same time I was serving as the dean and busily bringing in part-time teachers who happened to be in Washington to take a great part of the teaching load.

As for the students, the graduate students moved out very quickly. But the V-5 and V-12 programs saved the day as far as assuring us a continuing body of male students. Our teaching problems were exaggerated by the ambitious war contracts we took. For example, the one that led to setting up our human-resources project here and the one that produced the bazooka. We had to furnish staff to keep the projects going. That pushed us very hard, but it had its rewards.

My idea as to the climate of wartime Washington is more or less colored by my experience here with university students. There was a lot of suspicion in Washington. The atmosphere was quite taut. I can mention one case that would illustrate that. A brilliant lad of great literary ability, liberal in thought, found himself faced with the need to be a patriot. And yet he was documented because he had written in the *Hatchet* [the GWU paper] and was active in this, that, and the other. There he was. Military service comes up. He has a fine mind, and he of course wants a commission. All of his documentation is brought up. And I found myself in this case, and in many others, having to interpret not always to understanding people, what a good mind, a free mind, would do in an intellectual academic atmosphere, and what he would do when faced with the necessity for military service—convincing them that he could develop a sense of command and dedication that was not conditioned by what had gone before. Because he had been an intense believer before, he could be an intense believer now.

Then I was harassed by interrogators—FBI, Civil Service. They would pursue me to my house to get information; they'd come before me with these stenographer's notebooks they'd pull out of their pocket, and they'd begin. As I say, the wave of suspicion was terrible. I dealt with thousands of young men. When they were asked to give a reference, they'd put my name down, because they had taken, say, Ancient History with me.

I didn't know them half as well as I knew Nero. I'd never give any information over the phone. They'd say: "Oh, this is war, this is war, we haven't time . . . ." Oh, that pressure was awful. That's why my phone is still unlisted.

Nelson Poynter, then owner of the St. Petersburg Times, *spent part of the war as OWI's man in Hollywood. He said that* Variety *quickly named his office "The Little White House."*

I made it clear—and they were most receptive, because it was a very patriotic bunch in Hollywood—that our office had utterly no authority, that we wanted none, that they could make a picture saying this whole thing was a mistake and that Hitler was right and we couldn't do a thing to them, and we felt that was as it should be in this country, that during wartime we could maintain freedom of information. So they would come to me and say, "What can I do?" They wanted material from Washington.

I dealt mostly with writers and directors. They would have an idea and say, "Is this going to help the war effort?" Probably one of the most helpful things I was able to offer was reminding them that after the war the pictures they were making would have wide circulation all over the world. No other country could even approach the influence that Hollywood had over literally hundreds of millions of people overseas, dubbed in with the native languages or with just titles, like our early silent movies. So scores of times, in consulting with writers, I would remind them, "How is this picture going to look after the war when shown in Italy? Or in Japan? Or Germany?" For instance, Dore Schary had just made a picture with an American in combat with a Japanese, who said something about, "You yellow-bellied bastard." And I said, "You know, China is our ally." I saw him a couple of years ago in New York, and he recalled that simple, obvious thing.

I think Hollywood's impact on the war effort was very good. In the first place, entertainment was curtailed as soon as they put gasoline rationing in, and we went on twenty-four-hour shifts in our factories, making munitions and war materials of all kinds. In places like Detroit, motion picture houses were open literally twenty-four hours a day, so that people coming off the night shift, if they wanted to relax and go to the movies, could do so. And before they went on the night shift. This brought enormous prosperity to Hollywood.

There were amusing incidents—one small producer, I've forgotten his name, who specialized in B films, cowboy films, came to me and said, "I make cowboy pictures. Do you know whether the government is going to continue to let us have film to do this?" I said, "Of course. You're making some of the most fundamental pictures there are, because it always turns out that law and order will prevail against the bad guys. That's all this war is about. We're fighting for law and order, based on consent."

Evelyn Keyes was a young star, working for Columbia Pictures in Hollywood. Two years before Pearl Harbor, there was the premiere of MGM's Gone with the Wind, *in which Miss Keyes played the role of Scarlet O'Hara's sister.*

Once, right after Pearl Harbor, I was awakened in the middle of the night. It was pitch-dark, the light wouldn't go on, and I thought they had pulled the main switch in Los Angeles. Outside it was like a newsreel of the opening of a movie with big searchlights—light jutted up in the air, and I thought, "Oh, my God, the Japs are coming." I was seeing what I thought were parachutes hanging in the air; they turned out to be puffs of smoke. They were shooting at something, and so I grabbed the poker and I was ready.

I just worked almost steadily during the war. If it wasn't a picture, then it was in a portrait gallery making stills from pictures. They never stopped: War and star making—the war effort and selling bonds were a continuation of what we were doing. For publicity they'd send you out with other pictures, even if they weren't yours, just so your name got in the paper or on the radio.

There was a shortage of pickers for the crops, so they sent a bunch of us girls out, always combining getting your name in the paper and the war effort. We went out into the field and picked tomatoes all day. And the Mexicans complained because the girls were taking their work away from them. We gave them the boxes of tomatoes we picked so they could collect the money. But we did this with photographers clicking away.

We did what we were supposed to do. But we were so welcome everywhere and so eagerly sought. I spent a great deal of time in bathing suits for pinups. Even that was part of the war effort. It's funny when you think of it, because our careers were built on the war-camp walls.

We visited lots of army camps, saying hello or good-bye as they departed to go off to get killed. I was always escorted around by the brass—never an enlisted man. Once, I was supposed to have lunch in some mess hall; we got out of the car, went in, and there was a sea of black faces, because everything was segregated then. One of the officers escorting me said. "Oh, no, this is the wrong mess." The guys all looked up to see this movie star. "No, no, the wrong mess." We went out, and as we were going away, I felt guilty. I thought, is that why we didn't go in there, because they were black? Should I speak up, should I say "Look, here, men, don't do this; I'm against segregation. Can we go back there and have mess with the black guys?" And then I thought, well, who are you to think they'd want you for lunch; maybe they think you're a silly white thing they don't want to have any part of.

The hospitals were so depressing. I don't know how anybody could visit one in any kind of war. I went to one hospital, and they were all blind, not one single one could see.

I got a letter from somebody who had got his sight back— the first thing he did was to go see a picture of mine because he remembered my voice and he wanted to see what went with it. He told me how he got married, had children, got a job, and everything. That was nice.

When I was in California, I had a regular night when I went to the USO, and so did everyone else. Every city had a canteen, and so every time I went to a city, I would go to that too. The boys always behaved themselves. They treated us with huge respect. Since television, it has changed, because now they know you're real people. But at that time, you weren't quite a real person. You weren't really a girl.

Most of the movies we made then supported the war in some way. We also made some shorts for the Signal Corps. The message was "A slip of the lip may sink a ship," that sort of thing. I also did something about venereal disease, several of those.

The people in Hollywood wanted to help. If there were any

who didn't, they kept quiet. The whole country was for this war. The war years were exciting, very exciting. I guess it was a way of life.

The novelist James M. Cain was a scriptwriter in Hollywood. His novel Mildred Pierce *had just been published, and although it had not made as big a splash as* The Postman Always Rings Twice, *which was published in the mid–1930s, it was a best-seller. Cain was eighty-four when I interviewed him at his home in Hyattsville, Maryland, and he began by telling me that he was "in the First World War, when the bullets were really flying."*

I have no recollection what I was working on at the time of Pearl Harbor. I may have been working on a book, but I very quickly became chairman of some kind of local committee. God knows what we did—had to take courses under the Red Cross, some kind of air-raid stuff.

I think I was almost unique in the way I felt about [the war]. I think most of them persuaded themselves that they were doing a pretty important patriotic work and deserved a great deal of credit. There was not much talk going around about it. You have to remember that Hollywood is a very peculiar place. You can be having a conversation with a writer and compliment him on some war work he was doing, and he would be very pleased to hear what you had to say, and you would be sincere. And his wife would say, "Give me a light," and you'd light her cigarette, and she'd say, "My, but he's self-sacrificing—at three thousand dollars a week! My heart is bleeding!"

But the general atmosphere out there was pretty high-minded, pretty patriotic, and pretty quiet. Hollywood never played it noisy and never played it big, nor did they do any bragging. There was that general feeling about it. Keep it low; don't let yourself believe all the stuff about what an important guy you are because you work for pictures.

The only visible effect of the war you would see was, suddenly, every director, every writer had suede patches on his elbows. I was telling somebody about this, some writer in the course of writing me up, from the East, and he said, "Patches by Abercrombie."

The war didn't exactly impact on the industry: it impacted on nine hundred guys separately. For example, Clark Gable, he had the office up the hall from me at Metro, in the Thalberg Building, known as the Iron Lung. Gable was in a captain's uniform. I think, Air Corps. And he wanted to go to France and fight. But the government felt that he was so much more use being Gable for picture release and for publicity purposes right there at Metro than he would have been as one of a thousand combat flyers. There was only one Gable; making use of him was the main thing. Getting killed would have been very bad.

Most of them doing the pictures at that time were people like me—either too old or one way or another physically unable to take part in combat duty. You must remember that motion pictures had been declared an essential industry by whoever made the major decisions, the War Department maybe. They were so important for purposes of morale that nobody was knocking the picture business. But individual people in the picture business wanted to do their share. I knew dozens of guys that were commissioned, and some weren't commissioned, just enlisted. It left the picture business operated by older writers and directors and so on, and actors, of course, and women. There was no great excitement to it; you'd have scarcely noticed any difference in the way the lots functioned with the war going on.

I have to say there was some concern about the Japanese. They talked about the monstrous injustice of herding them into concentration camps, but they had themselves to thank. Before the war, if they weren't a nation of spies, they were giving a hell of an imitation of it.

I remember down in the Palos Verdes Estates, somewhere, there was a hilltop restaurant. And a lady and I were having lunch down there, and the proprietor of this place stopped by to chat. We were sitting there looking down at the ocean, perhaps a quarter of a mile away. Between us and the ocean were hummingbirds. Beautiful, shimmering in the sunlight and darting in and out at flowers. And he sat there chatting, and he had a thick German accent, and he excused himself and went off, and she said, "Did it ever enter your mind what entered mine talking to him?" I said, "You mean that if there were submarines out there, this would be a very convenient place to give night signals?'' She said, ''Yes, that's what I mean.''

I remember having the feeling out there that the Japanese were reporting an awful lot to somebody who was smuggling a lot of information back to Japan. It may or may not have been unjust and monstrous on the basis of abstract constitutional rights, as they would be regarded in peacetime. The war takes precedence over everything. There was a general feeling that the Japanese were doing a lot of spying, that getting them all bunched together in one place and keeping them there for the duration was not such a terribly bad idea.

The other bad idea was that when they were swept up and put there some people were profiteering with their property and taking advantage of them because they wouldn't be on the spot to look out for it. That kind of thing was very bad. But after Pearl Harbor it could not be assumed that an invasion of California was a farfetched, idiotic idea. Pearl Harbor was a farfetched, idiotic idea. But it put our fleet at the bottom of the harbor. So you couldn't take a chance.

Sid Luckman, the Chicago Bears quarterback, was married and had children. But he enlisted in the merchant marine after the season of '43.

Most of the great players who weren't married enlisted in the service or were drafted. So even though there were still a lot of very fine footbal' players around, there wasn't the caliber of football there was in the years 1940 and '41. The quality dropped.

The headlines every day were about the war, and people really needed an outlet. The outlet was to go to sports and to the movies to get their mind off thinking about what was in the newspapers. Football was very, very big in those years. A lot of people didn't want us to enlist because they wanted football to continue. But eventually, I guess, all of us thought it was an obligation to go and do our part.

Dr. Benjamin Spock was practicing medicine in New York City during part of the war years, when he also began work on his book, Baby and Child Care, *which was to help the nation's mothers raise the postwar generation of babies.*

As pediatricians were gradually taken into the armed services, it left more and more work for those of us at home to do. From the time I started practice in '33 until I went into the navy, in '44, I'd been only partly busy during all those pre—Pearl Harbor years. They were Depression years. In fact, it took me three years to earn enough money to pay my office and automobile expenses. Nobody needed a new pediatrician in New York at that time. But following Pearl Harbor, I gradually got busier and busier—for the first time in my career.

I was being called on for more and more work in my practice, but I wasn't thinking of the war years as a baby boom. I was thinking, rather, that other pediatricians were gone, so there's more for me to do. One thing I remember was how easy it was to drive around in New York City and to park the car. That was amazing. We got a C-card instead of an A-card. But still, they didn't give you a great deal of gas, and they asked you to conserve it. I was working also for the Public Health Department two mornings a week, holding staff meetings at baby-health stations all over the five boroughs.

I didn't have any experiences with women losing their husbands and having to adapt. It was late on when fathers were taken into the service. Generally speaking, the mothers and children made a good adjustment, I would say. I don't mean it was easy. But I think human beings respond to a challenge like that. It makes them summon all their resources. I saw how children reacted to the absence of their fathers and how good an adaptation most of them had. In fact, the adaptation that was harder was when the father came home. The child who had mother to himself from the age of one year to three years was outraged to have this ogre come home and take over his mother. That impressed me. In fact, the interesting thing to me was not only how much trouble small children had accepting a father who had been away but how many fathers went through at least mild depressions when they came back out of the armed services. All the years and days they had been dreaming about coming out and when will this damn thing be over. And then they came home and had depressions. Somehow it didn't seem as marvelous as they'd dreamed. It all seemed to be related to the psychic reaction to meeting challenges. I think what alerted me was hearing these reports, newspaper articles, magazine articles, about how neighborly, loving, and cooperative people were in England, where war was brought right to them. After hearing about it in England, I saw, at least in a mild way, that we had the same thing. People feel good when they're making sacrifices and being cooperative, whereas in good times, in a prosperous country, the majority—and I always say "for the majority" because there's a minority that isn't having a happy time at all—begin to feel guilty, and get greedy and selfish.

I think, as in most wars, mental health for the majority of Americans improved. During wartime there is less suicide, less crime. People were friendlier; they took care of each other. It's a horrid thing to realize that during wartime people are mentally more healthy than they are during peacetime, especially in a country where so many people live relatively comfortable lives. This kept making me come back to the conclusion that our species is designed to cope with adversity rather than take it easy. In the Depression, these same kinds of statistics prevailed: less crime, less suicide.

Judson Phillips, possibly better known to readers of mystery stories as Hugh Pentecost, was living and writing in Vermont at the time of Pearl Harbor.

At the time of Pearl Harbor I was writing magazine fiction: *Saturday Evening Post, Colliers,* and *American.* Those were your main markets. And I did a book a year at that time.

Everybody was urged to get in the war effort, and I tried to get into what was called Special Services. The air force offered me a commission as a major to go abroad and write letters home to the families whose fliers were killed in the war, and I said, "The hell with that." Because I was a writer, I suppose, that was all they could see for me. I was never able to get any other kind of an assignment, so I looked around to see where else I could be of service. I had a friend in the OWI and tried to get into that. It didn't work out, but he, in turn, got me into the Writers' War Board in New York, which was a propaganda agency.

One of my first assignments was to do a story on WAC camps. For the first time, women were in the army, so I was flown around the country in some kind of old crate with a bench in the back to write about WAC camps. As in most of the pieces I wrote for them, in the WAC feature I stressed how glamorous it was. The piece was placed in magazines and newspapers.

Then I got into something else. A friend of mine who was a radio announcer came up with the idea of doing a show about the great secrets of the war. And we did a show which went on every night from seven to seven-thirty called "Now It Can Be Told." We had a staff in Washington, and its job was to dig out the great secrets. Of course, we got stuff that was no longer classified. But nonetheless, we got a lot of interesting material about little-known stuff; and we did that right till the bomb. I regret to say this, and I would deny it with my last breath, but most of the stuff we had was pretty stale. But it did come out of government agencies, and much of it had not been revealed before, because nobody was interested. We made it interesting.

Unfortunately—or fortunately—it was a prosperous time to work. God knows. Except for people who had sons in the service who were in danger, it was kind of a lush time. Hardships were nonsensical. When you recall life in New York in those war years, you remember irritations, you couldn't get cigarettes. The deprivations, so called, that the citizenry had to bear were laughable. It isn't that you couldn't get cigarettes; you couldn't get *your* brand, and what you smoked was horseshit wrapped in paper.

Coralee Redmond lived in Beach, North Dakota. She had a large family—a husband, nine children, and several brothers. Eventually almost everyone in her family was involved in the war, some way.

The girls were in high school, the boys were younger. My oldest child was a son, and he went in right after New Year's 1942. He was out of college. So he decided he might as well volunteer. I was asked how I felt about it, and I said I thought the decision was his. I'm quite a military-minded person. I had a lot of military in my family, and I felt like the decision was his. But I felt that we had a duty also. I didn't want to make it one way or the other for him. He did go in, and my younger brother went in right after. And by March, my younger brother was already overseas, in Australia. He survived the war. And my older brother stayed in thirty years.

We quit farming about the time the war began because of my husband's health. So then when the boys left and went into the service, I had my older daughter, who was teaching, and we decided we should do something to help too. So we went to Tacoma, Washington, to work in defense plants, and we worked in the shipyards. I worked in the cafeteria and office most of the time. My husband was what they call a fireman in the shipyard.

I felt my family and I were doing our part with things that had to be done to help our boys that were in the service. This is what it meant to me. I didn't feel that it meant that much to some others. To them it meant a job. You remember, this came right after the Depression days, and people were thankful to have a job. And I would say the majority took their jobs seriously. They put in long hours and many hours a lot of times, because it was needed.

One daughter married, and her husband went in the service at that point. The other daughter was married, and she went with her husband, when he was stationed in Louisiana, until he went overseas. Then she came back to Beach and lived in our home. We owned our own home there, and kept it set up. The next-door neighbors checked my heat and such things in the wintertime. Usually in the summertime I took the boys back home because they were younger and I wanted them off the streets. But I kept my home there just so that if someone was coming home, for furlough—my son-in-law, my son—all they would have to do would be to get the key from the next-door neighbor. There was food enough to get by till morning if they came in at night. I felt like when the boys came home, it should be to the home of their youth, and not to Tacoma, which was quite crowded in the war days.

I had two other girls. One graduated from high school in 1943 and the other in 1944. One worked at the shipyard, and the younger daughter went to Boeing in Seattle.

And we all took our thing seriously. The boy who was in grade school picked beans and all that. The money he earned, we bought savings bonds for him. We taught him that he earned this money but let's put it in something that might help. He would gain from it in the future, but at that particular time, it might be helpful for the war. We all set aside a certain amount to buy bonds. The boy who was in the service—when he came out of the service, he was just out of college—he would be wanting to go into business or something like that, and that was our part in helping him have something when he came back.

They were busy times. The main thing that bothered me was the many hours I felt like I wasted waiting for buses because the buses would be so loaded. One would go by, and you'd wait for another one when you were trying to get home to get dinner for the family and to have time left to do some volunteer work. I felt that was needed, and the only resentment I ever had was having to wait for a bus.

Mary Dandouveris recalls campus life at the University of Wisconsin during the war and how the war helped her get her first postcollege job.

Because my family was a first-generation family from Greece, I had uncles and relatives in Greece who really felt the effects of Nazism.

But we didn't regard ourselves as aligned with the European side of the family; we just thought how important it would be for the United States to win. I do recall that my feeling was that this is our country, our home, and we felt sorry for those poor people over there, but we didn't feel like we were citizens of Europe. I mean, this was what we knew, and all we knew about Greece was what our parents told us.

I graduated from high school and was ready to go into the University of Wisconsin. I was a scholarship student, and it was easier for us to earn money to go to school because more jobs were available for students, as so many men had been drafted. A lot of the guys were gone, and women had their opportunity to take over in positions that formerly had been held by men. I was elected to the Student Council and was active in the War Council. We even had a woman who ran for prom king—Helen Finnegan. Prom king was an elected position on the campus: A man won, as it turned out, but the woman ran and had good support.

We never had troubles. I remember it as a good time— except the hours were very severe. It wasn't in the days of the liberated campus. Girls had to be in at ten at night on weekdays and midnight on weekends. But there were student lounges. They used to call them the Passion Pits because there was an awful lot of passionate kissing—not the advanced petting they have today. But the fronts of the dorms would be just jammed at quitting time, ten o'clock or midnight, with the sailors and the marines and the army people—whoever was on campus—kissing the girls good-night. But beyond that it wasn't wild. The troops that were stationed on campus were pretty well regulated. They had their own classes—they weren't mixed in.

The war ended in Europe while I was still on campus, and by that time some of the boys who had been in the war early had come back on campus. In my senior year I remember some of the journalism classes getting some of the vets who were back. It was a very interesting class experience because they were so much more mature. By that time all of us had matured because the war really impinged on us.

I don't really believe there was a fear of bombing, but we were right on the shores of Lake Michigan and the Great Lakes system, so there was a certain amount of concern that perhaps enemy planes could sneak across and over the Great Lakes, because this was an industrial section of the country.

When school ended in May 1945, I went down to Lake Geneva, Wisconsin, and took this job as news editor of the paper. I'll never forget the experience. It was a marvelous job, which I got because the fellow that had been doing it had been drafted.

Elizabeth Haslam spent most the war in Pensacola, Florida.

First I was teaching school—a first-grade class. Then I transferred to the naval air station and got a job out there in the educational department. I administered tests for the men coming into the service. We were a depot for men from Alabama, Mississippi, and many areas in that section. They had already been inducted into the navy, most of them drafted, and they were getting placement tests. We gave them tests on general knowledge, mechanical aptitude, math, and a test in vocabulary.

The war had been going on for a while, and we were beginning to get older men—men with families, men who had been working on war contracts in various factories. The pitiful thing about it was that they had a sheet to fill out first with background information on them, and we had quite a few men who couldn't read and write. They were making big money at the job they knew how to do at home, but they were not able to read and write, except maybe to just sign their name. And some of them were pretty homesick. A lot of those men couldn't write letters, so we made collect calls home for them and wrote letters for them.

Carey McWilliams, best known as the editor of The Nation *for many years, was in California at the time of Pearl Harbor.*

At the beginning of the war California had a unique agency. There wasn't anything like it in any state of the union. It was called the Division of Immigration and Housing, and it had been set up by a distinguished California social worker by the name of Simon J. Lubin. No one paid any attention to it until 1938, when they elected the first Democratic governor in forty years, Culbert Olson. Olson had been a state senator in Utah, had come to California, been there for perhaps a decade, ran for the state senate from Los Angeles on the EPIC (End Poverty in California) ticket, and was elected. And four years later he ran for governor and made it. But the point about Olson was that he knew very little about the state. So with his backers he was going through the various patronage jobs they had at their disposal. They came to this division, and they were at a complete loss as to what the hell it did or was supposed to do. George Kidwell, Olson's key labor advisor, said, "What about Carey? He's done a book about farm labor; he knows something about the background." I had been on one of Olson's committees, so he said, "Sure. Why not?" So I was commissioner of immigration and housing from 1938 to 1942.

After Pearl Harbor we had a great deal to do. A succession of things happened that raised consciousness of racial discrimination. One, of course, was the mass evacuation of the Japanese Americans from the West Coast, citizens and aliens alike, 126,000 people, with no justification, no security justification, in my opinion. I don't buy the argument that we were protecting the Japanese from the citizenry, because even in the wake of the shock of Pearl Harbor there were no incidents.

Furthermore we know that the Washington authorities shortly after Pearl Harbor had a very good report prepared, as I recall, by a man named Munson. He had cased the situation and didn't see any necessity for it. Naval Intelligence, which knew more about the West Coast Japanese than any government agency, because they had been watching them since the turn of the century, didn't think it was necessary. And the proof that it was not necessary really was what happened in Hawaii. If the Japanese were a security threat on the West Coast, they would be a much bigger security threat in the Hawaiian Islands. But there you had a district court judge who was a great man in my eyes—name of Judge Delbert Metzger—and he said to the naval authorities and the rest of them, "Nothing doing!" And they realized, when they came to their senses, that if they had tried to evacuate all persons of Japanese descent in Hawaii, they would have had no economy. So they just let them stay there. But this was near the end of Metzger's five-year term, and he was not reappointed, and this was the basic reason.

Anyway, the Japanese-American evacuation program put race high on the agenda as an important issue. Oddly enough, there's more interest in the internment program today than there was then.

Before the evacuation I had worked closely with the staff of a Senate committee in Washington that had been investigating farm labor conditions in California. That staff had moved to another committee in the House which was interested in migration, so I got in touch with the staff and said, "God, schedule some hearings out here under some pretext or other, so we can exert a quieting influence." There was political agitation to remove the Japanese, but I didn't detect any passion on the part of people to get them out. They were getting along reasonably well with their neighbors, and the agitation was largely a political thing. Because of a vague grant of jurisdiction to be concerned with the welfare of alien immigrants I had reason to go to the authorities and say, "Now look. I want to be heard about some aspects of this." They were delighted to listen, and I had excellent relations with the War Relocation Authority. The first director was Milton Eisenhower and the second was Dillon Meyer. When it was announced, some question arose as to who was going to have charge of this operation. Well, the army was going to have charge. This aroused great apprehension, and so we had to start a kind of agitation to set up a separate authority. Let the army move them out if you must, but we did not want the army running the camps. So they set up the War Relocation Authority, and they staffed it very well. It drew people who had backgrounds sympathetic to the idea of doing a good job, and I will say this to the army's credit, it handled the physical business of getting them out very well. But there is one very important thing to keep in mind. They never could have brought it off as well as they did if the Japanese had not been the kind of people they are. They were well organized themselves, responsible, cooperative, and they went along with it. To their very great credit.

After they had been removed, they went first to assembly centers and then into relocation centers which were scattered around—Wyoming, Arkansas, Colorado—and then at that point the then Institute of Pacific Relations commissioned me to visit the relocation centers, and I visited virtually all of the centers—all but two, I think—and that report was the basis of my book *Prejudice*. The camps were kind of chaotic, as you would expect; but again, the Japanese talent: They sort of found out what they were up against, and they adapted to it and began to do for themselves. And, of course, there were some problems. There were disturbances at Tule Lake in California, one of the relocation centers. There was some trouble there and one or two other centers, so it wasn't all peaches and cream. But by and large it went better than might have been expected.

And then came the final phase: At what point do you permit them to return? This was the hottest issue. [Gov. Earl] Warren said, "Not one should come back until after the end of the war, absolutely none." He said, "A Jap is a Jap." And so there was great agitation on his side to have many nationwide radio debates on the subject and so forth. My position was that they should be permitted to come back before the war ended. They should be processed through relocation centers, and those released should be permitted to return, the point being that there was a battalion of Japanese Americans from Hawaii. The senator, Inouye, was an officer. He lost his arm in that battalion. That battalion had an incredible record in Italy. Our thinking was to take advantage of that and also to take advantage of the fact that the war was still on. It's your patriotic duty to accept these people back rather than wait until the end of the war, when this agitation might start up again.

The final decision was that they could return. They began to return before the end of the war. Robert Kenny, an old friend, was attorney general. He was splendid. He called the sheriff and local police officers together and said, "Look. This is the way it's going to be. I don't want any nonsense." And to his great credit, Warren backed Kenny up. He was opposed to him, but when the decision was made, he said, "There's going to be no trouble." And with the exception of two or three very minor incidents, there wasn't any trouble.

Another problem that relates to this had to do with Mexican Americans. We had, you may recall, the zoot-suit riots in Los Angeles. The naval personnel would go into Los Angeles on the weekend—you know how navy people are on the weekend, looking for trouble—and they would go into these various Mexican settlements just to raise hell. The zoot-suiters were Mexican boys who wore long hair and extremely long coats and long, peg pants. They were kind of weird looking for that time, like the hippies were when they first appeared. The navy boys on leave would go after them, and the police would tend to side with the sailors. The attorney general was my friend Kenny, a Democrat, and the governor was Earl Warren, an old political opponent. At that time we didn't see eye to eye. He was not yet the Warren of the Supreme Court or we'd have gotten along fine. The question arose as to what to do about the zoot-suit riots. I got Kenny (I knew Warren would never do it on my recommendation) to appoint a commission, headed by the archbishop, to take a look at the facts of the situation. They issued a report that had a quieting effect. Many of their recommendations were carried out, and as a result, the Civic Unity Council was set up, and we were able to cope with some of the things that had caused the trouble and to quiet the situation down. As a result, we were commended by the officials in Mexico City for having played a constructive role.

At that time there were racial riots in Beaumont, Texas, in Harlem, a big one in Detroit, and others elsewhere. About a half dozen racial incidents. And the riots relate to the war in this way. It was not as some people tried to imply at the time.

It was not the result of any kind of agitation or anything of that kind. The minute the war started—any war will do this— you have a manpower situation. Then there was immediately an issue about segregated services. We've gotten over that now, but at that time it was a big issue. Segregation in the navy, segregation in the army, all the way down the line. And this began to raise the temperature, as you would expect and people began to say, "Well, we're fighting the Nazis you know."

Cathleen Schurr was born in England and was living there when the war began in 1939. She came to America just before Pearl Harbor.

I worked briefly for the Censorship Office. We were reading people's mail. Then I went from there to NBC. That was at a time when there were very, very, few females working in any of the media. It was considered that women's voices were unsuitable and that biologically and for other reasons we weren't able to work as reporters objectively. I was writing news in the foreign-news section, which was a special area. It was beamed overseas. I thought at that time, and looking back, that it was an opportunity for me as a woman which would not have opened up otherwise. I didn't have the patience to stay there, because women were still not allowed on the air. But if I had hung on longer, there probably would have been a better opportunity. There were many cases where women were practically conscripted into all kinds of jobs for which they had been considered biologically and emotionally un-suited. It's like men going into the army: Those women who had the opportunity and learned from it went on from there.

We lived in Greenwich Village, and you barely knew you were at war. I don't know when the rationing came in, but I never experienced the war in this country as being a war. I don't believe, living where we lived, in a major city, that we really had any intensive experience of war at all. Rationing to me was a joke. You had to save up if you wanted to have beef, but there was so much of everything else available. I don't feel eating fish and chicken and vegetables can be con-sidered a hardship, and there was never anything that we lacked. We had a car, which we simply didn't use, and there was no need for gas. We arranged our vacations so that we went by train or by bus, or we biked whenever we could. We had the sirens going from time to time, and we had signs up saying where the shelters were. A lot of people went around complaining. I never could understand what they were complaining about.

After I left NBC, I went to work for a public relations firm. I had gotten into doing industrial promotion, and that was when I really began to get close to industrial areas and production. I was the first woman ever to be on the floor of the open-hearth furnaces at Republic Steel. I did a lot of traveling because I had a lot of industrial accounts for a small PR firm that hired women because it didn't have to pay them much.

War industries had problems in their communities, and they had no sense of public relations.

Sally Knox worked for the government in the Midwest.

My job was to edit or prepare publications to be issued by the publications officer. I did that for twenty-nine years in various places.

I worked in Detroit for a year and a half, maybe two years and a half. Then I transferred to Wright Field, it was called at that time, later Patterson Air Force Base near Dayton, Ohio. Dayton was just coming out of a bad depression, and the war certainly started it up industrially. I think that many people in Dayton of the old line, the old society, were distressed to see so many war workers coming in. They thought it would spoil their pretty little town.

A man came to see me when I was in the Central Procurement District in Detroit. I don't know whether he was in uniform or not, but he held out his pass and told me where he was from and informed me that we were in a very serious war with the Nazis and we didn't want any Nazi spies around, and he wanted me to keep my eyes open and see if I saw anything of that kind going on at work. He may have been with the FBI or Army Intelligence, I am not sure. He gave me an address, and I was to write a letter to him every Sunday night, and I was just to talk about my girl friends and what I was doing, and if there was anything of interest, I was to put it in. So every Sunday night I sat down and wrote a letter, and I never had anything to report. I was never to tell anybody about it: I couldn't tell my mother. She wondered who I was writing to.

Charles Keller was a professor of history at Williams College in Williamstown, Massachusetts.

The first military program came here in January 1943. It was a navy V-5 program. It meant that a lot of members of the faculty had to teach navigation, physics, mathematics. Then, I remember clearly the great group that went down to Philadelphia and had a cram course in how to teach navigation. I was in that group. It was between Christmas 1942 and New Year's.

I was aware of the fact that I didn't know very much, and that I was going to teach something and not explain it. If anybody asked me how that formula was derived, I would tell them it wasn't the point. The point is to learn it. The group was here about three months. I did feel a little uncomfortable knowing that if these boys made a mistake in the course I was teaching and they were out over the ocean, they would be in trouble. I thought of that all the time. But for a group of non-professionals we didn't do badly. We had navy people who guided us. We had tests that were standard tests coming from Washington. We had strict marking, and if we seemed to be falling down, we were told about it. But on the whole, we had some pretty good results. From here, they went on to the next set of steps, which was more intensive.

It was hard to get teachers during the war years, but we had enough. We'd lost some members of the faculty, but a lot of the teaching was done by navy people, particularly in the V-5 program. And you had to do a real reshuffle. We'd get through a term, have about two weeks for exams and a break, and then begin the next term. That started in the summer of '42 and kept on accelerating through '46. I taught seventeen terms straight without any break whatsoever. This was my way of doing what I could. We were teaching because what else could we do. I used to teach four classes in a row on some days on three different subjects. And that was tough, so I would huff and puff and get through, but that was that.

6

"Don't You Know There's a War On?"

Of course, some Americans were more involved in the war than others. For a man with a physical defect, at the outer limits of the draft age, or with a wife and young children to support, the war did not have an immediate impact on him or on his family—especially if they did not live near Washington, one of the big industrial cities, or one of the many military installations around the country. Life went on as before, except for the shortages and possibly the concern about relatives or friends overseas. Millions of Americans were in this position. For them it was business as usual, except that every now and then someone would ask them—or they would ask someone—"Don't you know there's a war on?"

In Ocean City, Maryland, Jack Lynch, the owner and manager of the Commander Hotel, had his problems keeping a resort hotel operating during the war. He was married and had a family of four children, but he did take a job in a defense factory for one year, "just to clear my own conscience," as he put it.

We opened the hotel in the spring and closed in the fall. It takes a month to close it up, so when the war started, it was just about three or three and a half months since we had closed. Shortly after, we began to get submarine activity along the coast. We were put under the Baltimore region of civil defense. We organized a group of local people to try to work with the government and the region blacking out our town, because your being able to open the next season depended how you could black your town out. They felt that the lights from the various resorts would pinpoint everything for any submarine that might be operating offshore. A group of us got together and raised some money for the project by securing the Capital Theatre. The owner let us use the theater, and we showed the movie *Sergeant York* that raised something in the neighborhood of two thousand dollars, which gave us a little cash for the blackout project.

They were asking us to black out but weren't telling us a thing—there were no directions on it at all. After we organized, a group of boys went to the Jersey resorts to see if we could get any information about what they were doing before we started. Gee whiz, the theaters on the boardwalk in Atlantic City, you could almost see them in France! We didn't get any help up there.

Everybody had a front door opening out toward the sea, so we had to build a blackout and a turn. In other words, you entered and came out the doorway sideways and had to turn to the left, and the inside of it was all painted dull black.

Of course, that was before the days of air conditioning, so it was also quite a problem as to how you were going to have ventilation in a room with blackout curtains. What we did was to devise a standing rod which came out about six inches from the window, and hung a black oilcloth curtain. You didn't get direct ventilation, but you got ventilation coming in from the sides and over the top. We scoured the scrap heaps for number-ten vegetable and fruit cans, cut a hole in the bottom of each can, and did all the streetlights with those so there was no direct light shining; everything was right straight down.

I'll never forget one day during the war, on Good Friday, there was a lot of activity—planes and one blimp went by. A boat had been sunk the night before right off Chincoteague, Virginia, and the Coast Guard was called down there from

Ocean City to help pick up bodies at sea. They brought them back here, and they had them racked up on the stern of the Coast Guard boat just like cordwood.

Anna Mae Lindberg lived in the Homestead area of Pittsburgh, where her husband Russell worked for U.S. Steel's Irvin Works.

During the war Russell and I lived in a three-room apartment about ten blocks up the hill from City Farm Lane. He must have been in his mid-twenties—but he had a job in the mill.

I was a housewife during the war. I had worked before I was married, and I hadn't been off work very long. I had a secretarial job, but it was a political appointment. When your side was out, you were out too, and I was out at the moment. We decided to start our family. I don't know if this was ever in Russ's mind, but I thought it was one more thing that would keep him out of the war. It was something we didn't talk about, but that was my idea.

I don't remember when this happened, and if it was just social pressure or what, but my husband has a master's degree, so he applied for officer's training. He didn't discuss this with me—he just came home and said that he had applied. As it turned out, he wore glasses from the time that he was in high school, so his vision kept him out of officer's training. And I was so relieved. I can't tell you how relieved I was about that.

We did all the things us ladies used to do: went to the Municipal Building and sewed nightgowns. I get angry when I think back on those days—like having to save the tin cans and go out and collect milkweed pods because they were used to make life jackets. So we'd be out in the fields collecting these damned milkweeds.

The morale in our community was the same kind you get when you find out somebody has a terminal illness. You keep it to yourself—you try to cheer up the other person, and the other person tries to cheer you. So we pretended there was all this tremendous morale. I did not find the war years exhilarating and exciting. Never; not for me. I would question that very many women felt that way. They pretended. Men may have felt an excitement about it. Maybe it was just me, I don't know. Women go a little deeper into the consequences, the human. There was always that pinch and always that anxious tension.

Peter Scaglione was chief bartender in the Columbia Restaurant in Tampa, Florida.

I had some friends, young boys, eighteen, nineteen years old, who went to war and did not come back. I was 1-A myself, but they never did call me. I don't know why. They talked to my boss here. I don't know if he fixed it up with the board or not. Maybe he did.

When everybody was in uniform, we used to have a little more business on account of them. Sailors and soldiers would have a drink or two. Sometimes they'd fight, and I'd have to jump over the bar and get some of the soldiers out, because we didn't want no rough stuff, you know. I used to get my baseball bat and run them out. I didn't have much trouble, because they knew when they had a little too much. I wouldn't give them no more. They had to go somewhere else.

Harry Hahn, then a vice-president of the Hahn Shoe Company in Washington, D.C. and his wife, Elizabeth:

HARRY: Our shoe business was a Washington institution. It was family owned; I was the oldest of the third generation. We had seven shoe stores in Washington, and one in Baltimore.

I guess it was just after the war started that we got into rationing in the shoe business. We had no premonition of it at all. On a Sunday morning there was an announcement in the paper that shoes would be rationed.

ELIZABETH: You had to have coupons.

HARRY: Coupon number fifteen or seventeen in the sugar-ration book was designated as the shoe coupon. Leather was going to shoes for the military. The announcement came on Sunday, and on Monday morning, or evening, we had a meeting of all our employees and told everybody we had no idea what was going to develop. We had reasonable stocks of shoes on hand, but we didn't know how we were going to get more.

The problem was not in selling them but in getting them. You had to go to the factories, travel all over the country. But we never went into the black market.

ELIZABETH: I worked at the D.C. ration board, where they gave out the stamps. I think I did a volunteer job every day as long as I had a cook. We gave out all kinds of ration stamps—for gas, for meat. A lot of people exaggerated their needs for gasoline, but they were thoroughly investigated before they were given extra coupons. And I was very busy saving my gas for our car, because I had a little boy who was always getting into trouble, and I never knew when I was going to have to dash to the doctor's or the hospital with him. So I took the bus and saved the coupons to use for him and marketing and that sort of thing.

The one thing people would complain about was the meat rationing.

HARRY: Scotch was hard to come by during the war, too, scotch and cigarettes. You had to queue up for them.

ELIZABETH: Butter was difficult to get. And Harry said to me, "Don't you ever feed me margarine." I said, "I wouldn't dream of it." He'd been eating it for about three months and didn't know it.

HARRY: Business was very good. I was merchandising women's shoes, and we were on a gravy train. We were selling most of the WAVE's and WACs and marine girls uniform shoes. They had to have coupons for them. We all worked kind of hard. Later on, to compound the aggravations, we had not only the rationing but also price control. I think at that time it was desirable. We didn't care what we paid for shoes when we bought them. We were anxious to get any we could. If people would give us some shoes, we told them we would try to do business with them after the war. I opened some very important accounts and made some good friends on that basis.

ELIZABETH: We were never afraid to go out in Washington during the war. We worked at the Pepsi Cola canteen. Anybody in uniform could be served free, of course. I was a volunteer soda jerk, and I loved it. The servicemen were so wonderful; never any unpleasantness.

Newton Tolman lived near Nelson, New Hampshire.

I would say that, accumulatively, the effect of the war years on me was it aged me about twenty years more than I should have been; it confused my thinking.

Right after Pearl Harbor the government says my wife and small son and I had to be self-sufficient. The government says to raise pigs. So I got twenty-four hogs and plowed up six acres and got an old tractor, and Uncle Bill and everybody got into the act. I built a barn and got a stone and cut timber and spent altogether twenty-eight dollars on the barn. And then they said: "We have too many hogs." That knocked the bottom out of that, and we almost lost money on the twenty-four hogs, but we bought a cow and chickens, so that when I took off to save the country for democracy, my wife would be able to survive.

All the girls, including my wife, were in the Red Cross because, they said, "You got to be trained; the submarines are coming into Portsmouth." And they were all taught how to give baths. The whole thing was great. Crazy. Everyone was frantic.

Then gasoline had to be rationed. A cousin of mine was a big-time lawyer. He got sent to some place in Washington and came out a full colonel. But he didn't want to suffer for gas when he came up here, so he bought, surreptitiously, a five-thousand-gallon tank and had it installed below his house and filled it full of gasoline. Sometime in the next year or so it was discovered to be empty. The thing had a leak in it, so the gas all went down into White's Pond.

I had an old farm truck, and I took weekly pilgrimages to Keene—fourteen miles. Everybody would pile in the truck to save gas, buy their groceries, and come back. But the rich people could buy black-market beef, everything known to man. Mill owners in Keene, Harrisville, Swanzey, and all over were great patriots. Their mills were about to die, and some had been defunct for several years. Suddenly, they got a contract with the army and the navy, and so they were big patriots. "We wanted to go in the army, but we can't because we are essential to the war effort"—they all got out of it.

I was with the State Guard, working my ass off, as I said, not because I really believed in the war under Roosevelt or this or that. My own view was that, well, God, it's happened, so we have to do something about it. I just hoped to Christ

I didn't get into it. On the other hand, you have to follow the leader. I never told my wife, for God's sake, that I nearly broke my neck to get out of the navy deal. She probably wouldn't like it now, but I did. I didn't want to go. You have only one life to live, and if somebody wants to go and get themselves killed, well, let them go to it.

Helen Wilson spent the war at the University of Michigan in Ann Arbor.

We had a fairly normal world at the university for about a year, and then there was a sudden departure of all the males who had been in the freshman class.

There still were many young men on campus, because we had the V-12 program for the navy, and there were lots of boys in that. Then at the law school there was the judge advocate general's program.

I had a roommate who was a professional dancer during the summers. She worked at the Grand Hotel up at Mackinaw Island. I was also a dancer, but not as accomplished—my mother had really wanted me to be a Rockette; that was her ambition. We also had a very beautiful redhead roommate, so we put together a song-and-dance routine to sell war bonds and stamps. We'd go around to the various sororities and dormitories at dinner time, and it was great fun. I'm sure we weren't very good, but we were well received.

One thing I remember is the nuisance of rationing. I never understood the need for it. Why wasn't there enough sugar? Why were fabrics scarce? Why did we have to have coupons for meat? Was that much meat needed for the troops? There weren't any greater number of people. I can understand why there weren't consumer goods like washing machines or automobiles, but I never understood the shortages of food.

And I can remember the crowded trains. I never understood where everybody was going. It wasn't just military; there were just as many civilians. There never were seats on trains; I sat on my suitcase on the train between Ann Arbor and Kalamazoo on every trip for three years.

I did get a job in a defense factory one summer; that was my first and only war effort. I applied at the factory which made musical instruments. They were then making bombsights, and I had the job of soldering little hairs across the bombsight. I think I lasted about three days. The monotony of the work and the sloppiness of the work really concerned me. People were not really concerned about making good bombsights—just in three days I got that—it was making the good wages. As much as I needed the money, I really couldn't stand doing it eight hours a day. I had previously applied for a job as a nursery school teacher for the children of the women who were working in the war factories, and I was so happy when that came through. It was a much better job for me.

I remember summers in Kalamazoo, which was very close to Battle Creek, where a big veterans' hospital was always taking boys in and sending them back. Kalamazoo had a USO, and I went there regularly. Probably the biggest thrill of my entire young life was the night when a convoy from Battle Creek drove me home. There were six trucks that drove down the little street in Kalamazoo to take me home. I was very excited. It was like a scene from an Andy Hardy movie. I was probably a sophomore in college at that time.

I met a lot of soldiers in Kalamazoo. On dates then, the boys in the service were more demanding sexually than others. At that time, it's now hard to believe, we were really all very pure, and the sexual pressures were somewhat more than I felt comfortable with. There was a little of the attitude of "Well, I'm going overseas. I might be dead tomorrow," and some implication that you had an obligation because they were fighting the war. But surprisingly, the boys were either quite chivalrous or innocent themselves.

Arthur Edmunds began the war as a student at Fisk College in Nashville, Tennessee.

I was a History major, a Political Science minor, and considered myself very well-read. I used to read the *New York Times.* And I was a little bit amazed at the isolation of the students, at least the people that I came in contact with. Part of this was because we were in another world, so to speak. But I think, also, we were tremendously misled by our leaders and by the press. I would not have thought we were that close to war. Maybe it was a black reaction, I'm not sure, but there was no overwhelming desire to get a gun and go fight someone. Most of the students at the school were not Southerners. I'm not—I matriculated there from Iowa. We considered the Southern white to be as much our enemy as the Japanese five thousand miles away from us.

There was a notice circulated to all the men on the campus to carry their draft cards with them at all times. The Fisk campus is cut up by streets, and there are thoroughfares running through it. Police officers had been coming through and challenging students about their draft cards and roughing them up for not having them. I remember one student getting beaten for not having his card with him.

In the summer of '42 I worked with my roommate in a little bar on Washington Boulevard in Detroit. Several of the guys who came there to eat lunch were recruiting officers for the navy. The navy had two programs called something like the V-7 or V-12. They would give you two years to finish college, and when you came out of it, you became a gunnery officer, or a deck officer of some kind. By this time we were trying to analyze the war situation in relation to our own educational plans, and my roommate and I made the decision that we would try to get in this program. These guys had encouraged us, at least there in the restaurant, so we went down to the office and saw an aide there. The first thing that came up was "What school do you go to?" He named a couple of schools. We knew Fisk was an A-rated school, but there was not a black school on the whole list. And they would not take us. At the time the only blacks in the navy were stewards. So that put an awfully sour taste in my mouth for the whole damned military. I'm volunteering myself, and I'm rejected.

After I graduated from Fisk, I went back to Iowa and started some graduate study at Drake University.

Hezekiah Goodwin operated a dairy farm in the Canaan Valley just south of the Massachusetts border in Connecticut.

The war made hell with the help. Life as we knew it practically ceased. Oh, God, you have no idea. There were some wealthy people in the neighborhood, and they tripled the wages—more than we could pay 'em—and the supply of labor just dried up.

Well, we worked pretty hard, eyah, and we were able to get

piecemeal help. We could get people from the incorrigibles—drinking people who were really good and broke—and they worked pretty damned good until payday, then that was the last you saw of them. We had this fellow who had worked for us for forty years; all of a sudden he was a widower, and then he married a fancy woman and moved out.

Eyah, some were involved in war work, some weren't. We always thought the ones that were were crazy, because it meant a trip either to Hartford or Torrington to go to work, and it didn't make sense for economic reasons. You couldn't tell them that. We could offer them more net income without travel than they could get in a war plant. But hell, they apparently didn't want the long hours on the farm.

Our economic position early in the war was very poor, as was true of all farmers. The political decisions regarding the price of food and the price of milk were very detrimental to us. And with the increased costs and the poorer productivity, low prices were close to being disastrous. But we were able to ride it out.

The first sign of improvement economically was in 1944, when we began getting a subsidy on our milk prices, and the price firmed up a little. The butchers made their money on both ends. They were crooked as a ram's horn, but it was necessary because of the government prices.

Rudolph Spitzer in Kenmore, New York:

Like all parents, we were greatly perturbed. We have four boys in our family, and at that time three of them were subject to army duty. We were apprehensive and abhorred the thought of our boys being called to serve. These were anxious days and years, and gloom reigned over the entire nation.

Before Pearl Harbor I was in the sign and outdoor-advertising business. Almost immediately, due to the rationing of critical materials and curtailment of nonwar services, I had to operate on a very modified basis by using noncritical substitute materials whenever possible or available. The war practically terminated the sign business. The larger war plants had limited needs for signs and hired their own staff for this type of work.

Our whole manner of living took a disheartening turn. The

nation suffered a blow that reached most every individual to some degree, but mostly it was the family breadwinner in his own business who suffered. There was less of a problem for factory workers or blue-collar workers. To them the war was a gift from heaven. People who had been engaged in menial occupations, earning minimal wages, flocked to the war plants. Even some who could barely sign their name earned more money than they ever dreamed of. This sudden, easy affluence had some disreputable effects. As many of these workers expressed it: "I hope this war lasts forever, this is the nuts."

At this time, I operated my business on a part-time basis, but even that met with failure. I couldn't cope with all the restrictions involved. So, like many others, I went to work in a war plant—the Bell Aircraft Corporation in Niagara Falls. For commuting from my home to the plant I was entitled to gas-ration tickets, and from the very beginning I detested my job. I was placed on the 4:00 P.M. to 11:00 P.M. shift and eventually got used to it. But the strange activity, the unfamiliar surroundings, the misery of monotonous hour after hour doing the same thing, the confinement, all these things—so contrary to my previous way of life—sickened me. But there was nothing else I could do except long for the day that I could work my way out of this situation.

Three of my sons were inducted into the service. Fortunately, except for one son's bout with malaria, they all got home safe and sound. My wife and I suffered the usual anxious periods—a letter from one of the boys was like a gift from heaven. Naturally, we were aware that some of the boys would never be back, or be permanently handicapped or meet the horrible fate of being taken prisoner. When our boys came back, our feeling of relief was glorious and indescribable.

Rudolph Spitzer's son Richard was teaching high school English in Shortsville, New York, thirty miles south of Rochester. It was a small school, with probably three hundred children, in kindergarten through twelfth grade.

I was concerned that I would face induction, although the birth of our first child on December 9 pretty well eliminated that in the beginning. It wasn't until two or three or four years later that I was actually involved with it. My memories of the school's reaction to the war are very vague, but one memory has stuck with me. I went to that school in 1939, and somewhere I picked up some very handsome wall posters that came from Russia. They were beautiful pastoral scenes. I put them up on the bulletin board in the back of the room, and the principal suggested that maybe I ought to take them down because Russia was a Communist country. So with some misgiving I did take them down. Then, when this country entered the war, Russia became an ally. And the very same principal walked in one day with some posters. He said, "I thought you might like to have these for your room." When he walked out, I looked at them, and they were similar to the ones I had before. They were from Russia. I threw them out. Why? I just figured that if they weren't suitable two years ago, they weren't suitable now.

For a lot of the kids in the school, in the kind of community that I was in, the service really represented a great opportunity. Suddenly it was, as the military always is, a solution, or apparent solution. They didn't have to make any more decisions for a while. Many of them had a very limited view of their opportunities in the world. If you ask girls what they thought they might do after high school, the stock reply was, "Well, I don't want to be a teacher and I don't want to be a nurse and I don't want to be a secretary, and what else is there?" For the boys, it was a very limited choice of maybe the machine shop or farming. A very small percentage went to college.

I think the war times were anxious times. They seemed endless. You'd read about the progress or lack of progress of the army in Europe. You had the feeling that Hitler was monstrous. There was great empathy for the British. Ed Murrow had a great effect on me. I also remember sitting in a room someplace alone and Roosevelt announcing D day and this voice coming on the radio in the dark room telling about how this great assault had been launched and asking the people to pray for success. I remember the sense of relief when it was over. There was a feeling that something was accomplished. Hitler was destroyed, Japan would never again be strong.

Esther Benson lived in Newport, Rhode Island, with her artist-sculptor husband and two children.

We lived in a navy town, and I was well aware of what the war was going to mean to Newport, because everything was already beginning to show signs of speeding up. It became crammed full of people, and we had a tremendous shortage of housing for navy families.

My husband, who was an artist and had a very bad heart condition and couldn't, of course, be in the war, was worried all the time about getting work. In wartime there isn't much work for artists. So he went on with his teaching at the Rhode Island School of Design. And he started very early in the war running the power squadron, a civilian set of courses for men in small boats. They started with basic navigation and ended up with quite complicated navigation. The idea was to teach these men so that in a situation like Dunkirk they would be able to help.

We had a very active Red Cross in Newport. We had difficulty with some of the navy personnel, and I'm not talking about the sailors, I'm talking about the brass—people who were not knowledgeable enough about what the navy was. So many complaints, and their wives didn't have anything like a serious point of view about what this war was. I remember feeling that they should just be thankful they still had their husbands, instead of complaining about where they were living. Everything in town was crowded with people.

My street was on the way to the naval hospital, and there was an awful lot of walking traffic, sailors late at night going back. You were inclined to forgive the sailors getting drunk, because they were under such strain. I found out if I polished my doorknob brightly, then sailors would knock on it when they went by at night. So I finally left the knocker dull.

Rationing was awful, awful. I was always losing the ration books, and you just couldn't get anything good, even if you did have the ration coupons. I can remember thinking a can of corned beef was just marvelous. We ate a lot of Spam. The boys liked Spam, and it didn't require any coupons. I was not aware of any heavy black market, and certainly none of the people I knew were on the black market. Sometimes a friend would give us a dozen eggs, and that was about all. Of course, my husband had a little sailboat and caught a lot of fish, which was a tremendous help to us.

John R. Shepley, vice-president of the Saint Louis Trust Company:

I didn't figure the war would have much of an impact on our business, because we were primarily handling estates and trusts and things of that kind. I'd say, if anything, it improved our business.

I had two sons and a daughter, and the oldest son was a pilot in the air force, but my younger son was too young.

The principal effect on me was the inability to get enough gasoline. You see, we were at the bottom of the list, and I had a farm in Pike County, about 70 miles north of Saint Louis, where we always spent the weekends. I had a Cadillac at the time which had close to 100,000 miles on it. The tires weren't very good, and one of the most difficult things was keeping the car in tires. You couldn't buy any new tires, and I remember once I had a flat at Saint Charles, on our way up to the farm. I ended up going up some back alley and buying one of the most woebegone tires in the world. Beggars weren't choosers in those days.

In order to save gas, I got a Harley-Davidson motorcycle to go to work on. I rode it for over a year, and in that way we conserved enough gas to go to the farm on the weekend. It didn't have a windshield like the modern ones. It did create quite a stir around the bank. As a matter of fact, my brother, who was a bit more prominent in Saint Louis than I, was featured in the newspapers because he had a motorcycle with a sidecar.

At Leon Sylvester's gas station near Sedgwick, Maine, I asked two Down Easters, Forrest Eaton and James Saunders, about the war years.

EATON: I was lobstering some up here during the war. Lobsters was selling at thirty cents a pound in those days. People ate them as much as they do now; course, they were more plentiful then. There was a time when you were rationed on gas, had to have stamps. You were allowed a certain amount for your boats. There was a lot of black-marketing of gas— you'd get it any way you could. There was no rationing on lobsters. I don't remember that the war years changed things too much.

SAUNDERS: There's been a lot more changes here in the last ten years than there was in wartime. A lot of the boys did go in the service. I had two friends that never came back. They were in the Pacific. I worked down in Portland at the shipyard for about two years as a cleaner—got the ships ready for the painter. Things were tapering off and quieting down, so I thought it was time to come home. Life in Portland was quite more exciting than around here. There was a lot of girls; they had brothers, fathers, husbands in the service, and they did their part. The morale was very good. In the two years, there were sixty thousand people employed, and there wasn't too much drinking and carousing and stuff like that. People behaved themselves pretty well. Naturally, the men got interested in the women sometimes. That's only human nature. But it was not so bad. The women made the same wages.

EATON: I don't remember any hardships. Everybody had enough. Just didn't have luxuries. Most people fished for cod; you couldn't get deferred for fishing lobsters, because they were a luxury. So all the young fellows went trawling for cod—so they could get deferred from war. The war didn't have so much effect on this area as the Depression. We had a little place—an observation post—set up to watch for airplanes. But we never seen any. Never saw a German in the whole war.

Lillian Williams spent the war in Southwest Harbor, Maine, where her husband worked in the boatyard.

My husband was building PT boats. We had the Coast Guard and the navy there: everything was booming. We had a problem with gasoline, because people stole it all the time, siphoned it out at night. We had bought a new radio with shortwave on it, and we had it turned on in the evening. At a quarter past five every night it would come on that ''Oranges are orange: coal is black; mashed potatoes are white.'' They'd repeat it over and over and over. So about the third night my husband told one of the Coast Guard officers that lived right next door to us, and he looked into it. Somebody on the shore was repeating this so that the German submarines could come in and fill up with gas. They had big oil tanks in an old cellar. Enemy submarines were getting gas but they put a stop to it.

There were submarines sunk out there. One time they brought a lot of wounded soldiers into the harbor. They set up a place to give them coffee and doughnuts. Everybody was excited. Another time, on the back of the island some men were chopping wood when some German bodies washed up onshore. The men took their axes and everything they had and got out of there and wouldn't go back at all.

J. Willard Marriott was the founder of the Marriott Corporation. I interviewed him and his wife, Alice, in their summer home on Lake Winnipesaukee in New Hampshire.

J. WILLARD: The thing that worried us, of course, was using automobiles to get to our places. We were in a far better position for rationing and war controls than our competitors, like Howard Johnson. His places were all on the highway, and he was presented a real problem. He had to close up many restaurants. We had never gone to the highway business; we'd always gone after the suburbs, right around where people lived, so it never was a problem as far as we were concerned, getting to our shops. The big problem, of course, was rationing.

ALICE: In Washington more women worked than almost anywhere else, and I think they would stop on their way home from work or on their way to work. Because they couldn't get meat and a lot of things they ate out more than at home.

J. WILLARD: They were working on war jobs, so we had a real problem getting help. They were being conscripted for war, and it was very difficult to get shop replacements. The war took all of our managers and a lot of our personnel in the business, so we had a management problem. I wouldn't say it was boom times, but then I'd have to go back and look at my figures. Wasn't a growth period, that's for sure, because a lot of people were moving from one factory to another or from one city to another. There was all kinds of black-marketing; I guess everybody was involved with black-marketing to some extent.

ALICE: Sugar was the worst thing to get, sugar and meat. We had coupons for sugar—could only get so much a week.

I don't remember about the business, how they did.

J. WILLARD: I think that inasmuch as we were feeding the public and so many service people, we probably got more than some others, maybe. We were in a different area, and I think they rationed on the basis of need. But there were food shortages because they were shipping so much stuff overseas.

ALICE: It seems to me, Bill, that we put in a lot of dishes like macaroni and cheese and things like that because they didn't have to have meat in them.

J. WILLARD: The war didn't affect our way of life too much. We're not socialites; we're church people. I had a business that took a lot of supervision and really a lot of work. I was kept awfully busy.

ALICE: I don't think we noticed the war effort as much as people living out of Washington. There were a few things you couldn't buy and you had to do without, but I don't happen to think we minded that as long as we were trying to help out and do something for the country.

David Soergal was an engineering student at the University of Wisconsin when the war began, and, as he says, engineering students did not feel "involved" in the war. They were exempt from the draft and more concerned with finishing their education.

When the V-12 program appeared on the campus, the students who were in the army or navy would march up and down the streets of Madison, Wisconsin, singing.

The campus activities dropped down to a very serious tone. It was not all this frivolity. Most of the guys that raised a lot of hell around there were gone. The V-12s were based off campus. They had uniforms. They marched up and down the campus, kind of like ROTCs. The sports events were not as dominant. The people didn't go to football games as much, social events were way down. I remember some of the Wisconsin big gala events, like the Snow Ball, which had been a big thing in years gone by, were discontinued. We had a lot of turnover in our athletic groups because of the draft situation. But the engineering schools were doing their engineering as they had before the war started, and some of the poorer students did get drafted. I never had any discomfort about not being in uniform. Of course, I was only nineteen or twenty.

W. Clement Stone was the head of a selling organization—the Combined Registry Company, with offices in Chicago. It was an insurance agency. For Mr. Stone, who never had any trouble making money during the Depression, the years from 1942 to 1946 were mostly just more of the same—hard selling.

I had discontinued school at the age of sixteen and started to sell insurance. And I developed a system, which we call the success system—it never fails. In learning how to use one's brain power, particularly the powers of the subconscious, how to establish the right habits, how to aim high and to achieve high goals, it never occurred to me that we couldn't do as well at any period, peacetime or wartime, by turning a disadvantage into an advantage. Where others were having a difficult time during the Depression, I was, through my own personal production, earning in the neighborhood of three hundred dollars a week.

Our business was not especially affected one way or the other by the war. We take advantages of disadvantages—war, or boom times, or poor times—so, really, the external influences have little or or no effect because of the philosophy.

Of course, there were things like travel problems. Many of my salespeople traveled by car. But like everything else in life, one who has a positive mental attitude gets what he wants. For example, getting reservations and sleeping accommodations on a train: All you do is make a five-dollar bet with the porter that he can't find a berth for you in the next half hour—and for some reason you always lose the bet. You have to use your ingenuity. Under the gasoline situation, we did have a problem. So what we would do was have several men team up and use, say, one car. If we're selling in a place like Virginia, the group could go out, and one individual could be left off at one town, another at another town, and so forth. We use one car and therefore pool the gas.

Lois Raymond lived in Chicago and summered in Maine. Her husband worked for Swift & Company.

After you slaughter a lamb, you have a valuable commodity left over—wool. My husband would take the wool and sell it to the mills in various forms, depending on what kind of mill it was. He did a great deal of traveling.

Of course, his business was very good, because the synthetics hadn't been invented. I can remember that we had our first nylon stockings just about before the war. Most of the mills in the Midwest turned to making uniforms. A lot of them were blanket mills and were very busy making blankets for the service. He could sell all the wool he delivered.

My husband had been in World War I as an aviator and he had a 30-percent disability. He tried to enlist in World War II, but they said no.

Our daughter Barbara's fiancé, Paul, was a physicist. He was sent out to Alamogordo. I remember there was a test of the atomic bomb before the event. Paul wrote me a letter saying, "After what I have just seen today, I think all of us should become social scientists." But he didn't.

We knew that he was out there, there was no question about that. Also we lived right in the heart of the University of Chicago community, and half a dozen of my friends had said, "Well, we are going to have to go to Y-Town." It was a college name for Alamogordo. I remember having a dinner party and saying to Sam, "How is your cyclotron?" He said, "Oh, it is all packed up and put away." But we knew the Manhattan Project was going on. Famous physicists were coming from all over. There was a spontaneous code of honor in which you didn't spread the word around. You just knew they were with the Manhattan Project, although we didn't call it that.

The first war summer was 1942, and we decided to drive our car to our summer home in Maine. Gas was going to be rationed, and we wanted to get the car back to Maine because you can live in Chicago without a car, but it is almost impossible to live here without one.

On the fifteenth of May gas rationing was going to begin, and so my husband and I started on Friday night before that, driving at thirty-five miles an hour. They had asked everybody to drive at that speed to conserve gas. We stayed at that, plodded along, and arrived here on the fourteenth, in time to be available for our registration for gas for the car.

For forty-six years, Louis Speyer played English horn for the Boston Symphony Orchestra. I talked with him in one of the music rooms at Tanglewood, near Stockbridge.

I came to this country from France in 1918, during the First World War. We came for three weeks with the band. And instead of three weeks, we stayed about six months, wandering around everywhere, in hospitals, in camps, at rallies. So they got me a position in Boston, which was wonderful for me.

In World War II we were very lucky because we could get anything we wanted. It was nothing; we were here and safe. We played quite a few concerts for the troops, and some groups from the orchestra went to hospitals or camps and played for soldiers. The real hardship was for my family in France. I didn't know; we got some letters from the Red Cross. Of course, my father was dead already, my mother died during the war, and my sister was in the south of France, so she was safe there. But the rest of the family lived in Paris, and they escaped. I tried my best to send them something, you know, through the Red Cross, money or food; whether they got it I didn't know.

The war did not affect my life and career, because we were lucky to be with the Boston Symphony, and if you get in Boston Symphony, you can stay all your life. During the war, Mr. Perry, the manager, approached me and told me we have a black conductor—I wish I could remember the first name; the last name was Dixon—and he asked me, what you think, will the orchestra object to hiring a black conductor? We never had one before. And my answer was, they are sending black people to be killed in Europe, I think the orchestra can accept a black conductor. And then he was good. We liked him because he was good.

Jean Jepson spent the war years in high school in Bethlehem, Pennsylvania, and then at Smith College in Massachusetts.

When the war began, I was at Moravian Seminary, a Catholic girl's school. I remember a hayride that December, when everyone was home from school. It was a beautiful moonlit night, and I happened to be sitting next to a boy named Paul

Couch. I remember asking him how it would be to kill somebody, what would be his reaction? This was one thing that
really worried me about the war—you're going to kill somebody! I can't exactly remember what his answer was, but he
became a conscientious objector.

After high school I went to Smith College. One reason I
went there was because it seemed so lively, but by the time I
got there, it wasn't lively at all, because there were no boys.
But there was Westover Air Base. There was something about
the whole army thing that was a little different from getting
to know people another way. As the war was coming to a
close, a lot of the boys who had been overseas began to come
back to Westover, and we felt they were more interesting than
the guys who hadn't been away.

One guy I was involved with came back after the war—he
had been with the wave that went in for the Battle of the
Bulge—and I remember him telling me all about Holland.
They captured some Germans, and he told me how he inter-
rogated one guy and he just picked the gun up and he jammed
it down the guy's throat, and all the teeth went out. I was
dumbfounded, because this was somebody I knew exceedingly
well, and the violence wasn't like him.

*W. P. Laws and his wife owned a grocery store in Ocean City,
Maryland.*

The war meant different things to different people. In our
little church we were without a minister during most of the
war years, and we had student ministers, mostly from Princeton. One Sunday, there was one from over near Japan—he
wasn't a Japanese, but he had that coloring and features, you
know. He was attending Princeton, and he was very well educated, spoke excellent English and everything, but one of our
ladies had lost her son in the war, and just seeing him up there
in the pulpit, she almost had hysterics. Some people had that
attitude. They didn't send him back anymore, naturally.

We wouldn't have fussed about the hardships like some of
the other people. I thought about some of those people having
hysterics over butter and eggs. We managed.

Simon Greco is an Italian-born commercial artist who lived in Chicago at the time of Pearl Harbor. He is a conscientious objector to military service.

I was a commercial artist for a living, and a painter at my real job. Actually, I was doing maybe eight or ten days of commercial artwork a month. The rest of the time I was trying to learn how to paint. I wasn't selling any paintings at all, but I was becoming fairly successful as a commercial artist—a designer more than anything else.

How I arrived at a position of conscientious objector would be a little bit difficult to reconstruct. First of all, I think it had to do with my family. My parents were devout Christians. They're not very good Catholics in the real strict sense of the word, as most Italians are here. But they're very devout Christians. And I think that had a lot to do with it, and I think that being an artist had a lot to do with it, growing up trying to be one. Also, I think one of the things that probably led me to become a conscientious objector was a fight I had when I was a very small boy. I was going to be expelled from school because of the fight, and a very wonderful principal gave me a long lecture about what was the difference between me and an animal. That has always been in the back of my head. Men had an intelligence. They were made in the image of God and all the rest of that. Ironically, by the time the draft came, I didn't really believe in the image of God. The other part I did believe. Then, I think, it was the whole idea of who I was, what I was, what I was trying to do with my life. And somehow or other, killing people wasn't part of it. I really believed in the idea that somehow wars had to be stopped and that the only way they would ever be stopped is that the guy who had to fight them would simply have to say, "No, I'm not going to do it." I had a great admiration for Gandhi at the time and his pacifist method of trying to accomplish his ends. I did not think about being a member of a nation which was attacked. I think that that was not part of my makeup for the basic reason that I was brought to the United States when I was very young—three and a half—and although my father tried to make Americans out of us, he didn't succeed. I never really became an American in the real sense of the word, and ironically enough, I never became an Italian either.

I remember receiving my draft notification very vividly. Up to that point being a pacifist was a theoretical thing. And then, suddenly, you get this letter from Uncle Sam, and it's very real. I think that what most people don't realize is that you feel the weight of the government. Government is a really awesome thing when you're face-to-face with it. I remember that I filled out the questionnaire, but I didn't put it in the mail that day. I wanted to think about it because I realized what the consequences could be. I knew what the criteria were for judging conscientious objectors—primarily affiliation with a pacifist church or a pacifist organization, and I had none of these things. I had no record of being a pacifist anywhere except among a couple of people that I knew. So it wasn't a very encouraging situation that I was in.

At the same time I was being badgered by a friend who had signed up with the air force to be an art director and wanted me to be his assistant. He was very convincing about what a great time we would have, how we would never go anywhere but New York, how I wouldn't hurt anybody, and all that kind of baloney.

So another thing I learned very early is that being a conscientious objector meant that you had to make judgments almost daily. And I realized that he was asking me to make a judgment that really wasn't honest. If I were going to be an illustrator or designer for the air force, then I had no right to be a conscientious objector. I couldn't really play it both ways.

Finally, I sent the questionnaire, and I wrote them a letter. I had to give a reason for being a conscientious objector, and one of the reasons I gave was that I didn't really believe that I was put on earth to kill people.

Then I offered a deal to the government, because I realized I had very flimsy grounds in their eyes. I offered to go to war and do whatever they wanted me to do, with the provision that they would allow me to carry a gun after the war. If I were being asked to do what I considered committing murder in order to protect myself, I felt that after the war, if my existence was threatened by any enemy, even if he was the guy next door, I should have the right to shoot him down.

I felt the chances were better than average that I would end up in jail, but I really didn't resent the fact. I had a feeling— and this may sound like a contradiction—that societies are structured to protect themselves. If you're outside the mainstream of your particular society, it's your own hard luck. I also knew that if you want to make a stand for something, you really have to be prepared to pay a price for it. I was really quite surprised when a few weeks later I got this notification that I was classified as a conscientious objector.

Life as a CO in civilian clothes wasn't bad if you stayed away from certain places. The hard times came from civilians, the hard-hat type of personality. So you learned to stay away from those kind of bars.

The girls didn't give a damn about my not being in uniform one way or another. I never really had any problem as far as the women were concerned. They couldn't care less.

I think what resentment I encountered was not so much against me. A lot of people had an antagonism toward the whole idea of being forced to go to war or their children being forced to go to war and the inconvenience of the war. They couldn't say, "the goddamned government." So they would take it out on a guy like me, or get a poor 4-F and badger the hell out of him.

After a while, I got a call from the draft board to have a physical exam at an army induction center, and that was real rough, because we were spotlighted. We had a band on our arm that was marked CO—in yellow, of course. What else could it be? And a lot of the examining soldiers really gave us a hard time.

I remember two incidents. One guy, I guess he might have been an army doctor, got very violent. He was going to "kick the shit out of us" or something like that. I was getting worried. You know, you're walking around naked, you've got a towel around you, and these guys start crowding in on you, and they're going to fix you. I just finally said to the guy, "Now, I've had about enough of this. The first guy that lays a finger on me—I don't mean a punch or a kick; I mean just touches me—you're gonna have so many lawyers down here tomorrow, you'll never know what hit you, because I am not in the army. I haven't been drafted, and you guys have no authority over me. Now, either this whole thing quiets down or I am gonna just walk out of here, even if I have to walk out naked."

The other thing I remember is the psychiatrists—they were

really giving us a hard time. I don't know whether they were just trying to provoke us, but this one guy was particularly nasty.

He said. "Who do you think you are. Jesus Christ?" because I had a beard. Of course, in those days beards were very unusual. And I said, "No, I don't think I'm Jesus Christ. I've got a beard." And then I said something to the effect that "Seventy years ago it would have been weird not to have a beard. Today it's weird to have a beard. I just have a beard because I don't have to shave."

Finally, I got a letter ordering me to report to a conscientious objectors' camp in northern Michigan. I may or may not have gotten a ticket, but I know that we were not paid. All the expenses of being at the CO camp had to be borne by the individual if he could afford it. If he could not afford it, the Brethren Church, which ran the camp that I was sent to, fed you and found clothes for you. I shipped all my studio stuff home to Saint Louis and said good-bye to my two or three clients. I got an evening train and spent the whole night traveling up to this camp. It was a real bleak, deserted place, near Manistee, Michigan. These guys were standing there, and one huge guy—must have been six foot and a half—came up to me and said, "Welcome, brother. Are you saved?" And I didn't know what the hell he meant, am I saved? I thought, Jeez, I hope this isn't what I'm in for. The camp was an old CCC camp that had been used during the Depression. A bunch of us lived in one big long room.

We had army cots, and no privacy except what you could concoct with boxes or pieces of wood or whatever.

The Forestry Service was supervisor of the work the camp was supposed to be doing. Our job was to go out in the morning at, I think, seven o'clock and plant seedlings. Two days later it would rain and wash the seedlings away; we'd go back after it stopped raining and plant more seedlings. It really wasn't a real work camp; it was a jail. Let's not kid ourselves about it. We were incarcerated, and there was this mythology that we were doing work.

I did this maybe a month or so. Then the guy who ran the camp realized that I wasn't really fit for outdoor work, and so I was assigned to the camp sign shop. We made signs; we had a silk-screen operation; we did posters and things like that.

I noticed that almost every month when I first went there, they would send inmates to Detroit for another examination. What they were really doing was weeding guys out, sending them home. Another thing I am convinced of is that the army and the government really didn't want the statistics of conscientious objectors. I think they did everything they could to give you a 4-F—mentally incompetent or physically handicapped, or whatever it was, just so that they didn't have these COs on their list.

Finally I was sent to Detroit for another examination. They didn't change my classification—I was still a conscientious objector—but they sent me home.

I went back to Chicago for a while, and I decided I didn't want to stay there. I went home to Saint Louis for the summer. The afternoon after I got home the FBI was at the door. "What are you doing? Where are your papers? How do you explain this?" and all that baloney. Neighbors had called them up saying, "There's a young guy here. What's he doing home?"

My mother and father were the ones that really suffered. The people in the neighborhood where I grew up, most of them refused to talk to them because I was a conscientious objector. By that time my brother was a conscientious objector also. There were people that I had grown up with that wouldn't talk to me, relatives that wouldn't talk to me, wouldn't talk to my parents. The guy next door, who was like a second father to me when I was growing up, refused to talk to me.

Now I have had time to think about those years. When you are in your early twenties, life tends to be black and white, especially if you're my kind of person. As you grow older, you get all kinds of shades of gray. And I've given a lot of thought to why I did it. Had I taken up that offer of the air force, I'd have been a captain; I would have a pension now. I have thought many, many times over the years whether I really should have done it. Not that I've ever doubted that what I did was right—that I really believe. But the question that has cropped up is whether a person can cut himself off from humanity. Some days I think I should have been part of it. I'm still part of the human race, and I think the experiences of humanity cannot really be sidestepped. This is an argument I used to have with my brother and with a number of conscientious objectors, because there was always that line that had to be drawn. So you say I don't work for a munitions maker, I don't do ads for a company that makes bombers. But I do an ad for a company that buys something from a company that buys something from a company. What the hell, it's all inter-related! And pure isolation is never possible. If you pay taxes, you're helping the war. And they make very short work of you if you don't pay taxes. I don't regret what I did, but it's given me a lot to think about in the years since. I put this with the things I can't answer, but it's an interesting question.

7

Wives and Children

The war had a special impact on the wives of servicemen overseas and on all children.

Mabel Wiggins lived in Saint Paul, where her husband, Russell, was managing editor of the St. Paul Pioneer Press and Dispatch—*before he went in the air force. Her oldest son enlisted in the navy and spent most of the time on PT boats in the Panama Canal area.*

You really didn't let yourself worry too much about your husband being overseas, because everybody else was in the same boat, going through the same thing, and you wouldn't let yourself get down. I had three children at home, and I wasn't about to go to pieces. We had this mailman for several years, and then he stopped coming. I said to a neighbor, "Isn't that funny? I thought our mailman just had a vacation." And she said, "He couldn't stand all the women left behind who were always meeting him at the door and saying, 'You don't have a letter for me this morning?' He said he just couldn't stand all that worry, so he asked to be put in the office somewhere."

You kept right on doing what you had been doing, but adding more things to it. You helped in Red Cross. You volunteered wherever they thought there was something you could do; and the youngsters, too. It's quite fun to think how much really was accomplished. Saint Paul used to have a great big railroad station with a lovely big room and a big kitchen. Most of it had been taken out and turned into a nice recreation area.

I used to go down in the morning. I'd take that early shift because then I'd be home when the youngsters got home from school. And I would call home at seven-thirty to see that everybody was up and on their way to school. Of course, you had to ride the streetcars because you didn't have gas to trot back and forth. So, you'd catch the quarter-to-five streetcar, and it was perfectly safe. Now I think I'd be scared, because that wasn't exactly a pleasant neighborhood; there were a lot of warehouses down by the station.

When Russell was sent to the Pentagon, I went down to spend a day or two with him before he went overseas. They had to go in full equipment: the belt with the metal, the cuffs, the thing that opens for your plate, the canteen, full military garb, his typewriter, and one big bag that expanded. We picked up this young kid who was staying with his brand-new wife over in Georgetown. He came out looking just awful, weeping too, with all his equipment, and when I took them to where they would be dumped at the Pentagon, I said again, thinking this would cheer this poor boy, "You both look like little Boy Scouts waiting for the scoutmaster." The boy just looked at me. The idea of a wife being so frivolous was just too much for him. Russell said afterward he asked how long we had been married. I admit I had some tears as I drove away.

Jane Malach's husband was a doctor in the army, and she began the war in the Columbia School of Journalism in New York but did not stay there for long.

My husband had been called up the preceding June. I had been accepted for the fall at Columbia, and we decided that I should continue and that he would just stay and do his stint. We were both stupid, because we thought it would only last a year. That's what the Medical Corps man said at the time he went in—six months before Pearl Harbor. He decided that he would get somebody to cover his practice for him while he was away, and I would go back and stay with my parents and go to school. I kept commuting between New York and wherever he was stationed. First it was Tennessee, and then it was a lot of other places.

When this blast came on December 7, I had a very hard time trying to decide whether I should quit school and go down and join him. It was obvious then that it wasn't going to be just a year. What I finally did was go to the dean of the school, Henry Pringle, who was really great. Then I went to Carl Ackerman. By that time I had decided I had better go, so I said: "Look, I would like to quit now, not finish the first semester, and go down and join my husband." He gave me a long speech: "This is a great big war. Some of the men who have to go overseas may not come back, but we have our job to do here, and what our job is is to see that we keep things going so that this country is just the same—just as good when they come back as it was when they left. Your particular thing is to stay here and finish your course in journalism. Furthermore," he said, "if you quit now and go down and join him, I won't ever let you come back and finish." I thought about that and decided that I would stay and finish. Then I went and joined my husband in June of 1942 at Camp Forrest in Tennessee.

There is nothing more insulated than a New Yorker. When I went down there to live, it was really an eye-opener. When I first went there six months before Pearl Harbor, Tullahoma was the center of the First Army maneuvers. There were ninety thousand troops in the field in the area of Tullahoma and an explosion of wives and families. There was one little hotel in this town of about three thousand people, and people were sleeping on the floors, sleeping in the lobby. One of the things that shocked me was the fact that practically all of the women got married at eighteen right after they graduated from high school. It was an experience for someone who was as provincial as I was to meet people from Chicago and to meet the local people, really. I know this sounds absurd, but it was the first time I ever heard people use the expression "damn yankee."

After I graduated and came down permanently, I wrote to the *Chattanooga Times* and asked if they had any openings.

They said they didn't have anything regular but asked me to cover the graduation of the First Army Rangers School. That was fascinating, because it was the first guerrilla training. They had been trained in judo, so I read up on that and really learned judo. I was the only woman in the press group. The rangers and reporters participated in a graduation exercise. We had to crawl, and they shot rifles over our heads. That was my first newspaper assignment.

My husband was transferred to Camp Jackson in Columbia, South Carolina, and then into the hospital in Augusta, Georgia, and there I was in Columbia waiting for him. I went to the *Columbia State*, which was twenty dollars a week, but because I had a graduate degree in journalism, they paid me twenty-two dollars. My beat was the police department, which was absolutely wild. I was pregnant. I must have covered the Police Department for about five months. When I appeared the first time and said I was the police reporter for the *Columbia State*, they all dropped, but they were very gentlemanly. I had to go over there every day; it was part of my beat. By the time I came back the second time they had cleaned out the jail—they really scrubbed it out. I think they were very careful that nothing happened while I was in the department; they felt I wouldn't know what in the hell to do if there was a murder, anything. They were darling, just darling! I was the first woman police reporter in the South. I was also the music and ballet critic.

Anna Katherine Siemers had a husband on an LSM in the Pacific. "Number 242, I still remember," she says. When I interviewed her at Leisure World in Silver Spring, she brought out the letters from her husband she had saved and her old, mostly empty ration books. Her husband was dead.

At the beginning of the war, right after the Depression, my husband was working in New York City. I was working as a secretary for an engineering firm. We were living in Richmond Hills, Queens. My daughter was born in May of 1943, and my husband was drafted right after Christmas of that year. We probably would never have had a baby if we had known he was going to be drafted. We were both in our thirties, and we had kept postponing it because we didn't know whether he would be called or not. Finally I said, "Well, they are not calling anybody over twenty-nine." But it didn't work out that way. Of course, I am very glad we had the baby.

We lived near a railroad yard, and it seemed all I was doing the whole time was scrubbing. That's what I remember most about the war. I just had my hands full existing. I still have my ration books. We would trade stamps with our neighbors. I didn't care much for sugar, so I would give my neighbor the sugar stamps, and she would give me coffee stamps. That is how we got along. I really felt the burden, besides not knowing where my husband was. I think that really was the worst thing—the uncertainty of everything. But he did survive the war. He said he was lucky; the fellow next to him had his head blown off at Iwo Jima. He said, "I guess it wasn't my time." They never talk about it too much when they come back. About that side of it.

ViCurtis Hinton was a student at Howard University in Washington, D.C.

I don't remember that the war affected my college life too much, but it affected the fellows who were in college. They were really afraid of not being able to finish; everybody was running to the draft board trying to get deferments.

In Washington I used to work with the service clubs. We had a little group that would go to entertain soldiers here, at Fort Belvoir, Fort Myer, and different clubs. We were trying to keep morale up. Some boys were in good spirits, some were really antiwar—but not as much as they were about Vietnam. The majority of them seemed happy. Some of them were bitter that they didn't have the opportunity to stay in college like others did.

My husband and I were married in '43. The night of my wedding reception he got his telegram for the army, which I'll never forget. He had finished medical school and had just finished interning. And all the fellows from the hospital . . . oh, they were so delighted to bring him this telegram!

When my husband went in the army, he went first to Fort Huachuia in Arizona. It was strictly an army base, in the middle of nowhere. That's where they sent most of the black officers. Everybody you ever knew at Howard University eventually got to Fort Huachuia. My husband was with the station hospital there. They had a party at the officer's club every Saturday night, and you just knew everybody because you'd been at school with them. The wives had a good time. This is terrible to say, but we had cars, we had coffee sessions every morning, we played cards all day while the fellows were working; it was a lot of fun.

I was interested in medical technology, and they didn't teach it at Howard at that time. So after my husband went overseas, I went to the University of Minnesota. It was really quiet in Minneapolis. In Washington you did get a little activity, but out there it was like nothing. You didn't get as much segregation there. The black population was small. One girl who was in school with me said I was the first black person she'd ever seen.

Heli Swyter lived in Houston, Texas. She and her husband were Dutch. He left her to join the army in Holland in April of 1941, while she was pregnant, and she did not see him again for four years.

We came to the United States in 1938 because of my husband's job with Dutch Shell. He was a research chemist, and they wanted to use him either in the Dutch East Indies, the United States, or Saudi Arabia. We said, "Why not America? A new adventure for both of us." So we arrived here in May 1938, and in April 1941 he joined up. We weren't even fit for our first citizenship papers when he shipped out. He had already decided to become an American citizen when he was here only a half year, because he liked it so well. I said, "Yes, I like it in so many countries. But it's not enough for me to become a citizen. It's not like taking off a jacket and putting on another jacket." So he said, "If you don't want to become one, why, just stay what you are, and I'll be married to a damn foreigner!"

I only decided to become a citizen when he came home alive. The war wasn't over, but he was called to this country to train the Dutchmen who had escaped, hundreds and hundreds, who had escaped Holland. Most of them didn't know a word of English, and they needed Dutch officers to train them, so he had to change uniform for the second time and became a captain in the Marine Corps. Our child was going on four when he came back.

One problem in raising the child alone was that I had no money. He started as a buck private. The Dutch government was in such a mess there in England, he didn't even get any pay. And so how did I have to live? The Shell Company, who knew about this, sent some delegate to my modest little apartment, and they told me I could borrow as much money from the company as I wanted, or needed, for my own upkeep and my baby's, but that it was a loan and later we'd have to pay it back. When my husband was commissioned, he was able to send some money home, but it still wasn't very much because he wasn't paid by the American government. It was still Dutch.

So I went back to my art; I began making portraits. The trouble was, it was ten years ago since I had done that, and in those ten years I had lost the sight of one eye. It's a terrible handicap to have to make the portrait with one eye, because you don't see depth any longer; you only know that by estimation. You don't know how far the nose sticks out. But I had adjusted myself, and I did pretty good. How to get known, though, because I wanted to sell the things that I did. So, through a friend who was a Russian artist and photographer I did a portrait of Judd Mortimer Lewis, the president of the *Houston Chronicle*. He wanted to buy it, but it was the only thing I had to become known. It was shown in the Houston gallery, and then I got commissions after that, mostly friends of mine. It didn't help much financially, but the main thing was it helped me from being blue, morose, pessimistic. I was really feeling very low that first year.

I lived completely for my child. I felt the responsibility of having to be not only a mother but also a father. I noticed that, for a boy, he was oversensitive. He was not an aggressive child. Of course, there are aggressive boys and nonaggressive ones, but with him it was definitely a matter that he had never had a man around to play rough with him. When his dad came home, he noticed that right away too. He wanted his son to be a real boy, so he started to wrestle with him, and slowly he became a different boy. I think he needed his daddy very much.

While his father was away, it was hard for the boy. He used to play with the other children in the neighborhood, and they would talk about their daddies and how they were going to see them at suppertime. My boy would come in around five o'clock and say, "Where's my daddy?" I used to say to him, with a bright face, "Your father is far away, son, but he will come home. He is on a boat, that's why he can't come home so soon. That boat is far away." How many pictures he drew of the boat! And he used to say, "When I get bigger, I am going to swim out to that boat." I sent the pictures he drew of the boats in the letters to my husband. The letters from him took so long to come—six months, more. And they were so censored. And what kind of a censor that was! My husband was not a fool; he didn't give me any information about where he was.

When my husband finally came home, I got a wire which said, "I'll call you from San Francisco." I hadn't heard his voice in so many years. I just about died! I couldn't say anything. I went in the car with our boy to the airport in Houston, and when the plane finally came in, from a distance I could see my husband come out of it, and I thought, is that him? He looked so much bigger in the uniform. When he came real near, I said to my little son, "There's Daddy." And he ran to meet his daddy, a strange man—but he knew him from the pictures. I had put in the back pocket of the little suit he was wearing, a package of Lucky Strikes to give him, and I said, "Don't forget to give Daddy his cigarettes." My husband picked him up, and with him on his shoulder he came to me and said, "My, I don't seem to be a stranger to this little fellow."

I was always very proud of the hair of my son. My husband never had very much hair. It was not curly or wavy, but my son had it from my side of the family—soft texture, plenty full, and it was curly—and I had always snipped the curls myself to make it kind of boyish looking, I thought. He'd never been to a barber. In these days it would be normal, but in those days, when the boys always wore the hair short, he must have looked to his dad like a girl, because the first thing he said after they became acquainted was, "Why don't you have his hair cut like a boy's?" I said, "He has such pretty curls, he is just so young, not even four; that can come a little later." My husband said, "That can come right now. He's a

boy, my boy." And the next day he took him to the barber,
and he came home like a little boy.

*Regina Wilk lived in Albany, New York. Her husband was in
a First Army antiaircraft unit. She had a son, born while he
was away. Her son was later killed in Vietnam. She was first
national vice-president of the Gold Star Mothers of America,
when I interviewed her.*

My husband was overseas at the time our son was born; he
landed on Utah Beach, and he was in France, Belgium, and
Germany. That's why I went to work; I wanted to get that off
my mind. I worked in the payroll department of the New York
Engineer Depot. I was one of the civilians working on a military base, and the morale was good. We had a job to do, and
we had to keep busy. My mother took care of the child.

We all took the shortages in stride. I don't remember any
complaints. I was married rather young, and maybe I really
didn't get full realization as to what was going on. I had a son
killed in Vietnam, and I think this war had more of an impact
on me than World War II. It's closer to me. I suppose if my
husband, God forbid, had been killed, I'd be feeling just the
same way as I do now. But unless something affects you very
closely, you just go on your merry way, which is an awful
thing to say. I think I did worry about my husband being in
the service, but it's not the same as the actual loss.

*Mary Devereux Crist is a member of a Marine Corps family.
Her brother was Col. James Devereux, who was captured at
Wake Island. Her husband was a Marine Corps colonel who
spent twenty-nine months in the Pacific.*

The first thing my mother said after Pearl Harbor was,
"What's going to happen to Jimmy?" My brother was captured on the twenty-third of December 1941, and held as a
prisoner of war for four years. A lot of people criticized him
because he didn't go down fighting with his men, but he was
in command, and he had all the civilians under him, and he
thought it was a better thing to do.

When my husband was sent to Camp Nyland in California,
I drove out with the three children.

After he left Camp Nyland, the Marine Corps paid our way to any spot in the U.S. that we wanted to go to. I had been in contact with a very good friend, and she suggested that we come to Clearwater, Florida. And I decided that the government might as well send me as far as they could. So I got on the train with the three children; copious tears at leaving. We landed in Clearwater with no place to stay, but we had one friend there, and she finally found me a house. My children were ten, five, and nineteen months. After a while the oldest boy got to be too much for me to handle, so I sent him to a prep school in Dade County, Florida, which was about a three-hour train trip away. I think the main problem was just growing up with female companionship alone.

One year I sent my boy to Porter Military Academy near Charleston, West Virginia. I came from Clearwater up to Charleston to see him one weekend, and the headlines were all "Marines Land in Bougainville and Iwo Jima." I remember this woman who was in tears, an employee of the hotel where I was staying. Her son was in the Marine Corps, and we figured out that he was with my husband, and I said, "Well, at least you know he's under somebody who has had a lot of training." At the hotel they said they didn't have any rooms at all, and I said, "Well, I'm just going to sit here in the lobby until you find me some place to sleep." Then I thought of a marine wife I had known who had made her debut in Charleston. Her husband had gone overseas, and I presumed that maybe she had come home, so I called the society editor of the paper, and she traced this woman to where she was rolling bandages. She made a phone call to the desk clerk at the hotel where I was, and he gave me a choice of rooms. So it just showed that if you knew the right person, you could get anything you wanted. Anyway, that morning they went into Iwo Jima, and I was able to comfort this woman employee at the hotel a little bit, though I was scared to death myself. My husband did see the raising of the flag—the first raising—remember there were two; one staged and one for real.

More and more wives who were in the same position I was in came down to Clearwater, and it ended up there were thirteen Marine Corps war widows down there, all with small children. We got as much liquor as we could. Not that we were alcoholics, but we certainly had our drinks in the evening.

I was down there for nineteen months, when my husband came home on emergency leave because his father died. I remember when he called me and told me he was on the West Coast. The phone rang at two o'clock in the morning, and of course I screamed bloody murder and woke up all three children, and we all got on the phone and talked to him. He came to Clearwater, and one night he asked all the wives out for dinner—took eighteen of us to the country club. There were some Army Air Force men sitting at the table next to us, and they wanted to dance with us, but he said, "No, you can't dance with my girls. I've been out for nineteen months without anyone at all." Then he broke down and let them dance with them.

After my husband's leave was over, he went into Guam, and that's where he got hit. He was sitting in a deep cave, way in the back, so he thought he was safe enough. He took his helmet off and was sitting on it when a piece of shrapnel exploded just outside the cave, and it came back and grazed his head. I received a telegram—the telegraph office got mixed up and put the four black stars, which meant death, on his telegram. I was hesitant, to say the least, about opening it, and then I found the message was, "YOUR HUSBAND HAS SUSTAINED A WOUND OF THE HEAD," so I called Washington to try to get some word. I had a brother-in-law stationed at the headquarters in Washington, and I got him to try to find out out how serious it was. He did finally, after several days, and said it was not a serious wound in the head. But you can imagine what was going through my mind. He was not even hospitalized.

I lived in Clearwater for nineteen months, then moved to Park Fairfax, Virginia. To tell you the truth, the people up here were still having a good time, and they certainly didn't talk about the war much. No one ever asked what I heard from my husband. They seemed to have the same cocktail parties. Life went on pretty much as usual. Gas rationing didn't seem to affect them much, as I remember. If they had enough money, they would have two or three cars, and they would buy the gas.

The war years were like a haze. I think I was restless for something to get my mind off it and see new people or cry on my mother's shoulder and let her cry on mine.

Celeste Kavanaugh, now living in Bradenton, Florida, was just finishing at Florida State College for Women, in Tallahassee.

I remember Founder's Day at the Alpha Delta Pi House. We had a beautiful lawn party, and all the girls dressed in long dresses. That was in May of 1942—it was so peaceful and so lovely, and yet there was this overtone of all the girls trying to decide whether they were going to go ahead and marry the boys they were pinned to or whether they were going into the war effort or what they were going to do. It was such a contrast, because May in Tallahassee is so lovely. I remember the phonograph was playing "Don't Sit Under the Apple Tree With Anyone Else But Me," and I said to myself—and I've thought about this so many times—"Will life ever be like this again?" Things were so different after the war. It was never the same again.

One thing always amused me, looking back. I was a Political Science major, and I had been reading *One World, Union Now With Britain* and all these books, and I remember before Pearl Harbor—it must have been, maybe, the first part of the 1941/ 42 school year—going to the president of the college with several f·· nds. We wanted to organize a One World movement, and he looked at us very peculiarly and stopped it in a hurry. The war came so closely thereafter that it's really strange to think that you still were idealistic about the world.

There were lots of air bases around Tallahassee, and the officers would fill the sorority houses. They were always there, coming and going. I had some good friends at the Jacksonville Naval Base who were learning to fly; they were cadets. I remember one boy who was killed in training—by his friend, incidentally. He was following too close behind the other plane. His plane was hit, and he couldn't open his parachute in time.

I took the civil service exams for administrative assistants before I graduated in May. Then I went to Fernandino and was waiting for an assignment—I had no idea it would take so long in coming. It was a year and a half before I heard from the exams. My father was in the marine hardware business, and he was flooded with forms to fill out to requisition materials for the fishing and shrimping fleet there. I helped him with his office work and helped with the civil defense in Fernandino.

They were exciting times. You would just see uniforms everywhere. In trains you'd sit in the aisles on suitcases because the trains were so full. You weren't supposed to travel unless it was necessary. There were signs Is This Trip Necessary? everywhere. It was exciting. We were very united then. Everyone was doing anything he could to help, no matter what it was. Whether it was rolling bandages or addressing envelopes, civil defense, or anything that came up, everybody was pitching in, going about cheerfully, not complaining, patching up old tires, stretching the gasoline, going without sugar; because everyone had part of his family in the military. They were doing it not just for the country; they had a personal stake in it.

Everything was very uncertain—what the news was going to be from overseas, what you were going to be allotted, whether you would find what you wanted at the stores, food or anything else. You just sort of adapted to it and accepted it as it came, but still you never quite knew what was coming next. And I remember that every night when Kaltenborn came on, everybody listened. His voice was a very caring voice, and the overtones of sorrow were so strong. Any family that had sons or sons-in-law in the war were so concerned about any news from day to day. I remember hearing Kaltenborn on the night that Dunkirk was being evacuated and what a terribly depressing time that was. But it was also exciting, you know, hearing about the boats and how many of them were going to get there and worrying about whether those little boats were going to get back to England loaded with men.

Eunice Yoakum lived in Chicago. Her husband, a retired minister, was too old for the military service, but he wanted to do something for the war effort, so he went to weather school and then taught weather at Chanute Field in Illinois. She had a young son, Robert, who could not wait to get into the air force. She took a job working for Liberty Mutual Insurance Company.

Bob was in college at that time, in his second year at Northwestern. Very soon after the war began, he called up one night and said he wanted to enlist. He was an only son, an only child. It was, I'd say, in January or February 1942—before the school year was up. I thought that was terrible, but his group was very patriotic. His whole crowd of friends enlisted in the Air Corps. When Bob went away to school, I was very conscious of the war coming on, and I wanted to do something, so I took a secretarial course, a whole-year course, and then I went right out and got a job. I could have had every job I applied for, but I took this job at an insurance company. My work really didn't have anything to do with the war, except that they did need help. I had two girl friends who were also working in the insurance business, and it was really loads of fun. I was on my own in a way I hadn't been since I'd been married. We did everything together. We took in shows when we wanted to, and it was a very independent life. Except for worrying about Bob.

The war had quite an impact on the company. We had a great deal of trouble getting help, and what help that did come was very mediocre. The good ones were leaving because they were all getting jobs that paid twice as much. The starting salary was $18.50 for file clerks. I guess it was $21.50 for typists. You could get double that in the defense factories. So the average efficiency was down because of the types of people we had to hire.

I was constantly worried about Bob, just constantly. I would wake up in the morning with an awful feeling that something terrible was going on; and, of course, it wasn't just poor Bob, it was the whole situation. But being the only son, my whole life, almost the only time I had him off my mind was when I was working. That's one of the reasons I was very thankful to have a job; I could forget about it all through the day. I think any mother went through that. I had one real scare—the Battle of the Bulge. He had written to me where he was, and when we heard about the Battle of the Bulge, we looked on the map and knew he must be in that territory. That was terrible. It seemed like at least six weeks, but it was probably three weeks, that we didn't hear a word from him. Then he finally wrote from Paris that he was having a wonderful time. He met Moira Shearer—the dancer in *Red Shoes*, the ballerina. He had been sent by his colonel to publish a little pamphlet on what they were doing in the Nineteenth Tactical Air Force. So there he was, having the time of his life in Paris, and I'd been worried about it.

Gertrude Blassingame lived on Anna Maria Island, near Bradenton, Florida, with her daughters, Peggy and April.

My husband, Wyatt, came home and said he had applied for a commission in the navy. April was born in January 1942, and I don't think Wyatt told me about this until after she was born. I was mad; I guess it was a woman's normal reaction. We had very few conveniences, and the pay for a lieutenant in the navy was very small.

I felt terrible. I felt alone. But I would say it was one of the best things that ever happened to me, because I learned to depend on myself. About a year and a half later, Wyatt was transferred to Quonset Point, Rhode Island, and I just walked in on him with the kids. He didn't have any place for me to stay, but I was going to be with him if he was in this country, so we slept in pretty crowded quarters, the four of us. When his training there was up, he was going to South America, but he went someplace else first. So he said, "Look, I'll pay your fare back to Anna Maria if you promise me you'll stay there for the duration." Wyatt was sent to Hawaii, just living it up. But he made up for it in Okinawa.

I followed the war by listening to three commentators. I didn't want to get confused with too many people who had different points of view so I kept to about three that I respected—H. V. Kaltenborn, Edward R. Murrow, and I can't remember the other. I followed the Battle of Okinawa on the radio. It was my first experience with following a map. When the radio would announce where there had been a battle, I'd say, "Well Wyatt was just there." I thought he must still be alive, and he was. Of course, I was worried, but I think I just believed. I remember one time I sent him some martinis. They weren't supposed to receive alcoholic beverages, but I went to the canning company here in Bradenton. Two quarts and a pint bottle just fit in the package, so I made the martinis, put them in the bottle, and then the bottle of olives fit in the side, and I took it to the canning company. They sealed it for me in the form of a can of orange juice—Tropicana. The man that is there now would not have approved of it, because he's a teetotaler. Wyatt received it, and he was sending his men out on a mission that night to bomb Shanghai. It was just enough to go around, and the mission was successful.

I remember some things with pleasure. I had no fear; I didn't feel like I feel now. We didn't even have a house key. We had a radar station up on the north point. I think they may have had about eighty men there. They'd come to my house, and if I had beer, they would drink it. I finally made it clear to them that they were welcome, but beer was scarce, so they'd have to bring their own, and they did. They were nice, and there weren't any older men—I was in my thirties, and you didn't have to fight off passes or anything like that. We'd have parties, and they would come to our house on Christmas and any holidays. That part of it was good. I found out that if you don't want to be lonely, you share your facilities with other people. I learned to be cautious, but not to be afraid.

Her daughter, Peggy, was eleven years old at the time of Pearl Harbor. Then her father went into the navy.

He was a lieutenant in the navy. I remember thinking how wonderful he looked in that white uniform. I don't remember thinking necessarily of his being a hero. He was home one Christmas, and that was a dismal time, because he must have been leaving immediately, maybe the next day. So instead of being happy, I felt low. I couldn't take the day for what it was worth; I was too worried about tomorrow and having him go back again. I missed him very much, and I got along with him very well—at that time I got along with him better than with my mother. Now, in retrospect, I see that so much of the irritability that she had and her terrible tension was due to the fact that they were separated and that she had to fear for his safety.

I was too young to have any personal friends who were servicemen, and when strangers would whistle as I went by with my girl friends or they'd come up and say something, I'd want to slug them with my pocketbook. I could romanticize about them as heroes, and it was all beautiful.

The war years had a tremendous impact on young Herbert Collins. He lived in Bowling Green, Virginia, a small town about thirty miles north of Richmond. Camp A. P. Hill was nearby, and he remembers the war years and what they meant to his town.

Camp A. P. Hill took over one-third of Caroline County area; it moved in in 1941, and that made a real impact on me when that happened. I had relatives there, and it displaced them. The army bought up land in adjacent counties as settlement land for people who were dispossessed and couldn't find houses of their own. People don't realize that happens in the twentieth century. They moved all those families at A. P. Hill, and I remember them moving the bodies. They moved every cemetery out of there at the time. They found one casket which, they said, was filled with silver. It probably was buried there during the Civil War, when a lot of silver was buried like that.

I remember the USO clubs at Bowling Green. They were segregated at the time; the black USO club was down by the black high school, and the white USO club was up in Bowling Green, the county seat. Many of the old maids at home who went to these USO clubs met service guys and married them. On weekends the troops completely took over Bowling Green. There were no bars, but restaurants served beer. Here was a little town with five hundred people, and you couldn't even get your car through the streets; both sides of the streets were just lined with army trucks and jeeps and all kinds of army vehicles. Even tanks would be driven in, so that you felt like you were in the middle of warfare. This really made an impression on me.

War is a time of social change, and the girls were supposed to be nice to the service guys. They dated a lot of the local girls. You know, you didn't have that attitude that was felt after the war: "No sailors or dogs allowed on the grounds." That's more of a peacetime thing. Soldiers had real support and backing in World War II.

We had a lot of patriotic songs, "Nathan Hale and Colin Kelly, Too," "There's a Star-Spangled Banner Waving Somewhere." That was one we used to sing all the time. "In a distant land so many miles away, / Only Uncle Sam's great heroes will ever get to go there, / How I wish that I could also be there one day," and it just goes on and on, and it lists all the patriots, from the Revolutionary Army on.

I remember the gas rationing, because we were on the farm at the time, and the school buses had to consolidate routes. Children had to walk several miles to board a school bus, and I was very fortunate, because the pickup point for the children was at my house.

I think the gruesomeness of the war certainly made an impact on the children at the time. I saved a clipping about how they had taken the Jews and burned them in Germany, and they had heaps of ashes with bones all mixed in, and I saved the picture as a child because that made an impression on me.

I also learned who the generals were. I went to war pictures and saw the newsreels. You had this growling lion head that would come on before the news, and then the news would come on, and they'd tell what was happening in the war, and then they'd go on to the movie. I went as much for the news as I did for the movie because we didn't have any radio at home.

Congressman Norman Mineta (D-Cal.) was ten years old at the time of Pearl Harbor. He was a Nisei Japanese living in San Jose, California.

My parents were born and raised in Japan. Dad came over in 1902 as a boy of roughly fourteen years. He and my mother were not American citizens because the laws prevented Asians from becoming U.S. citizens. The Chinese weren't able to get their citizenship until 1944; the Filipinos didn't get theirs until 1946. The Japanese got theirs in 1950. We were leading a comfortable life; we were not a wealthy family, but I think we were above average.

Immediately after Pearl Harbor a curfew was imposed on all people of Japanese ancestry. You couldn't travel in groups of any more than five, and you couldn't travel distances of greater than twenty-five miles without permission from the FBI. My sister got married in February of 1942 in San Francisco, and so we had to get a permit to go to the marriage ceremony. My brother had to stay home because if he had gone, there would have been six of us.

My father's business just went down. His clientele was 100-percent Japanese, anyway, and at that point the insurance companies would not insure anyone of Japanese ancestry either. On the nineteenth of February of 1942 the president signed Executive Order 9066, which established zones in Washington, Oregon, and California and indicated that within thirty days those people in zone 1 would have to be removed to camps. The army took over racetracks, and the early ones being evacuated from their homes had to go and live in stables.

We were fortunate in that we were able to lease our home to some friends. My dad had just purchased a 1941 Packard—he had probably bought it for fourteen hundred dollars, and he had to sell it for seven hundred dollars. There were other people who had businesses and grocery stores. What do you do with a grocery store? In thirty days? A lot of them just padlocked their businesses and had to walk away from them.

We left San Jose on big trains and were taken to Santa Anita, a racetrack in southern California. We were fortunate in that we didn't get placed in one of the horse stables; we got put in barracks buildings that had been built in the meantime. In a room about the size of this [a Congressman's office, which is not very big] there were six of us. We were there from May until October of 1942. They tried to keep friends and families together as much as they could. From Santa Anita we went to a camp at Hart Mountain, Wyoming. These camps were all barbed wire, guard towers, searchlights. They were concentration camps. There's no question about it. In roughly May of 1943 my dad got a job teaching at the University of Chicago, teaching Japanese under the Army Specialized Training Program, so he was able to leave Hart Mountain, Wyoming, and go to Illinois. My mother and I stayed at the camp. Camp life was a very Spartan kind of existence. Morale was low. But, you know, despite what happened here—to show the resilience and the loyalty of the Japanese Americans—at Santa Anita they were making camouflage nets for use by the troops during that whole time. Behind barbed wire enclosures and in a concentration camp, American style, they were still making camouflage nets.

These places, where the camps were, were not vacation spots. In the summer they were extremely hot and in winter extremely cold. They put them in isolated spots so that even if you jumped the fence and got away, you'd still be twenty miles from any community. We stayed there until the latter part of 1943, and on Thanksgiving Day of 1943 we were able to leave and go to a home my dad had rented in Evanston, Illinois.

In Evanston I think we were treated as well as could be expected. There was always that curiosity among the kids at school about whether or not I was Japanese. I remember during the war they said things like, "You can always tell a Japanese because they can't pronounce their v's and their l's, because v's come out like l's and the l's come out like r's." So the kids would try these rhymes on me, and I'd go sailing right through them pronouncing the l's and the v's, and they'd say, "Are you sure you're Japanese? Are you sure you're not Indian?" Evanston being a university community, I think there was more tolerance in our being there.

My brother-in-law was in the army with the 442nd Regimental Combat Team, the most highly decorated outfit of its size in the annals of U.S. Army history, and my brother was learning Japanese to go to the South Pacific. So as a twelve-year-old boy, I followed the war, read the papers, and watched the maps of the battles. I remember following those things very closely.

Hugh Sidey was in high school in Greenfield, Iowa; population, 2,500.

We had a boy in town who was killed at Pearl Harbor. He was on one of the battleships. His mother worked for my mother. So, instantly, the war was brought home. And I think the mothers understood it, but we kids didn't look that far ahead. When my brother turned eighteen he enlisted, ended up in the medical corps, and was over in Europe in field hospitals that followed the troops. It was kind of exciting. I didn't really understand it, but it began to come home. We had a bunch of fellows that were lost. Red Oak, Iowa, nearby, lost more men than any single town of its size per capita or per unit than any other place in the United States in World War II. Their boys made up a good part of the 34th Division that was hit hard in Tunisia. That was our National Guard division.

This little town was all you had. In many ways it was a marvelous life. We made kites; we'd buy a nickel orange crate and cut the lumber up and make model planes; hiked; we swam in the old creeks around there. We were totally happy, but there was no money. Out of that we just went from one kind of restriction to another—gas rationing. I remember we canceled some football games. And we canceled music contests; and there were no vacations. You stayed right there. Our diet was affected a little, not much, but you had the rationing—meat stamps, shoe stamps, sugar stamps. My dad had a pretty good gas ticket—a B-sticker because he was a country editor and got to drive around. But in those small towns, you walked or rode your bike; it didn't have that much impact on us. We never went anyplace anyway. So we didn't feel deprived.

My father's newspaper business was good. We began to come out of the Depression because of the war contracts. So now it became very difficult to get help. He needed linotype operators; he had machines that broke down, presses, that sort of thing. But he was a handy guy and he improvised a bit. He had to work awful hard, but he made more money, and one of the reasons he made money was that there wasn't any help to hire. I worked at the paper in the mornings and after football practice.

I took pictures of all the draftees leaving and by this time, when I was in high school, they were friends—only two to three years older than I. The old Trailways bus would come to the hotel, which was right beside my dad's newspaper, to take the draftees into Des Moines, and Dad insisted on a picture of every guy. Almost every day, it seemed, there would be another ten or fifteen, and they all lined up in their farmer's clothes with their cardboard suitcases. I'd go out there with my speed-graphic and shoot a picture of them lined up. I'd see them go off, and a year or so later, in some instances two years later, suddenly would come news that so-and-so was lost in a bomber over Britain or killed in the Pacific.

So I was very much aware of the war. The social mores were also affected. There were sexually deprived women around and there were some wild scenes. Young wives, with their husbands gone, took the boys in high school out and introduced them to the joys and sorrows of sex. There were divorces after the war; there were bizarre and exotic tales.

Then there were the boys coming home. They'd come around to the high school, and oh God, we thought they were the greatest guys in the world. There was even a flyer or two who came back and buzzed the high school—and then they'd write about it later. Airplanes were still novelties, and everybody would go out to look at these guys flying over. One guy flew over in a B-25. They'd be ferrying these planes, and they'd come low, you know, circle a couple of times. It was a marvelous thrill.

We did have a little bitterness in our part of the country. They deferred farm boys. A lot went, but some took those agricultural deferments to work on farms. Quite legitimate, but it caused a bitter feeling, no question about it.

There was a sense of exhilaration during the war that brought people together. There was no problem except for those families that lost sons. Even there, there were some people who took that as part of their duty, the lost sons. It was a sense of pride, in some way.

Anne Relph remembers what it was like to be evacuated from her home in California and go to another country—Louisiana.

I was in an elementary school, and soon after Pearl Harbor my mother got very worried about the possibility that the Japanese were going to attack the coast of California, because a submarine was sighted or something like that. So she sent me to stay with relatives in Louisiana, in the little town of Bogalusa, which is about eighty miles outside of New Orleans. As a child, I didn't realize why I was being sent until I got there, because my mother was so frightened about this that she didn't even tell me. She simply said, "You're going off to spend a vacation with Aunt Gladys in Louisiana."

My mother brought me home in about six or eight months. Of course, it had become obvious that the Japanese were not circling Los Angeles and were not going to come and drag us all off. But the psychological effect of that attack on Pearl Harbor created a kind of war hysteria that took a while for people to get over.

We lived in North Hollywood, and they had big searchlights on those hills, I guess to look for aircraft or something. I can remember going up and taking hot coffee to the soldiers in uniform. I was a member of the Civil Air Patrol, which was something they organized for kids. We bought WAC uniforms from the army surplus and were given wooden guns to drill with, and we were taught Morse code and the different kinds of airplanes to watch for. We were never actually used, but we did have a sense of being prepared for something, for some time in the future. That was the only time that to me the war seemed real.

Ray Hartman lived in Chicago, where his father was in the restaurant business. He says, "I was probably his number-one dishwasher, on a part-time basis."

Everybody was campaigning to sell war bonds. The school set a goal. They were selling stamps. Each kid would buy stamps and try to fill books to get an $18.75 bond. We were using our allowances and paper drives and whatever way we could to get money to purchase the stamps. In those days we were going around selling war stamps similar to the way children now sell chances on raffles. We'd go door-to-door and ask people to contribute dimes and quarters and fill up a book of stamps and buy the bonds. The goal of the school, I believe, was somewhere in the seventy-nine-to-eighty-thousand-dollar range, and we were told that this would be sufficient money to purchase a P–38 fighter plane. We reached the goal. I was the student chairman of the drive, and after probably eight or nine months of work, we were successful, and there was a P-38 named after the school. Alphonsus was the name of the school, but they named the plane The Spirit of Saint Al's. We went to some Douglas Aircraft Company when they painted the name on the plane, more or less christened it, took pictures. I was thrilled, being the chairman of the student drive. I did the ribbon cutting or something like that. We received a letter of commendation from some general for the school. There were pictures taken with a couple of air force men who were pilots dressed in their uniforms, so it was a thrill.

Tony Taylor was only twelve years old at the time of Pearl Harbor.

During those times people looked at soldiers like saviors of the world and they got away with a lot of shit that nobody else would have gotten away with. I think there were a lot of times when they were very lax.

One thing really stands out. Where I lived, it's about a block from the railroad, and, man, we used to always see the trains come through. During the war it was the troop trains, and sometimes they would have to stop in our area. All of the families, man, like my mother and our neighbors, would always take things to give the guys. There was a very strong feeling when they saw a soldier, and he didn't have to be their son, because they are thinking like he's somebody else's son. And I think that made people come together, made people come out of their shells a little bit more, be more aware of other people. Everybody's relatives were going into the service somewhere. I lived in a predominantly black area, and on most of the troop trains that came through, you know, there were more whites than blacks. But it ain't none of that bullshit. They just went on out to the train.

You see, it takes a major disaster to make that kind of thing happen.

Richard Lingeman was a ten-year-old boy growing up in the little town of Crawfordsville, Indiana. Many years later he would write a book about the home front in America called Don't You Know There's a War On?

My father was a doctor. He was too old for the service but was quite active in community affairs that were war related, not all with a specific civil-defense organization or anything like that, because it was a small town of about ten thousand. And he took over from other doctors who went away, which was an added burden for him.

He also helped start recreation centers where young people could dance and play pinball. There was one for soldiers and navy boys in town, too. There was an ambivalent view regarding servicemen. I remember having Sunday dinner for a soldier. It was a great thing, and we would do that for navy boys, too. At the same time there was a dislike of the servicemen, especially among the high school boys, because they were taking away the girls.

The sailors had a sort of risqué image, anyway, and the girls who went out with them were looked on as sort of bad girls. These were college boys—V-12 students at Wabash College—who would probably go out as officers. It was a small town, and they were sort of foreigners. At the same time people would have them over for dinner.

My mother was not much of a participant of community groups, but she did join the Motor Corps, driving a car around, learning how to change a tire; ferrying people to give blood donations was one of the main projects they had. I think the community was pretty much in support of the war, but there were certainly isolationists there. And there was dislike of Roosevelt and criticism of the way the war was being run. Even in Sunday-school class there was talk about Roosevelt being a Jew, this sort of thing—pretty far out.

Necei Degen was a fifteen-year-old girl living in Malden, Massachusetts, a suburb of Boston.

I was a plane spotter at the local school, where I spent every Saturday morning with a telephone that never rang and with maps that were never used. After the first year I began to look on it as a bit of a joke.

At that time I met a lot of young people who were in the navy, and that was a very interesting part of my young life. There was a great sense of danger and a great sense of romance in the immediacy of the moment, the kind of thing that ensues from a wartime climate. I remember having a tremendous number of dates with young men from all over the country. It was interesting and exciting, if you could put that apart from the actual war, which was far away.

My mother's family was in Lithuania. She did manage to get one brother to Canada a year before the war, but the rest of them—six or seven sisters and brothers—were all lost in concentration camps during the war. They had been communicating up until 1939, but after that no word was ever heard from them again. We lived with that very big worry in the life of our parents.

The radio was the main line of communication. We listened every night. Radio had a much greater impact on our lives than TV does today. You were removed from having to contend with the faces and interpretations that are forced upon you by TV. They gave you the news, and so much of it was imagery for yourself to develop. I think TV has taken away, what shall I say, a good bit of the thought process that should go into interpreting the news yourself.

We also used to go every week and visit young men in the hospital who were seriously wounded. That was very sobering.

Sally Lucke remembers the things she did for the war effort in Columbus, Ohio—and how it affected her attitude toward the Japanese.

I spent all my waking hours outside of school collecting tires and organizing the whole neighborhood for collection of scrap materials, and my parents very kindly put up with all the miscellaneous objects in our garage for quite some time. I don't know whatever happened to all these objects, but we certainly had the spirit. Also, we collected all kinds of magazines and books for the Red Cross. The only real awareness of the war was in blackout curtains.

My feelings for the Japanese people had been very loving. We had had one Japanese houseboy before the war named Kay, who loved to take his camera all over the United States, and we often wondered if he could have been a spy and if he was as friendly toward our family as he appeared to be. We have no way of knowing whether he was a spy. He went back to Japan, and we only heard from him once, so I still have doubts. I think the war made me want to understand how a people could be so sensitive in their art and culture and still commit atrocities.

At the time of Pearl Harbor, Erwin Hargrove was nine years old and living in Saint Joseph, Missouri.

I got the idea that people might get conscripted to work in war production of various kinds and that I might have to go off and be separated from my family. My mother had died about three years before; I had a stepmother, and I was very concerned about losing my family. But it took the war to project that into a kind of anxiety about the family being broken up. This was in Missouri, the middle of the country: The thought of the enemy coming never bothered anybody. I had no immediate concern about my father going to war. He was in his early forties at the time, and I had no brothers or sisters.

We had a Victory garden that almost killed my parents. I can remember to this day my father out there on a summer evening in the dusk, staying to the very last minute. He had to do everything after work, and he was working himself to death on this big, stupid garden. My father also ran the USO in Saint Joe. He found a building, leased it, and hired a director.

I remember knitting squares. I think, maybe, they were used to make blankets. I don't know whether they were for soldiers or refugees or Bundles for Britain, but I remember learning to do that, and it was a big deal. All the boys were learning to knit. But the thing I remember most vividly was getting out of school to go on scrap drives. That was the thing that was the most fun. You would take the wagon and go pick up scrap—old newspapers and things like that.

The war was really fun for a boy. We used to follow it in the paper and the newsreels and on the radio. I remember Lowell Thomas. We followed the movement of the troops and all the war movies. My God, the number of John Wayne movies I must have seen.

The war brought Eleanor Neuland romance; a husband, Edward Kuhne; and a new way of life.

In 1941 and 1942, I was living with my father and mother in Glover Park in Washington, D.C. I was working as secretary to the vice-president of the gas company.

A lot of my friends and acquaintances had gone into military training. My parents became very active in feeding and housing problems under civil defense. They helped form a unit with the neighbors to list available emergency sleeping spaces and arranged for using the basement of an apartment nearby for a feeding center. Everyone contributed coffee, canned goods, coffee urns, and other equipment.

I did not have a serious boyfriend at the time. I was kind of between romances. A friend of mine in the office was going with a boy named Mickey, a marine at Quantico. That was how I met my husband. She would meet Mickey at Quantico on alternate weekends when he couldn't get leave to come to Washington. She asked me if I would like to go down with her one Sunday. Her friend knew me, and he would get me a date. Of course, this was very easy to do at the marine base. They met us at the train. We went across the parade ground to the Hostess House, where they served food and drinks and the servicemen could take guests. When the four of us went in, there were two Marines sitting across the room, and one was definitely my type. Mickey said, "Hi, Ed." So I whispered to Marie, my friend, "Let's sit with them." There was no reason for us to sit there since there were plenty of empty tables, but she whispered to Mickey, "Eleanor says let's sit with them." So he took us over and introduced us. I sat right down next to Ed as fast as I could and started talking to him and he to me. The boy I was supposed to be with finally got up and left. It wasn't very nice of me treating him that way, but we had nothing in common anyway. Anyhow, poor Ed was not financially prepared for an unexpected date, but he didn't seem to mind too much; he borrowed some money and we went on from there.

We spent the rest of the day together, and he kept saying, "I'm snowed, I am." At that time I was not bad looking. I had golden-red hair and I was dressed in a matching "Eleanor" blue dress and coat, and a white flower hat. He was taken with me. He put me on the train at midnight, but we had been talking so much that he had forgotten to ask for my phone number until the last minute, as the train was pulling in. So I wrote it down quickly, with the paper against a rough brick wall. He put it in his pocket without looking at it. The next day, he was going to call me, and when he got the paper out he couldn't read it. He called what he thought the number was. It was the wrong number.

I waited for him to call for three days, and all this time we each thought the other had been handing out a line, so we both were very depressed. Mickey finally talked to Marie about what Eleanor had done to Ed, and she straightened things out. Ed called me, and everything was lovely from then on.

We had only about five or six dates before he had to go overseas. We were very much in love, but I knew that Mother and Daddy wouldn't have any part of me getting married when he was on his way overseas.

He was away thirteen months, in the Ellice Islands. They were without adequate supplies and the food was very poor. Ed was a big fellow—six feet and heavy chested. He went from about 250 down to 165 pounds.

I signed up to be a lady marine while he was overseas the first time. I took the aptitude test, passed, and went down to be sworn in. There I was in my mink scarf and high-heeled shoes, and the man said, "Are you sure you want to do this?" I said, "Yes, I am sure." So I was sworn in, which meant I would have to go into training camp. I barely got home when there was a letter from Ed's buddy saying that I might get a big surprise. Of course, I knew that meant that Ed was on his way home. I had to get out of the marines as fast as I could. My uncle knew somebody who knew somebody, and they finally got me out of it. I hadn't actually gone to boot camp, or I never would have been released. I was in the marines for three days.

When Ed came home, he was assigned to San Diego as an instructor in communications. We were married there in the marine base chapel by the Catholic chaplain. Ed was not a Catholic at that time, but he had arranged everything. I was so blithe. At that time, I wasn't afraid of anything. But when the time came to get married, I began to shake. I had little curls on the back of my head, and my mother said they were going like steel springs. The more scared I got, the calmer Ed got. He took my hand and steadied me, and we made it through the ceremony.

Ed was there for ten months. When he went overseas, I didn't have any social life. I just wrote letters. I didn't mess around. If I had been younger, I might have been tempted to, but I was twenty-eight years old—I had gone with a lot of different boys, and had found the one I wanted. But many of the other girls, with their husbands overseas, did mess around. People react differently to war. Sometimes they can't adjust to it, that's all.

8

The Home Front

With the Atlantic Ocean between us and Germany and the Pacific Ocean separating us from Japan, America was never in any real danger during the war. But we could not be sure. The civil defense units organized as if attack were imminent. Elaborate systems for spotting enemy planes were developed. Coastlines and big cities were blacked out, and coastal waters were watched for enemy ships and submarines, which we knew were out there from the number of ships that were sunk off our coasts. And we had our hardships. There were shortages of almost everything—food, clothing, houses, gasoline, tires, and services. This led to rationing—and consequently black markets. And every backyard, vacant lot—and occasionally even window boxes—had a victory garden. Some people remember life during the war as being hard and unpleasant but something we had to put up with "for the duration." Others recall their tribulations as something of a joke.

Ann Hoskins in Lakeville, Connecticut:

I was always writing letters to the government, because I got very teed off about a lot of things—including the observation posts. They were absolutely ridiculous. We'd get up at dawn to go on down there, and we'd do our level best, but Stewart, my husband, was hard of hearing, I was nearsighted, and between us it was the best of luck that we would recognize a plane, whether it was his, hers, or ours. The dear woman who took over after us in the morning was eighty-six years old. She couldn't read a menu her eyesight was so poor. They made no attempt to screen or train people. So I wrote to the government and said, "If this is as important as you say, why don't you train a few people to come into these towns and pick people who have all their faculties, their hearing and sight and everything else?" I got back a stiff little form letter saying that it was very important.

We had air-raid wardens who were very strict. Boy, they never missed a trick. If we were at a town meeting or something and the siren suddenly went off, which meant a blackout, we would race home, because the kids would be alone. Right next door to the house was the church that rang its bells when there was a blackout alarm. The bells made a heck of a noise, and we were afraid that they might be afraid, so we would drop everything and run back to the kids. Usually, they would sleep right through it.

Alida Pierce was working as a secretary in the chamber of commerce in Dunkirk, New York. When I interviewed her, she had a scrapbook from the war years, which included copies of letters she had received while she was with the rationing board.

Almost immediately, we were involved in administering the rationing program. A chairman was appointed, and we organized committees, made up mostly of businessmen in town and chamber-of-commerce members. Soon we were swamped and had to take over larger headquarters because we had thousands of volunteers working for us. Whole plants, their office staff, would come in for an evening. We interviewed people almost every night of the week on fuel oil, foods, or shoes, or whatever was being rationed at the time.

Of course, our board had a soft heart for the boys from the service, and sometimes they managed to get extra stamps. One of the most interesting cases involved a full-blooded Indian from Oklahoma who came every summer to sell perfumes and this type of thing. He told our board that he would have to go back to Oklahoma as a permanent move.

Rationing and its supposed hardships made up a lot of the conversation. You would hear this sort of thing: "Thirty-five cents for that little basket of grapes? Ridiculous! They were grown right here in Fredonia, weren't they?" Or, "My neighbor just *drove* to New York, all that way. *Where* did he get the gas?" And, "I thought they were checking on prices, but my wife paid $1.86 for three dozen eggs. Who's checking?"

And so, on and on. Let me read you a couple of the letters I used to get. I think you will enjoy them. I had a few of them reprinted for a speech I used to give to Rotary clubs and places like that.

Here's a letter and bill from an indignant farmer who suffered a loss because his request for fuel oil was delayed two days:

Dear Miss ____

We received no certificate so we could buy kerosene for a stove to warm a house in which to keep little pigs. The pigs were born last night; they are all dead. Enclosed you will find a bill to cover the loss. We hope and pray you may influence the board to grant us our request for kerosene to keep the house warm for the other sow who will have her pigs during that week.

We are sorry your board was delayed in their acting on this, for it means eight pigs that will not be raised to help win the war. Please act as soon as possible.

Yours truly,

Rationing Board
Dunkirk, New York
To: Mr. ____

| 8 pigs | at | $7.50 | $60.00 |

$7.50 is the price these would have sold for when old enough.

Balance due $60.00

And what would you have done if you were a board member and received this letter:

Dear Sirs:

This morning a card came to my home stating that my husband may have booklets for more gasoline. I want you to know the truth. My husband does not need more gasoline. He takes the bus to work on his day shift. When he works nights, he uses the car only three times a week; on Tuesdays and Thursdays he drills at the armory and works days. You can figure out for yourself if three gallons a week is enough for twelve miles. The reason why he needs more gasoline is for pleasure. He likes to go out with women. I'm sorry to tell you this, but I'm sure you will help from breaking my home. You can come to my home anytime and talk to me personally. I am keeping the card. If he appears before the board, you can show him this letter. He will tell you I'm crazy.

Sincerely,
Mrs. _____

P.S. I will probably get a beating for this, but it's the God's truth.

One lady even sent us a poem:

I can't send my husband to market—He'll order some meat for a stew,
And then when the points are requested, insist they be torn from the blue.
Or if it's canned soup he has chosen, or pineapple, ketchup, whatnot,
He'll count up the number of red ones he plans to give up for the lot.
He'll pick up the greatest collection of vegies, in big cans and small,
Although I've repeatedly told him the fresh ones aren't rationed at all.
And when from those rules he's untangled and able to just muddle through,
He's likely to offer some coupons from strips which have not yet come due.

I carefully list all the items, essential we need to replace.
And then he buys plenty of extras he wants to have handy
    "in case."
I can't send my husband to market—he worries me into
    a huff,
For when he adds points up correctly, he never has money
    enough.
So now we've a frank understanding; he's "sorry" (the
    wily old elf)
He stays home and plays with the children, while I pull
    the boners myself.

Amy Bess Miller lived in Pittsfield, Massachusetts.

We had to be careful of food, so I plunged into working on
a war garden. We had more than an acre under cultivation at
our house; we supplied five families, plus ourselves, plus providing space for other people to have gardens, plus growing a
lot of material to be sent up to Canada to be canned. Then we
sold our surplus, and during the summer the children had a
little store on the street to sell eggs, honey, and all kinds of
things. That was the first project, to be able to feed people.

Freezing was in its infancy then—but we managed to get
hold of an ice-cream freezer, and whenever the power went
out, as it did often, it seems to me, we'd have to bicycle up
and get dry ice, because our gas was rationed. You should
have seen us biking with a huge parcel of dry ice and trying
to see over it! And transportation was funny. Sometimes the
buses didn't run.

We had guaranteed to supply fourteen acres of carrots,
beets, and beans to the Canadian government. They were going
to send flatcars for them and can them up there. The vegetables
were just in marvelous shape, all ready to be called for on the
first day of September—and we had a killing frost on August
26! The beans were ruined and the beet tops and carrot tops.
The following business day, we got a letter from the Canadian
government saying, "Sorry, we can't send our flatcars." What
were we going to do with fourteen acres of produce?

We thought it was a crime to deprive anyone of all that
food, so we got in touch with hospitals and that sort of thing,
and they said they'd buy it at cost. So we didn't have to plow

it all under, just what had really been damaged.

After the war started, I joined a group to sell war bonds. We had our monthly quotas, and if I found that the business sector was not meeting its quota, I'd try to prime it. At one of the meetings, I'd have a banker stand up and say, "I want five thousand dollars, worth of bonds." And the businessmen would, hopefully, follow suit. A good meeting would produce five or six thousand dollars, and we'd have something like six meetings a year.

During the war I think everybody ate better and fared better, because the emphasis was on keeping the home front healthy, not being a drag. I don't see how the doctors managed, so many had to go to war. That's why they taught us preventive medicine. If a neighbor was sick, you went right over to see what you could do about it so she wouldn't have to call a doctor. There were a lot of babies born at home.

The most dramatic thing about the war was D day. The office in Washington got in touch with me to say that when it was known that we had landed, they wanted me to notify the clergy—all the churches in Pittsfield. They thought people would want to go to the churches and pray for success and pray for the lives of the boys on the front. The call from Washington came late at night. I called our minister, Mr. Hayden, who had agreed to notify all the others, and at 5:00 A.M. all the church bells rang.

Paul Kneeland, a reporter for the Boston Globe:

The mechanics of black-marketing were no different then than they are today. Seller A wants to get a good price for some beef or nylons. Remember, we had price controls then, and you couldn't get more than x cents for a pound of butter or x dollars for a pair of nylons. Buyer B wants the scarce item—butter, beef, nylons, whatever—enough to pay two or three times the controlled price for it. The distribution is usually done privately, not in an open store, and you hear about it word of mouth.

With rationing it was a common sight to see people waiting outside the stores where they had scarce products for sale. Butter was a scarce commodity, and the word was quickly passed from person to person: "Come down to Cowles' Grocery; they have butter!'' Immediately there'd be a line of shoppers who'd come from out of nowhere—sixty, seventy-five, or one hundred people—with their ration coupons, waiting for an opportunity to buy a pound of butter.

Something I'll always remember about the war were the air raids in Medford and how strictly they were enforced. There was no such thing as not pulling down shades or not dousing lights.

I remember when there was a false air-raid alarm in New England and we were listening to the radio. My mother was in tears; my aunt, shivering under the dining room table in our house, said, ''I hope if it hits, it hits us direct.''

Lillie Bernstein had four sons in the service, and she knew what her duty was.

I was born and raised in Chicago, and I'm in the Hall of Fame in Chicago for sixty-four years of community service. During the First World War, I remember my next-door neighbors were a senator and his wife whose son was killed in action. That was supposed to be a war to end all wars. She would talk to me about it frequently, and I said, ''Thank goodness, when my boys grow up, there won't be war anymore.'' I had four boys, and I never dreamed that they would all be in the Second World War, but they were.

At the time of Pearl Harbor my sons were thirty-one, twenty-nine, twenty-seven, and nineteen. They all went into the service, and they were in every spot that you could think of. My youngest son was in the third contingent to land in Europe. My second son, a civil engineer, was a lieutenant commander in the Navy Seabees. They sent him first to the Aleutian Islands. My next son, Sheldon, was a special assistant to the attorney general of the United States when he enlisted. My oldest son had already gone overseas, and so I said, ''Three of you are gone already; you're the fourth. It wouldn't be so terrible if you didn't go.'' But he went anyway. He thought any day they were going to send him overseas, but they never did.

I was on the management committees in the Chicago USO and of the Jewish Welfare Board. I'd start out early in the morning and wouldn't get home until midnight every blessed day of the week. I worked day in and day out. My husband would meet all the trains that the boys came in on, and I would work at the USO. You know, Chicago was called the serviceman's city. They got everything free; they didn't pay on buses or streetcars. They could go to any show or any restaurant in Chicago if they'd just come and ask me. A number of them would say—it seemed to me that nine out of ten were from Brooklyn or New York—"What can we do to repay you?" And I'd say, "One thing you can do. When you get back home, you can tell your parents that everybody west of New York isn't an Indian."

I didn't realize how weak we were until I went to England— we'd cry if we couldn't get an extra piece of butter. We're so spoiled; we're so used in this country to having everything, we take everything for granted. When I went to England, I saw everybody getting along on practically nothing, and nobody was complaining. That was immediately after the war, and they were still being rationed. One piece of meat a week per family—they could make it go so far—and one egg a week, and here we were crying because we couldn't get a little piece of butter or something else.

But I don't know, there's something in the American spirit that when the need is there, they all come and get together and do something about it.

At the time of Pearl Harbor, Herbert Collins was a nine-year-old boy in Bowling Green, Virginia. My interview with him took place in his suburban home in northern Virginia. It began with him showing me his collection of souvenirs and mementos saved from the war years.

I was in the fourth grade in 1942, and we would all buy war bonds and war stamps to support the cause. When you filled a 25¢ defense-stamp album, you'd turn it in and get a $25 war bond. I think it cost $18.75 at the time you bought it. The school-bus driver would take orders from the children who wanted to buy war savings stamps, then go to the post office up in Bowling Green, get our stamps, and bring them back to us the next day. He did that to encourage the schoolchildren to buy war savings stamps.

This pledge on the stamp book says: "To every soldier,

sailor, and marine who is fighting for my country. For you there can be no rest, for me there should be no vacation from the part I can play to help you win the war. I therefore solemnly promise to continue to buy United States War Savings Stamps and Bonds to the limit of my ability throughout my summer vacation and until our victory is won." It is signed Herbert Ridgeway Collins and witnessed by Cora V. Kay, my fourth-grade teacher, May 29, 1942. At one time I had it in a little frame on the wall.

Then there were war ration books. You had all kinds of rationing—meat, sugar, gasoline. I remember going down to my great-aunt's, and she would say: "You should bring us a sugar stamp." It was very embarrassing to visit more than once or twice and not take a sugar stamp. I also remember going into restaurants, and they'd have signs up that said, "Use little sugar and stir like hell. We don't mind the noise."

Different-color stamps stood for different products that you bought. If you didn't use the whole stamp, you got back little red tokens and little blue tokens, depending on what type stamp you used. Each member of the family had a ration book.

During the war a lot of people had this little button. It showed Uncle Sam, and when you pulled a string, Uncle Sam pulled Hitler up on a tree limb and hanged him. The slogan was: "Let's pull together." You'd wear it on your lapel like a campaign button.

Newton Tolman in New Hampshire:

We had this one fellow who had a row with the mailman shortly after gas rationing came in, and he said, "Don't bring the mail. I will get it in Marlboro." So he got extra gas rations from our friends down there in Keene, and for the entire war he would drive, not once a day, but usually two or three times, twenty miles to get his mail at the post office because he didn't like the RFD fella. While everybody else was breaking their asses really living up to it and using as little gas as possible, he's going twice a day at least twenty miles to get his mail because he doesn't like the mail carrier. But he was telling everybody, "I'm all for the war!"

Everything was regulated by the government to some extent. The county seat, Keene, was the center of distribution, so that's where everything went that we raised—to the market there to help the war effort. At the market where all the mill owners and the wealthy people and everybody else dropped off their things, here were these guys making a million dollars selling black-market beef. People were really cashing in on the war. Everybody was for big, fat wages and everything, except for the poor buggers who were out there getting killed. I never bothered with the black-market beef. I'd go out and shoot a deer every year and use that, but the black market, no.

I was interested in the State Guard, because I knew a lot of these young kids who had never gone through the sixth grade, and I thought, "Jesus, they'll get drafted, and they don't know how to kill or drill; they don't know nothing." So I went all over the area, not only in my town, telling the young kids to get into the State Guard. They'd say, "What for?" And I'd say, "Well, you're going to get drafted. Don't you know there's a war on?" Well, I talked a lot of them into it. A fellow who was here this morning got into the marines; he has only one eye now. He had a terrible time, but he made out. If he hadn't had this State Guard preliminary training, he wouldn't have. These guys could hardly read or write or anything, but they learned to drill, they learned the routine, principally the phony part of it, the military, but you have to learn it. Once a week we'd have encampments, and then we'd go out three or four nights and have sham battles in the woods and that kind of stuff. All the officers got drunk as hell. These kids remember that training to this day. I saw one yesterday who I hadn't seen in about fifteen years. He said, "You know, you saved my life with that State Guard thing."

Martha Wood lived in Raleigh, North Carolina, with her husband, who was then a professor at North Carolina State College.

We were restricted socially. I remember that we had a LaSalle sedan, and because of gas rationing we sold it. Dr. Wood rode a bicycle to N.C. State, and I was working within six blocks of our home, so I just walked.

The couples formed a neighborhood Victory garden, plowed up the backyards of three houses, and planted beans, corn, tomatoes, okra, squash, and all the things we could use. When the crop came in, the two wives who were not working used a pressure cooker and canned all day. I'd come home at five o'clock, fix my evening meal, and then I was given the pressure cooker. So I was canning until midnight and later, night after night, and I frequently said, "I wish I had Hitler in that pressure cooker."

We raised chickens in our yard, too, for the three families. At noon it was my duty to walk home and make the warm mash to feed the chickens. We didn't have home freezers at that time. We had a community freezer, and on Saturdays, when the men would kill the chickens, we'd help pick them and clean them; then they'd take them to the freezer. These three families shared everything.

My husband plowed, because his classes would be over early, and the other two men, who were working for private industry, didn't get home until late in the afternoon. so he was the chief farmer.

The morale was real high in Raleigh. Rationing was hard to live with, particularly silk stockings. I can remember that if you had a run in your stocking, you took a needle and thread and worked it back up, because there was no chance of getting any.

We took vacations when we could down on the coast of North Carolina. The family we stayed with had to black out the house at night. We ate our supper by daylight and didn't even turn on a light at night. German submarines had been spotted within sight of that house. Of course, the area was always patrolled by the Coast Guard, and it was an eerie feeling. Everybody was suspicious of everybody else. My husband would walk at night to a little grocery store at the crossroads to hear the news on the radio, and until they knew that we were from Raleigh and that he was a professor, the men in the grocery store were a little apprehensive, because we were strangers.

Jack Altshul, city editor of Newsday:

Miss [Alicia] Patterson decided it was time that *Newsday* grow its own Victory garden. Assigned to the job were two staff photographers who knew nothing about gardening, which was the idea of the whole thing. Herman Klappert and Jim

Martenhoff were to go out like Mr. Average Nassau, buy seeds, plant them in a small plot, and watch the tomatoes, corn, radishes, and cucumbers grow. They were to photograph the progress, and the end result would appear in a weekly page of how-to-do-it pictures.

The idea was a wonderful one, and one ghastly incident would have been averted if the war had not worn the photography department so thin. Since Klappert and Martenhoff had been allowed to work on their garden on office time, there wasn't a photographer in the office one noontime when Harold Davis got a call from Miss Patterson that she was the guest of the president of Arnold Constable at a country-club luncheon and wanted a cameraman to record the event.

Davis got Klappert at his home, the backyard of which was *Newsday*'s Victory garden. He told him to drop everything and shoot over with Martenhoff to get a group of pictures at the luncheon. Klappert tried to explain it would take some time, because both were dressed in dirty flannel shirts, jeans, rubber boots, and chicken manure. The managing editor had no time for argument. "Get over right away or else," he screamed through the phone.

They looked at each other. "I will if you will." Off they went to the country-club luncheon, following instructions about not bothering to change.

They walked solemnly into the impeccable grill of the club and up to the U-shaped table, at the head of which sat Alicia Patterson and Isaac Lieberman, whose department store had recently signed *Newsday*'s biggest advertising contract.

Noses wrinkled and heads turned away as the photographers wended down opposite sides of the table to the head table. Miss Patterson blanched as she saw her men, but remained poised, though cold. When the photographers finished taking the pictures, Mr. Lieberman turned to her with obvious distaste and asked,

"Who were those men?"

"I never saw them before in my life," Miss Patterson replied, deadpan.

I remember one thing that shocked the hell out of us, and the paper made a big crusade out of it. Some socialite in Garden City was marrying off her daughter. She was marrying a Philadelphia boy, a mainliner, society people. One of our society reporters who was covering the wedding called the managing editor and said there were an awful lot of big limousines from Philadelphia over there, and where did they get the gas to come to this wedding? This wasn't a military wedding. We looked into it, and it turned out that, sure enough, the father of the bride had influence, and he was able to get gas stamps. This was the kind of story newspapers kept their eyes open for.

Monday morning the story broke on a gas-pinched public, complete with copies of telegrams sent by a senator and congressman who had told the local rationing chief it was okay, the official wording of the rationing law pertaining to weddings, and pictures of many members of the wedding who had been invited to attend and told not to worry about rationing restrictions. Some whose licenses were taken by the police eventually forfeited their ration books and blamed it all on *Newsday*. The paper accepted the blame—and the flood of congratulatory letters from readers who had no friendly senator to get them special gas privileges.

Dean Elmer Louis Kayser in Washington, D.C.:

I remember rationing, but I must say that it never made it impossible for me to get what was adequate for my needs. It did lead to some very strange incidents. I might mention one: My daughter was married to a marine officer just at the end of the war, when rationing was still on. And for the reception at the Mayflower I wanted the traditional wedding cake, of course. My friends on the Mayflower managerial staff said, "We can't give you a wedding cake. We haven't any sugar." So I began going to places where you would normally go, and finally I got hold of Clement's, a very good confectioner, and they said, "We'll make you a cake if you'll get us the sugar." I got the sugar. I like sugar myself, and when I was sure that was one thing that would be difficult to get, I built up a supply of it. And that supply of sugar made possible my daughter's wedding cake. That, I think, is the most grotesque of my experiences. I'll tell you, I had a very good technique on gasoline. I live on a hill, and I mastered the technique of coasting down Wisconsin Avenue to the station at Q Street. That saved coupons.

Fourteen-year-old Peggy Blassingame, living on Anna Maria Island in the Gulf of Mexico, did her duty.

We always would hear nice, delightful, scary rumors about somebody seeing a U-boat out in the gulf. For a while my girl friend and I were plane spotters. The plane-spotter station, which looked like a fire-watching station, was built right up on the gulf. We had a special assigned time, I forget how often it was—a couple of days a week for two or three hours, I think. We were given charts and taught the shapes and silhouettes of the planes, and we were supposed to tell how many miles away they were. It was terribly confusing in the beginning. At first, we were lucky to distinguish between an airplane and a seagull. But eventually we could identify every plane we saw. We learned to estimate distances and direction—north, east, south, and west. I never had the remotest idea which was which before, but we learned it fast. As soon as we saw a plane, we instantly reported the type and direction. We were certainly under the impression we were watching out for a possible enemy plane that might have infiltrated our airspace, but of course, we only saw domestic planes. We would have recognized a plane that was not American. We were terribly confident.

Before my father went into the service, he was one of the air-raid wardens. He would patrol the beach every night to make sure everything was completely blacked out, and my mother would walk with him. One night when he was doing his patrol, he saw a glaring light; he hightailed to it as fast as he could go, and the closer he got, the more he began to realize it was our house, and I was the culprit. I was home with my baby sister, and I had left the bright bulb burning in the bathroom with the shade up. The only light on the whole island! It was the first time I ever remember his being angry with me. He was furious. I was forbidden to go to the movies for months and months. During that time *Mrs. Miniver* played and I never got to see it.

Max Bassin was the proprietor of the famous Bassin's Restaurant, on Pennsylvania Avenue in Washington, a block from the Treasury Department.

I wasn't drafted. I had children at the time and a business they felt was essential. There were a number of times when I felt uncomfortable not being in uniform. Being in the restaurant business was hectic. You couldn't get any labor of any consequence. We were working so hard that subconsciously I wished I had been drafted. I had two brothers-in-law working with me. They went in, and two brothers went in. One of the brothers-in-law was a partner, so I had to take over his portion of the restaurant and run the whole thing during the war. I used to average twelve to fourteen hours a day working. With the rationing and the stamps, it was a very complicated process just running the business.

A situation came up that was very peculiar. When I started making sandwiches for the army, I went to the local OPA and told them what I was planning to do—open a different place, put my manager up there, and run the sandwiches out of this one shop, on Georgia Avenue, called B & B Commissaries. They told me that it would just be a continuance of what I had been doing and gave me a letter to that effect, so I could use the volume I had there to get the stamps. Ration stamps went a lot further when you just served sandwiches than when you served steak. It took ten, fifteen, twenty times as many stamps to get steak as it did to get sandwich meat. After I had operated the commissary for six months to a year, I got a call from the head of the main office of OPA, and when I went up there, they told me I wasn't handling it right, that I had to have institutional stamps for one and regular restaurant stamps for the other. I explained to them that I had cleared it with the OPA before I even opened the place and had a letter to that effect. He said, "Leave the letter with me, and I'm sure we can get it straightened out."

About six months later I got another call. Come to the OPA. Same thing all over again with somebody else. Explained it to them, and they said, "Oh, we'll take care of it." A little while later, I got a third call. This time I was told they had no record of the letter, no file on the case, and according to the law, I had to close both places until I had absorbed the hundreds of thousands of food stamps that I used and they said I wasn't entitled to. So I asked if it was about time I got myself an attorney. The fellow I was talking to said, "Yes, you ought to." I said, "You don't happen to know anybody that's familiar with this thing?'' He said, ''Yes, there's this Chinese who's familiar with the operation. He's a very good man.'' So I went to my attorney, and he said I should go see the other one. I did and was told it would cost fifteen hundred dollars as a retainer and an additional fifteen hundred dollars if he got it straightened out for me. He did. I got a call a few weeks later saying it was all straight. I suspected something fishy, but couldn't say anything about it. There's no way to prove it. But as soon as I went to this attorney, there were no problems. I sold the commissary on account of that. There was so much aggravation going through those things, being threatened with closing both businesses, so I sold it.

Hezekiah Goodwin, a Connecticut dairy farmer:

A lot of people cleaned up. The black-market activity around here was considerable. We never traded with them. They would come out and prey on the local farmers, who would butcher the legitimate quota and kill the rest in the woods, stamp it, and peddle it. They used to do it pretty openly. I was kidding a fellow one day, and I said: ''John, I'd like to get a nice quarter of beef tonight.'' He said, ''Hessy, I can give you any kind of meat you want,'' and he pulled out a five-gallon pail all full of rubber meat stamps: Swift's, Armour, all government inspected, choice. It didn't faze him a bit to take a Jersey carcass and stamp it ''Choice Swift.'' It was a great business.

Potatoes were high at certain times and hard to get. I'll never forget, before the war we had a nice crop of potatoes, and they didn't sell very well. Hardly any customers; nobody had any money. I stopped at this old Italian food store where we traded, and I said: ''Mrs. Divarre, could you use a few nice potatoes?'' And she said, ''We got Maine potatoes, and the Maine potatoes are nice; the potatoes around here no good.'' So, needless to say, she didn't buy any. Then sometime in the middle of the war I was in there, and she said, ''Mr. Goodwin, you got any potatoes?'' And right in a flash it occurred to me I got a whole cellarful, and she didn't have a damned one. And she said, ''Would you let me have a few bushel?'' And I said, ''Well, Mrs. Divarre, I'd like to, but I can't. I have to think of my steady customers—you know, the people who bought potatoes from me years ago when they could have bought Maine potatoes." And I got her so mad she was jumping up and down.

Pauline Christensen, a widow with two young sons, worked in the educational publishing business in Chicago. Her contribution was to drive for the Red Cross.

I was a member of the Red Cross Motor Corps and spent a good many thousands of hours convoying. Of course, I was working, but on weekends and evenings I would go into Chicago and spend whatever time I could driving convoys. The young recruits would be sent from one camp to the other, and we would drive them from the train, as they arrived, to Lake Bluff or into some of the other areas. We'd also drive the blood bank, entertainment buses, and things of that sort. Or we would pick up an admiral and take him wherever he wanted to go in the Chicago area for a whole day. I don't know why that was a Red Cross responsibility.

When we were on duty, we wore our Red Cross uniforms. That protected us a great deal, because we were all over the city, back into some of the areas I had never known were there—the Polish community, the Greek community. Sometimes it was a little bit scary, but the uniform protected me. We drove all hours of the night. There were some black and white problems in the area at that time. Once, I knew someone was following me as I got off at the station in Evanston on my way home. Finally the person caught up with me—a young girl who said, "Oh, ma'am, you walk so fast, but I knew if I got close to your uniform, I'd be safe."

Mary Devereux Crist, whose husband was in the Pacific with the Marine Corps:

I was up in Washington one time visiting and wanted a ration book to get some liquor because I was going to see a friend in Virginia. I went into the ration board, and they said, "Sorry, we can't give you a ration book when you're just visiting." I said, "Well, nobody wants a visitor who has a drink or two if he doesn't furnish his own liquor in this day and age." They said, "Well, haven't you got a letter addressed to you here in Virginia, or anything that would show that you are going to be here awhile?'' I said, "Yes, I have. I've got a ticket from a shoemaker, where I've taken my daughter's shoes to be resoled.'' They said, "That's enough to get a ration ticket for the whole month, because you'll never know when you'll get those shoes back.''

In wartime Washington, the worst thing was the cigarette shortage. I remember one time standing in line with this little baby of mine and after three hours getting up to the head of the line and being told they didn't have any more cigarettes. I got in a cab in tears, and the cab driver gave me the rest of his pack. He had only taken about two cigarettes out of it, and I've never been so grateful for anything in my life.

9

The Ultimate Cost of Victory

War may not have affected America the way it did other countries, where the battles were fought. But the loss of a son or a husband in the war is the ultimate hardship and something from which some people never recover.

Jack Altshul, city editor, Newsday, *Long Island, New York:*

The most popular feature on the paper, which almost broke your heart, were the casualty lists—every day a new casualty list. And often you had to send reporters to families who had just received the news that their son was lying on some beach, or whatever. It was a tragic period, and it did get to you. It got to me. I hated to read those casualty lists for fear of finding friends on it. And you often did.

Betty Bryce had two sons, Dalton and Kenneth, when the war began. She lived in Mount Pleasant, Michigan.

Dalton was eighteen years old and valedictorian of his class. He had an American Legion scholarship, but he went down and applied for immediate induction as soon as he graduated from high school. He went overseas—I think he was gone seven months from the time he enlisted.

I was out raking the yard when I got the telegram. The man who brought it went next door to my neighbor and asked if she would come over with him, because it was the third one he had delivered that day in our town. When he handed me the telegram, I just looked at it. He said, "It's bad news." I guess I was kind of in a state of shock, until I read it, you know, seeing he's gone, that was it. The police went to the high school and brought my younger son, Kenny, home. We had a terrible time getting him calmed down, and of course, my ten-year-old daughter took it awfully hard.

Dalton was home once after he went in. I knew, when I put him on the bus, I'd never see him again; I just had this feeling. And while he was home, he got rid of everything in the house that belonged to him. He must have had a feeling too. He received the Silver Star, and there was a citation that came with it which told about it. They were in Germany, six miles past the Remagen bridge. He was a medic; he went to help some fellows in a burning tank and was killed by a sniper on his way back. It took me about a year before I could really get ahold of myself. I think I cried day and night for three or four months. It was a terrible thing to happen to anyone. He was so young.

My youngest son went into the paratroops, and while he was still in training, I wrote to the adjutant general in Washington, D.C., and had him transferred out of that. I just felt that I couldn't take a chance with him, too. I didn't want Kenny to be where he would be in danger, and so they put him behind a desk, which he didn't like. He never talked about his brother, never even mentioned his name. He just seemed to clam up inside, and he's never unclammed. I think it had a tremendous impact. We mention Dalton's name real often; we talk about him a lot, but Kenny doesn't. And yet, when his son was born, he named him after his brother.

Mary Moore Lacey was the wife of a naval aviator assigned to the carrier Yorktown. *After the* Yorktown *left Norfolk, and later San Diego, early in the war, she settled down in Coronado, California. She had two small children.*

We had built a small house in Coronado, and I was glad to have a place that I could call my own—sort of as though I had roots. It was not long before we heard that Jack had been lost in the Battle of the Marshall Islands. They didn't know what had happened, so he was declared "lost" all during the war.

My son was a year old when Jack was lost. My daughter, Sandy, was born six months later. Occasionally a friend of Jack's would come through and take the children to the beach or something like that, but there wasn't a lot of masculine contact. We were all in the same boat in Coronado, and it was comfortable for me, because I didn't have to keep explaining. When I went into family situations, I got a lot of "you poor dear" kind of stuff. I found that very difficult to take. I understood that I needed to be real about what was happening and say that it hurt and, yes, it was hard. But the minute I began getting sympathy, it made me feel awfully sorry for myself, and I'd break down. It didn't seem to heal anything. It just opened the wounds.

The allowance Jack had allotted wasn't enough for me to live on. Everything else was frozen, so I went to the officer's club at North Island and worked. My job was making sure that the kitchen staff had food ready for service at the snack bar. I was also a Red Cross nurse's aide and worked in a civilian hospital in San Diego and in a military hospital at North Island. In nursing duty I felt very much part of the war.

Patricia Megargee in Pelham, New York:

I had one boyfriend who was killed. He flew a torpedo bomber, based on an aircraft carrier in the Pacific, and I really expected him to come home. He hadn't been reported killed: he'd been reported missing. It took me about a year to get over it.

Another one wanted to get married before he went off, and Mom said she thought I was too young and he was too young, and, really there wasn't a lot of point to it. It was kind of a panic situation as far as he was concerned, I think. His parents were divorced, and he just wanted something that he could hang onto. He finally married someone he'd known just for a very short time. I heard from his mother later that he too was killed. So it was really good to work, I think, and have something to do. When you weren't working, it was very depressing.

The Reverend Harold Toliver and his wife, Elva, in Pittsburgh:

ELVA: There were tragedies. One of the cases in the congregation was very pathetic. We had a young couple, and the husband went to war and became what they called a "basket case." He was in a hospital in Washington, so depressed and bitter that he didn't want anyone who had known him before to see him.

HAROLD: I had performed the marriage several years before he went into the service, and they were happily married. When he came back, he would not see his wife. We never found out whether it was just his physical condition—impairment from all his injuries and all that—or whether it was something deeper than that. I don't know. He wouldn't talk, and I never got down to the camp to see him or get to talk to him. They eventually separated.

ELVA: He told her he wouldn't have anything to do with her, and she got a divorce and went on and carries the name. But she grieved just terribly. She was brokenhearted.

Governor Leverett Saltonstall of Massachusetts:

I had four children in the service. One son was killed—in Guam—after Guam had been declared safe. He was with the marines who landed on the island and was put in charge of a patrol. They were supposed to be safe, but there were still several hundred Japs hidden, and they fired. Two were killed, and three got back. My son was one of those killed. It was three o'clock in the afternoon when I heard. They always sent the top Western Union fellow up, so when I heard he wanted to see me, I knew it was trouble. It was hard, especially for Mrs. Saltonstall.

Mary Speir lived in Westminster, Maryland. Her only son enlisted in the air force when he was a sophomore in college. Her husband was also in the air force.

At that time I had a different feeling than I have now. I thought maybe people should go, but I didn't want my son to go. My husband also went, but he was a grown man and knew what he was doing, and that was different. I had a very bitter feeling about taking these college boys and not training them, which they didn't do for infantry. My son was only in the infantry six weeks when he was put in the lines, which I thought was very bad.

When my son enlisted in the air force, he went to McDill Field in Florida. So I went there until he shifted to the infantry and was sent to Fort Gordon. Then I came back to Westminster, which was a big mistake. I should have stayed in Florida. I found that people who didn't have someone overseas were not too concerned. They were interested in bacon and sugar and gas, which I was not. I even had people make remarks to me that we ought to do war work because we had men on the front. I felt the others lucky enough not to have men on the front should be doing it. However, I did a lot of war work—not after I came back to Westminster, but when I was at McDill, I worked in the hospital and at the USO. In fact I got decorated for the work in the USO in Tampa.

I started to do some volunteer work in Westminster, like rolling bandages, but I couldn't make it. The people I was doing it with were not in my situation at all. They were more concerned with what they were having to give up than with what was happening in Europe. I had people call me up and ask, "Do you have coupons? We can get butter tomorrow." I never stood in a line for a thing. I thought that if the men could do without it, so could I.

I was alone and was terrifically upset the morning the Episcopal rector arrived at my door and said, "I have very bad news for you." I said, "Has my son been killed?" He said, "Yes." He was twenty—my only child. It ruined my life. I can assure you of that.

I hadn't seen my husband for nearly two years; he had been overseas. He was able to get leave for fifteen days when our son was killed. The minister who brought the telegram was young enough to be in the service. Instead of trying to be of any help to us, he wanted money from us. He even came and asked me for money as a memorial to my son before my husband got back from overseas. I nearly left the Episcopal church; in fact, I didn't go to church for five years after the war. I had been on airfields, and I knew they needed chaplains, and I didn't have much respect for him for staying out. I told him so.

Four boys who had been with my son during the war came back, and we call them "our boys." They've been very close to us.

Sally Lucke in Columbus, Ohio:

My cousin was in the war in Europe. He was badly wounded in the Battle of the Bulge and died soon after the war as a result of those wounds. When we would visit him when he was home on leave, sometimes we would be awakened in the middle of the night by his screaming in German. From his death, his father had a heart attack, and from his father's death, his mother became ill.

Dorothy Whitaker's brother was on his way to the Pacific when the war started.

We didn't hear much from him after Pearl Harbor, which upset the entire family. Several months later we learned that he was at Corregidor. Then we heard from the government that he was missing in action. They were pretty sure he was a prisoner, but that's all the message said. Then we got two letters from him over the next three and a half years. He said he was in prison, but his letters were so censored that they didn't make much sense. Eventually he was transferred from the Philippines to Japan, and I don't believe we got any more information. The worst thing was that when the war was over and the peace treaty was signed, we still didn't know anything. That looked bad. We had gone to meetings set up by the Red Cross, and the boys that came back from Germany told what they knew of prisoners still over there in Germany, but very few had any knowledge of what was going on in the Pacific. None of the prisoners in Japan had come back. We kept calling the Red Cross, and they contacted the government; they were doing all they could, but they couldn't locate an awful lot of them.

It had a very bad effect on my mother. She tried to have a

good outlook and did, but it affected her more than any of the rest of us. She was sort of withdrawn, not herself.

It affected me, too. You just went from day to day wondering if it was ever going to end so you could stop worrying about it. You didn't indulge in your usual pleasures; you were just thinking about the war all the time. I about gave up hope for my brother for a while; my mother never did, but I think my dad and I were prepared for the worst.

We didn't have a telephone, and my mother wanted one installed so the Red Cross could call as soon as they heard anything. Finally, when they did get news about him, they called, but they wouldn't talk to anybody except my father, and he wasn't there. They wouldn't tell Mother anything. Evidently one of the rules was that they could give the information only to the person whose name happened to be on their list, and that was my father's name. Finally she called back and said, "Look, this is my son. I've been waiting to hear from him all these years, and I am entitled to know one way or another what has happened," They said, "We can't give you that information, but we will tell you this, he's all right."

Elva Newman in Washington, D.C.:

My son went to England and took all his training there. I heard from him regular, and, of course, they weren't supposed to tell where they were, but in my husband's family, way back, they had a saying that his great-great-grandfather was chased out of England for stealing sheep. So, when my son wrote, he said, "I'm in the same place where my great-great-grandfather was chased out for stealing sheep."

He was there until the D-day invasion, in the 115th Division—I think the 116th went in first, and then the 115th followed. That was June 6, and he was killed on June 12.

I heard the news by telegram, but I wasn't at home at the time. My mother had had a stroke, and I was taking her home by ambulance that day. The ambulance came in the afternoon, and right behind it I recognized the cars from my home. My husband came, and the children who were at home, and my son-in-law, who was in the marines stationed in Washington. I wondered why they were coming in two cars, but thought, "Well, I guess they want to leave one here for me." But they came to bring me the message that they had gotten the tele-gram that morning. He was killed instantly. I heard from one of his buddies. They used to correspond with me. He was buried temporarily in France. Later they asked whether we wanted him brought home, but we decided not to, and he was buried in Saint Laurent, in the Normandy cemetery.

Ten-year-old Ray Hartman had an older brother whom he idolized.

My brother immediately volunteered for the air force, and, I believe, he failed his first entrance examination because he was lacking in math. So he went back to school and took several courses in math, which probably took about a year. Then he took the examination again and successfully passed as an air force cadet.

On August 24, 1944, we got a call saying that he had one more practice mission to fly and then he would get a furlough, before going overseas. He was in the Eighth Air Force. We were elated that he was coming home.

The following day when they took the last training mission, there were one hundred planes flying in formation; two of them locked wings and tore each other's wings off. Both planes just crashed to the ground with no survivors. We got a telegram around four o'clock in the morning. I was sleeping, so I heard about it in the morning. It was quite a shock to me. I was about thirteen, going on fourteen, when that happened.

Naturally, being a young boy, I blamed it on the war, on the Japanese and the Germans, because if it hadn't been for them, we wouldn't have been involved, and he wouldn't have been killed. I did idolize anybody that was in the service—my heart went out to them.

Helen Wilson at the University of Michigan:

I was concerned about a boy I was interested in, because he was with Patton's army. They were always moving into the fore, and anyone attached to that group was in danger most all the time. I remember giving him a sort of a macabre gift before he went off—a lighter that smoldered rather than flamed, so you wouldn't be seen. Thinking back on it, it was really a terrible gift. But it did save his life. He was carrying it in his breast pocket when he was shot, and the bullet was deflected off the lighter. He was a delightful, gentle person, and I doubt that he ever got over the effects of combat.

Herbert Collins, who was nine years old at the time of Pearl Harbor:

Raymond Barlow got killed in service, and I remember going to the funeral as a young boy. I expected the body to be there, and instead they had Raymond's picture up on the communion table, with flowers on either side of it. It struck me as being very funny that they didn't have the body there. Then they had a second funeral when the body arrived, and it seemed odd to have two separate funerals for one person. I remember the curiosity we had about the bodies when they were brought back. In some cases they wouldn't let the undertakers open the caskets up—they said for health reasons. There was much talk in the neighborhood that they just put sand or rocks in the coffin and didn't have bodies in a lot of them because there wasn't anything to put in. So people whose loved ones were brought back always had a doubt as to whether there was anybody in the coffin, indeed, and if it was the right person in there.

Eleanor Kuhne was married and living in California. Her husband, Ed, was overseas.

I was very worried about Ed all the time he was overseas, although he never did get wounded. Twice I saw pictures in the newspapers of someone who was wounded, and I was positive it was him from the back. But I think that is what everybody went through. Looking back, it seems everybody has a tendency to remember the good parts. Ed would never tell me about the dark parts; all he would tell me about the service are the funny things.

It was a horribly lonesome time—the anxiety, the worry about Ed, wondering whether he was dead or alive, and all the other people that were hurt, wounded. So many of my girl friends lost their husbands and boyfriends. And others came back so changed. Marie, a friend of mine, was engaged to a boy who was in Guadalcanal through the whole thing. He went away a carefree, handsome, laughing type of Irishman, and he came back a wreck. I think he went into a mental institution.

Leo Hershfield in Washington, D.C.

In December of 1944, they were busting out of the Bulge. My younger brother, a pfc in the infantry, was killed in action on the twenty-fifth. Sam had gone after the job. He could have had himself rejected for active service because of an eye problem due to an injury in a Golden Gloves match. But he volunteered. I'll never forget the phone call from my older brother in Chattanooga about the War Department telegram.

A few weeks later his widow received a letter from the colonel commanding the 290th Infantry and one from his good friend and sergeant, who described the action. He said, "Sam was very cool-headed and brave" and that they had "wished each other good luck and Merry Christmas" before moving out.

Mabel Wiggins in Saint Paul, Minnesota:

I remember going to a luncheon, and one of the guests was late; she was on Red Cross duty. The hostess had just started serving a lovely casserole when this lady opened the door and said, "I'm sorry I'm late! Have any of you heard the news?" The *Royal Oak* had blown up in the Pacific, and no one was saved. I was sitting at the right of the hostess, and I could see her hand shaking. She went on serving and said, "I have two nephews on the boat." It was shocking. But she changed the subject, and that was it.

The fellows were so nice. Whenever anyone came back on leave, to be transferred someplace else, they'd put in long-distance calls to all the wives. I was awakened so many times at three o'clock in the morning—my *W* was down on the list—and someone would say, "I had dinner with Russell two nights ago, and he's just fine." One day the telephone rang, and the operator was so gay. She said, "Mrs. Wiggins, where are you?" and I said, "What do you mean, where am I?" She said, "Are you sitting down?" She wanted to tell me my husband was calling from the East Coast, he'd arrived; they had such times, she said, with people who'd faint. And they used to have an older man who had some understanding and sensitivity deliver the death notices, the telegrams. They couldn't do it over the telephone, because people just fell apart.

In Fort Collins, Colorado, Dorothy Schenck's war years were dominated by the fact that her son had been captured on Bataan.

He was in any number of camps there, and then, eventually—it must have been a year or so—we got the austere, typed card that said "I am well" or that sort of thing. But it was his signature. I knew it. And we were allowed to send one box to the Red Cross. Some of the boys who came back said that he had shared some of the things he had.

I think I was practically the only mother in town who had a son who was a prisoner of war. I did get one letter. It hadn't been opened—there was no cancellation or anything—and I always had a feeling that it went out with MacArthur when he left there.

It wasn't until after the armistice was signed, quite some time after, that I had word that he had been killed. The Japanese were sending the prisoners of war by unidentified ships to Japan to work in the mines, and they were bombed by the American troops because, naturally, they thought these were Japanese troops. They didn't have them identified as prisoners of war when they were transferred. He lived through the bombing of the first ship, one of the boys that came back said, and everyone who lived through that was put on another ship, plus others. They couldn't sit down; they couldn't lie down; they were just body-to-body standing up. The boy who came back told me that. It was January before I was notified that he had been killed.

War ages you very fast, I can tell you that. You go through a nervous strain. No night did you sleep, because you knew your son was a prisoner of war.

Lillie Bernstein was living in Chicago, Illinois.

One of my daughters-in-law said to me, "Mother, do you see anything different in Sheldon?" He looked good, he's a very handsome man, and he looked the same and everything. I said, "What do you think? How can a man who has never hurt a fly kill people?" A kamikaze attacked them, and the first person killed on the ship was the doctor, and my son had to cut off legs and do other things that he never dreamed of doing. How could it help but change him? But only a mother and a wife would know it. It surely harmed their nervous system—every one of them—I could tell it.

I'll tell you, the war work helped me keep my mind off my sons. My husband was so beside himself that his four boys were away that in order to brace him up, I was very courageous. Of course, I had a four-star flag in the window. I had to succumb to it, or rise above it.

Henry McMurria, in Columbus, Georgia:

My brother was a prisoner of war in the Pacific, and the government didn't know where he was. One night, a Sunday night, about midnight, the night editor of *The Enquirer* called. The day editor had gotten a bulletin about a British ship going into Rabaul and taking off a number of prisoners, and it mentioned my brother's name. He didn't read the article, but he slipped it back into a drawer so the night editor would find it. When he did, he called, and that was the first we had heard. The war had been over for several weeks, and that was the first we had heard. My father just put on an overcoat over his pajamas and went down to the paper and got a copy of it. Of course, the story came out in the paper the next morning, and we had friends coming in before breakfast.

Martha Wood in Bradenton, Florida:

My husband's brother was sent to Europe and ended up with the OSS on the island of Corsica by the time the war came to an end. We never knew where he was. Several times he was sent out from a camp and didn't come back. So they sent his clothes home twice to his mother in Birmingham, and, of course, that terrified her. But when she would get in touch with the Red Cross, they would tell her that everything was all right. We can laugh about it now, but at the time it was not funny.

We were in Raleigh, North Carolina, when the news came of V-E Day. Our church was open for prayer, and that day I went in with a woman who said, "My son is in Europe, and I'm just happy to come today to pray." He was killed the next day, because the war had not actually ended in some of those remote areas. I remember that woman well when she prayed that day.

Mary King was president of the Gold Star Mothers of America when I interviewed her.

My son loved the navy. I really think he would have stayed in after the war. He would love to have made it a career, because he was trying very hard to get a rating and go right up. He wasn't one of those "ninety-day wonders." He was working his way up, and I don't doubt he would have done it, because he was a very smart young fellow, if I can say so.

I first got a telegram that he was missing in action; that's the way it came through. And it came to me at a very bad time. My daughter was making her wedding gown to be married to a man in uniform, and here I was reading this, and it wasn't sinking in for a while. You know, you read something and you don't read it. Then suddenly I broke up, crying.

He lost his life on March 19, 1945, on the U.S.S. *Franklin*, fifty miles off the coast of Japan. All the boys were ready for a takeoff when this lone Jap—how he got there nobody knows—a kamikaze, hit the ship, and all of them, there were four hundred and some, were lost. There was a book written about the U.S.S. *Franklin—Big Ben* they called it. I have turned the pages to read it, but I just can't go far, because my son's picture is in there. He was taking his initiation as chief petty officer, going through this foolish ceremony where they had dirty whites on and they had fellows kneeling in front of him. I never saw him with the uniform on.

I have two other sons. They took it very hard. And, of course, my daughter did too. She thought I was going to stop the wedding. I debated in my mind, should I, and I thought: No, if she had it all planned, then let her go through with it. But it wasn't an easy thing to do.

Since I've been in the American Gold Star Mothers, I have really felt that I am not alone in the world, having lost a son.

Back home in Rhode Island we have one mother who lost three sons. You have a different outlook belonging to this, because you just try to forget. We try to brush it off, and I feel myself that would be as my son would want me to be. We all have something in common: We don't have to go around bewailing ourselves.

One of the things that used to annoy me during the war was that there was lots of work going on, people were getting good money, and when it ended, some wished we were in the war again for the money they made. That was the attitude of the working class. It really was an awful thing. The fellows would go out there and lose their lives, and then for some people to feel that way. That hurts.

The Reverend Edward G. Latch was the minister at the Metropolitan Memorial United Methodist Church in Washington, D.C.

I tried to keep the war, as such, out of the pulpit, because I felt people had read enough and that when they came to church, they wanted something with meaning to their life, something that would support them, some idea they could use during the week in this state of confusion and uncertainty.

Any number of my people had folks in the service—always hoping things would turn out well. All I did was try to be a steadying factor, persuading them that God is good and not that he was on their side or the other side; I avoided that; I just stressed that his will will be done, with truth and goodness coming out of it.

Once in a while I would have a call in the middle of the night if a family had just learned of a death. But usually they would wait until morning, and I would go and just let them talk. There is nothing much you can do.

Most people took it exceptionally well, tragic as it was to them. The church plays a very important role in a moment like that. People need someone to turn to, someone to talk to, someplace where they can come.

War begins to turn you against the fact of war because of what it means to people and what it does to people in terms of personality problems, domestic problems, neighborhood problems that arise out of war. You begin to see how, actually, in the long run, war is useless. But I didn't find many people opposed to the Second World War. Pearl Harbor came, and people thought there was only one thing we could do and that was stop them from doing what they were doing.

10

1945—The End

The year 1945 was possibly the most significant year in American history, certainly in the twentieth century. In April, President Franklin D. Roosevelt, who had been president for twelve years, longer than any president in our history, died. It was not only a traumatic experience for many Americans, it symbolized the end of an era. And his successor, Harry S Truman, symbolized the beginning of a new era. In May, the war in Europe ended, and with it the most destructive human force in modern history—the German Nazis. On August 6 and 9 the United States dropped what, by today's standards, were small nuclear bombs on Hiroshima and Nagasaki, and on August 14 the Japanese surrendered, which ended one era and launched a new one. Some of the Americans we have heard from in this book recall their reactions to the events of this momentous year and to the two men who dominated it—Franklin D. Roosevelt and Harry S Truman.

THE DEATH OF FDR

Jack Altshul, at Newsday:

I personally thought President Roosevelt was a hero. I thought everything he did about the war was right. You couldn't understand how these Japanese, who didn't consider themselves our military equal or threat, could wreak the havoc they did. All of a sudden, for the first time in our generation, we were underdogs. You didn't know what was going on about Roosevelt's conduct of the war, except that after two or three years all of a sudden we're getting those islands back and we are winning battles on the seas and we're landing in Italy, and then, of course, D day. I will never forget that.

Hezekiah Goodwin:

We hated him, Roosevelt, because we saw what he was doing—this went back before the war. He had nothing to offer us. He had ability as a war leader, but we certainly hated him and his ideas on domestic affairs.

Melville Grosvenor:

I was not a Roosevelt man before the war, but he converted me when he started the lend-lease assistance to Great Britain and followed with the deal leasing fifty destroyers to England. Being a navy man, I knew that was a particularly intelligent move. Britain was in danger of losing control of the North Atlantic to German submarines.

Francis Martin:

I had no use for Roosevelt. None whatever. He caused class distinction in this country. And when he met with Stalin and Churchill over there! When Roosevelt sold out to Stalin, it was too bad, because they should have let Patton go right on through. I think that was most people's opinion.

Rep. Wright Patman (D-Tex.):

On January 20 of that year—1945—at the time of Roosevelt's speech to Congress, he came in on the arm of James, the oldest boy. And instead of going up the ramp to the podium, as he had done in the past, they went up in front of the Speaker in the aisle that led to the Senate. And as he took his seat, he said: "Well, I guess you fellows have wondered all the time that you've seen me walk in here under surveillance how I could possibly get along so long? I carry 112 pounds of steel on both of my legs, and that's quite a burden for me, which you realize. But I've enjoyed every bit of it, for I felt like I was doing something."

Gov. Leverett Saltonstall of Massachusetts:

The last time I saw him was when he came before the joint session of the Congress after his trip to Yalta. He came back and spoke from a wheelchair in front of the podium. He looked an awfully sick man.

Marquis Childs:

I remember the last private phone call I had with Roosevelt. His assumption, partly spoken, but implied, was that he would be around to mastermind the peace. It was just exactly one year almost to the day he died. He was then, I think, a tired man; I remember his hand shaking when he was lighting a cigarette.

Bryson Rash:

He had the ability, and I've seen this seldom in men, to come into a room and, depending upon his mood and attitude, light it up like an incandescent bulb or throw it into complete gloom.

Toward the end of his life Roosevelt lost weight. He looked terrible because his clothes didn't fit properly as they had before. I was talking with Adm. Ross McIntire, his personal physician, and told him the president didn't look too good. He said, "He really is in fairly good shape, but he's a stingy Dutchman, and he won't buy any new shirts. The result is that he's wearing all these old shirts, and they're too big for him, and his neck looks dreadful. If I could get him to buy some new shirts, he'd look a heck of a lot better."

I had seen him the night he left for Warm Springs. He made a little speech in the diplomatic reception room, which is a relatively small room. He came in with three dogs—Fala, and Elliot's mastiff, and another big dog that looked like a Labrador. He was in great spirits, he really was. I went to him and said, "Mr. President, let's get these dogs out of here, because if you're on the air and right in the middle of your broadcast, these dogs get into a big fight or we start a big barking contest, it's going to sound dreadful." He said, "That's great. Let 'em bark. I think that would add a great deal to the broadcast."

Bill Gold in the WINX radio newsroom in Washington:

I was standing in front of the line of Teletypes in our newsroom urging my newscaster to please look at the goddam copy before he went in. It was twelve minutes to six; he was going to do the big evening newscast at six o'clock. Lou Aiken was a hell of an impressive newscaster, but I couldn't get him to look at the copy before he went in. I was standing there saying, "Lou, for God's sake, will you look at that copy," when the INS machine stopped, which indicated that a bulletin was coming. Somebody said, "What's this going to be now?" I said, "Oh, probably an announcement of how many tons of shipping MacArthur's air force has sunk," since that report was about due. The machine remained stopped for a few seconds longer than I could stand, so I kicked the leg of the thing and said, "Come on, idiot, tell us something!" And it did. The bells began to ring, and it said, "FLASH, FDR DEAD." Boy, you should have seen that newsroom at that point. Oh, man! Everything went out the window, and we got on the phone to the White House to confirm.

By the time we got confirmation from the White House, all the wires were carrying it. Now you could take your six o'clock newscast and throw it in the wastebasket. We had eleven minutes in which to get up a new newscast—a brief summary of all the other stuff, and almost all of it on Roosevelt. In the meantime I was sitting at a typewriter, writing just as fast as I could, and somebody was taking it out, putting it into some semblance of order, fitting in the other stuff, and carrying it into the man while he was on the air—and he was doing a beautiful job of figuring out what went where. I know I was crying as I wrote; the people on the desk were crying; and the newscaster on the air—although he wasn't crying, he was shaken.

Leo Hershfield:

I was down on the Potomac River at the boat slip, and somebody had a radio going, and it came over like that. I dashed back to the house, then went into town and did a drawing that evening of the vigil—people in Lafayette Park just standing there looking at the White House. It was very moving.

Jack Altshul at Newsday:

Roosevelt's death broke after our last edition was out, and I felt like sitting there crying. We had to get out an extra edition of the paper, and all our carriers were out with the earlier paper, but we went back to press. God, there were people in the office who were professed Republicans and may have come from stockbroking families who have never forgiven Roosevelt and still, during the war, were blaming him for bringing on the war, getting us into it. But I can remember going with some of those guys to the bar where we used to hang out after we put out the new edition, and the guys were crying.

Kay Halle, working for OSS in Washington:

I was walking home from Q Building, near the old naval hospital, where we worked, with Geoffrey Hellman, another

OSS colleague. We were crossing the park at Dupont Circle when a friend approached us shouting out the news. We couldn't believe it. Odd how everyone remembers exactly where they were at that moment.

Ann Hoskins:

I was coming home from the office in the late afternoon. It was one of those lovely spring days, the children were biking up and down the street under the elms, and suddenly my little girl, with her pigtails flying, came running up, and said, "Roosevelt's dead, I just heard it on the radio." I felt as if the bottom had dropped out of me, and I couldn't imagine what was going to happen next. But it never occurred to me that he wasn't mortal.

Tony Taylor, a young boy working in the Cosmos Club in Washington:

I remember the night Roosevelt died, because all the news commentators were coming into the Cosmos Club. They were shocked, crying, screaming. It was really an unbelievable thing. And you know how everyone felt about Roosevelt if you was a black person. He was a savior, man.

Anne Relph:

That was a terrible, terrible afternoon. I can remember riding my bicycle back to the playground after school, having just heard on the radio that Roosevelt had died and feeling, as a child, that this was going to be the end of the world, because he was the only president I'd ever known. I was almost not aware that there could be another president. He had always been THE PRESIDENT, in capital letters.

Mabel Wiggins:

Somebody told me up here [in Maine] that when she heard President Roosevelt had died, she rushed home to tell her husband so they could celebrate. Just cruel, sick people.

Lillie Bernstein:

I was on the corner of Wabash and Randolph Street in Chicago, and I stood and cried my eyes out. I thought the world had come to an end.

Studs Terkel:

I remember meeting with a sponsor in the Stevens Hotel; we were having some drinks, and somebody said, "The president is dead." I didn't know what the hell he was talking about. "The president's dead." "What are you talking about?" "Franklin Roosevelt." Everybody left. I'm walking south on Michigan Boulevard, and I can't stop crying. Everybody is crying. I was doing a series for Mutual of Omaha called "Freedom of Opportunity," dealing with Americans—John Huston, Ring Lardner. Somebody said do a program on Roosevelt, and I said, "I can't." It was too much. But I did do one finally, for my news program. I may have played some music.

Mary Punderson:

I was reading College Boards at that time, and I remember coming out—I can see the surroundings of buildings and trees and things—and hearing that President Roosevelt had died, then meeting someone, looking rather gray and grim, and saying, "What do we have; who is Truman?"

TRUMAN BECOMES PRESIDENT

Marquis Childs:

I think it was one of the great moments in history. I will never forget. I got home, and the office called to say a bulletin had just come through that Roosevelt had died. And I thought, "My God! Harry Truman is president." I had known him through his whole career. I had known his connection with Prendergast and how Prendergast had made him a senator sort of by accident and all the rest of it. And how his first election was one of the most rigged elections in American politics.

Kansas City always waited until the rest of the vote came in, and then they voted as many as were needed. I had had a casual enough friendly relationship with him on the Hill, and I was dismayed. But I came to feel that he was certainly doing the very best that he could. That he had not been clued in to anything.

Richard Spitzer:

In the beginning, I thought, my God, this is the end of the country—this poor political hack who was part of the Prendergast machine, who couldn't make it in a men's clothing store, is president. I had this feeling for a long time; then I began to gather some respect for him.

Alison Arnold:

Like everybody else, we thought he was a little necktie salesman. Everybody had the same idea.

Helen Wilson:

I remember Truman taking over and what a pitiful sight it was. I must have seen it in the newsreel. He just seemed so inept and struggling for help. You could tell. This man was not prepared to take over as president. You had the feeling that Roosevelt obviously hadn't prepared this man, even though he must have known he couldn't last another term.

Bill Gold:

People thought that he was a small-town politician, a Prendergast man who just couldn't cut the mustard. Well, the war was pretty well won, and I think from the moment Mr. Truman came in, he began to project an entirely different image to the American people. I remember at one of the very first press conferences, Merriman Smith asked, ''Mr. President, are you going to go to a conference with Mr. Stalin?'' And Mr. Truman pulled his arms across his chest very complacent, and satisfied. He wasn't at all impolite about it. But it was just beautiful the way he said, ''Why, the president of the United States would always be happy to see Mr. Stalin if he came here,'' turning it around very adroitly. And we began to get a sense that this was no little country boy, he was a very solid citizen.

Edward Stuntz:

A lot of newspapermen knew Truman as a senator, and they knew that Truman was one guy who said what he meant and meant what he said.

Stephen Ailes:

I was greatly sympathetic to Truman, as a guy who was in a mile over his head, to all appearances. It's always been my view that there was a rare form of patriotism which you find in congress—guys like Sam Rayburn—who really are concerned about the future of this country. I always put Truman in that category.

Frank Waldrop:

Truman was a relief, because you can't imagine the intrigue. God, talk about a corrupt court. You see, you had a president who had been sitting there a long time, and it was rather like Versailles in the last six months of old Louis. So Truman was a breath of fresh air, a great relief to everybody. We got along with him fine. He was, in every way, a better president for the time at hand than Roosevelt.

V-E DAY

Paul Kneeland in Boston:

On V-E Day everybody was covering it. It was really great. Every reporter took off. We were all out getting color stories— interviewing girls who had taken off their blouses, taken off their shoes, were dancing, standing on their heads, hanging out of hotel rooms, sitting on ledges of hotel rooms fourteen flights up and waving down, pouring water down. Crazy. World gone nuts!

Ann Hoskins in Salisbury, Connecticut:

On V-E Day the church bells rang out all over town, and everybody dropped what they were doing and went to whatever their church was. And those who didn't have a church went to any church. They came in overalls, they came with babies in their arms. And all they did was just say a few words and sing a hymn, the choir kneeling, and it was one of the most moving, simplest services I ever heard. I'm not much of a churchgoer but this did me in.

Anne Relph:

I can remember being on a train with my grandmother and hearing bells ring as we went through little towns in Louisiana. I didn't know what was going on until the train stopped, and someone told us that the war in Europe had ended. There was rejoicing, people sort of dancing in the street and church bells ringing in every little town we went through. In New Orleans people were literally dancing in the streets. They were singing, dancing, jumping in and out of fountains, and people were kissing and hugging each other. It was like Mardi Gras, and just this incredible sense of relief that part of the war, anyway, was finished and that people would be coming home again.

Anne Rippery on the New Jersey shore:

We were at our beach house. My aunt was a nurse in the army and had been sent back to the United States. She'd gone home and found out we were at the beach, and just as the news came, Florence came up the walk to the house. That was such a sheer delight for the whole family. We were in the midst of celebrating, when one-half of the family we worried about so much just walked in the door.

Don Baldwin:

They had a major disturbance in downtown San Francisco on V-E Day. Servicemen particularly, but also some civilians.

They really ran amok, broke windows and looted right down at Fifth and Market around the Emporium and that area. I went to work at about midnight, and it was really exciting. The police had made one of these cordons. They had some armored cars, and they were just sweeping Market Street. Servicemen and civilians—just sweeping them ahead with all those big bullhorns: "Break it up—Get off Market Street." It took them the better part of the night. People turned over streetcars and some taxi-cabs. And of course, all the liquor stores had their windows broken.

THE BOMB

Tom Page at the Office of War Mobilization:

We had a request once, related to the refinement of rare metals in Germany. "Rare metals?" we all said, "what the hell are rare metals?" Well, they said, things like plutonium and uranium and named four or five rare metals. We started calling around the country and went to see metallurgists who we knew were familiar with occupied Europe. And we'd get answers like "We can't talk about that. Why are you asking about that? You mustn't go around asking questions like that."

Actually, we were asking about the atom bomb, but we didn't know that. We were asking guys who were working on the Manhattan Project about the refinement of plutonium and uranium, and Christ, they wanted to get under the bed, they didn't want to hear any part of these questions. After we went through this, a guy I was working with said to me: "You know, there's something about these rare metals—honestly, if I had any money, I'd invest it in rare metals!"

John Lacey, who worked for the Johns Hopkins Research Laboratory:

I remember attending a meeting down at the Office of Scientific Research and Development, and something was said about Oak Ridge. When I said, "What's Oak Ridge?" everybody sort of recoiled in horror, and somebody said, "Oh, it's just a wide place in the road down in Tennessee." I got the message.

Rep. John W. McCormack (D-Mass.):

I remember being in FDR's office on some matter. We knew that the Philippines had been recaptured, and there was some organized resistance on the part of minor segments of the Japanese army. A mopping-up process was going on. FDR said to me, "John, I have before me now three plans from the Joint Chiefs of Staff as to our next military campaign, and I've got to make the decision in the near future." Two of them were in different parts of continental China, and the other one was through Japan. And he said, "If I make the decision that the next campaign will be right straight to Japan"—and I knew he would—"the Joint Chiefs of Staff have estimated that there would be one million American casualties." That was what faced Harry Truman when he dropped the bombs on Hiroshima and Nagasaki.

Horace Hubbard, an engineer with General Electric:

We knew we were working on something unusual. But at that time I did not have a feeling of the devastation of this weapon. And when the bomb was dropped, I had a feeling of satisfaction that what we worked on apparently produced results. It seemed to me at that time that, regardless of the subsequent criticism, the United States had almost no alternative but to use it. I don't know if that was any worse than a whole lot of other things that were going on.

R. W. Danischefsky, with the Defense Plants Corporation of the RFC:

I worked on the Manhattan Project for about eight months and didn't know what I was doing. Nobody did—the greatest kept secret in the world. I was helping to equip plants to make small parts in Detroit. All we knew was that it was for the Manhattan Project, and nobody knew what that was, and there was no way you could find out.

Marquis Childs:

I had known about the building of the bomb and had written a column saying that, of course, the United States and Germany are competing to see who will come out with it first. I was in the dentist's chair, I remember, when the censor's office called up—maybe it was the head guy himself—and said, "This is very bad, you will have to kill that," which I proceeded to do.

Jerome Thirion:

I had a friend who worked at Los Alamos. The power of the bomb was made clear to us through him. When he visited us, he brought us samples of the tower—they must have had a huge tower that they had set off. The samples he brought showed just how this tower melted right into the soil. It was highly radioactive, but it was permissible to bring it. It was a souvenir encased in plastic. It made me realize what a thing the bomb must have been.

George Garrott, working for OWI in Washington:

I was called at home to get over to the White House for an important announcement. I think it was about noon. So I got over to the White House, and we waited around. Nobody knew what was coming until finally the secretary came out and just handed us a mimeographed announcement which said that the atom bomb had been dropped, and its force was twenty thousand tons of dynamite. There was no briefing of any kind, but they did give out the so-called Groves Report on Atomic Energy. We looked at it, and it was just so much flute music, fanciful mathematical writing. So we did what any newspaperman would do—wrote a story saying the report was out but that it was very difficult to understand and then quoted two paragraphs from the frontispiece by the author of the report, and that was the official story of the first atom bomb.

Gus Robbins, editor of the Hopewell *(Va.)* News:

I was in the back shop when my girl Friday came running back and told me they had dropped the bomb on Hiroshima. I stood there with my mouth open, and I said, "Oh, my God, they've destroyed the world." I remember those words just as well as if it happened yesterday. You see, I had a brother-in-law in the Manhattan Project, so I knew what was going on, and I was praying they'd never do it.

Judson Phillips, who was writing a news program for radio station WOR in New York:

The day that the bomb was dropped I had already written my show when the radio station called and said: "You've got to change the show." I asked them why, and they said: "Come down here. They dropped the bomb on Hiroshima." So I went down, and they had listened to the tapes. I had no more idea what they were talking about than the man in the moon, but, for a show that had to go on the air at seven o'clock, I wrote a story about the dropping of the atom bomb, not having any idea of its dimensions or its importance or anything else. The people at WOR didn't know what the hell it was, but they figured it must be important, so much was being made of it. I guess the show I wrote was the first dramatized program on the air, because it was three hours after it happened. And I never had a tape of it. At the time, it didn't seem like anything. We weren't really aware of the significance. Truman's speech seemed like double-talk.

Dorothy Whitaker, whose brother was a prisoner of war in Japan:

It just left everybody in a state of shock. It was so foreign to anything we had even thought about. It left everybody wondering, what next? When we got the pictures, it was sickening. But at first everybody thought, "Oh, this is great! We've got something the others don't have, and it's enough to stop the war." I was thinking of my brother and all the other prisoners and those boys who were over there getting ready to go into battle. It seemed like such a great thing to have it cut off just like that. The churches all were open that day, bells rang, and everybody left their shops and jobs and went to church. My brother was in Osaka at the time, and it sounded so much at first like Nagasaki.

Helen Wilson:

It just seemed like another weapon; nothing particularly traumatic about a larger size weapon.

Anna Mae Lindberg:

My husband's parents had a place in the country with no electricity, no water, no nothing. Consequently, we had no radio or telephone. Every day we would go down to the village and buy a newspaper. Well, the day the bomb dropped on Hiroshima, we were isolated. We had no visitors, so we didn't know anything about it when we bought the newspaper. I don't remember exactly what the headline was—but 100,000 people killed by a bomb! But I could not absorb that, getting it for the first time on the written page. I thought, this must be a joke newspaper or a misprint, or the headline is wrong. I couldn't conceive that 100,000 people would be killed in one blast. They were the enemy, but they were people. And actually, they were innocent people, the same as if they were to drop that bomb on Homestead [Pennsylvania]. You could put yourself in their place, because if they dropped a bomb on us, then it would have been me.

Celeste Kavanaugh:

When I look back on it, I'm rather ashamed. One of my dear brothers was in the Philippines, getting ready to invade Japan, and I knew that it probably spared his life. I had another brother in China at the time. After four years of wondering from day to day where they were going to be, it was a great relief to know that things were speeding up. It was a terrible way to end it, though.

Hezekiah Goodwin:

We thought it was great.

Newton Tolman:

Christ! Oh, my God, don't ever mention it! I haven't been sane since. Hiroshima to me was the most total defeat of the whole progress of humanity that I have ever seen. I'm a pessimist—that's why I'm happy.

Well, anyhow, my reaction to that—I remember so vividly, more than any day in my whole goddamned life—was, this is the end! This damned stuff can't be! Jimmy Doolittle's best lifelong friend had come back from the Greek army, and he was all excited. "Isn't this wonderful! Jimmy has done it!" Well, Jimmy did it all right, but Jimmy never knew what the hell he did. It was disaster. Don't mention it.

Frank Waldrop:

About dropping the bomb—I felt just like everybody else did who had any sense. I didn't give a damn how many Japanese were killed; it was Americans who made the difference. And if the Japanese didn't want to get bombed, they shouldn't have started the monkey business they did. The president of the United States has an obligation to the corn farmers in Iowa, never to mankind. Nobody knows who mankind is; that is one of those great big juicy generalities that is an alibi for not doing your job. Yet he knows who the people of the United States are, and it was their sons who were out there getting killed.

Marquis Childs:

I remember the next-to-the-last session we had with Marshall, in which he repeated what had been the provincial wisdom of the attack on the Japanese mainland: It would cost 500,000 American casualties. The Japanese—man, woman, and child—would fight with pitchforks or guns, or whatever they had. I think that was probably a terrible overstatement of the situation at that time. The Japanese were beginning to make overtures for peace. And I thought Truman was so unwise when he was interviewed by Murrow, remember? Truman said: "I would do the same thing tomorrow."

Arthur Edmunds:

I reacted to the dropping of the atom bomb almost exclusively on a black-white issue. It was dropped on colored people, not on white people. I tried to accept the rationale of the leadership at that time that if we had not done that, it would have cost so many of our soldiers lives, and so forth. And I have some appreciation for that. But I never quite understood it.

Mary Devereux Crist, whose husband was a Marine Corps colonel:

I was delighted. There are very few service people who would say that. I have a good friend, a writer, and a retired marine general, who thinks it was perfectly awful that we dropped the bomb. But he was not out there when we did it, and I felt: Why shouldn't we? My husband and I discussed it many times after the war was over, and he said, "Well, if it hadn't been for that, I would have made the landing in Japan. We were all prepared to make it."

Tony Taylor:

Dropping the atom bomb didn't scare me, 'cause I said: "Now, wait a minute, these people are fucking around over there, you know. Like, let's end this shit and just drop a bomb and wipe out a whole lot of people." But then, later on, my Christian side came out. I said: "Hey, I could be very aware of those people, the innocent people over there. They don't want bombs dropped on them." I almost feel that the tempo was such that Americans wanted to show their dominance at that time. They had all the technical know-how, and they wanted to really display it. I think that everybody thought the same way. They didn't look to the other side, the Christian or humane side of it. They thought: "Hey, we're being faced with something, and this is a shortcut, and if this bomb is dropped and we let those people know how powerful we are, we can end it right there."

Necei Degen:

The dropping of the atom bomb was a question of morality. It was an immoral act, as far as I am concerned. I knew that day something ungodly had happened. The American government had unleashed this vile thing, and it has haunted me personally from that point on.

Studs Terkel:

Well, this is my moment of confession. At the time, I felt—wow—the war would be over. I remember that night I was on the radio, and I said, now the war would be over. Later on—the horror hit me! Remember when Einstein heard the news, he is reputed to have said: "I wish I were a locksmith." His secretary said on a program many years later that she met him coming down the stairs, and he said something like "oh way." She wasn't Jewish and, of course, what he was saying was "*oye veh.*"

David Soergal, an electrical engineer:

My reaction was then and still is that I don't know why we didn't tell the Japanese we'd demonstrate this thing at some unpopulated island, and they could come over and watch it. I don't know why we didn't do that instead of kill over 300,000 people. There's no point in using science to kill people. Science can do wonderful things, but it can do a lot of bad, too. There was a great revulsion among the leaders in the atomic energy business at the use of this thing. Robert Oppenheimer got labeled as a Communist just because he was philosophically against it.

Lillie Bernstein:

When Truman dropped the bomb, I thought it was the most courageous thing. I felt terribly bad about the people in Japan.

But I felt that it took a lot of grit and courage to say it should be done. At that time, two of my sons were en route from Europe to go to the Orient, and it looked as though there would be millions more people killed.

Anne Relph:

A very terrifying thing, the feeling that the world had somehow changed and that it was never going to be the same again, that some kind of scary, terrible force had been set loose that nobody had any way to contain. I can remember having bad dreams about it for weeks—about building shelters in case of an atomic attack and there not being any place you could go to escape. I was old enough by then to be going to movies, seeing newsreels, and being aware of what was going on, rather than having it filtered through the grown-ups. My family tended to keep a kind of optimistic attitude about things, but I think this was one of those secret terrors that children have that the world had changed, that there was no way you could ever go back to the time before that bomb had been dropped.

Jack Lynch:

Whether you liked Truman or not, he made many good decisions, and probably the most debated one was the decision to drop the atom bomb. I agreed with him 100 percent, 1,000 percent, because I think he saved many thousands and thousands of American lives. We didn't start the war. If they paid a price, I think it was their own indebtedness.

Peggy Blassingame:

I didn't think of it as horrible. I thought of it as being fantastic—this means the war is going to end. Of course, I didn't understand the destruction. But today I still refuse to feel the sense of guilt that some Americans feel simply because it happened, because of the number of people who died. I agree that it was terrible, but, God, how many more would have died had the bomb not been used?

The Reverend Edward G. Latch:

My reaction to dropping the atom bomb was that it was a tragic thing to have to do. I question, sometimes, whether we had to do it, yet who am I to know? I can't answer questions like that. I'm just an ordinary citizen like anyone else. It took a lot of lives, but it saved a lot of lives that would have been taken if the war had been prolonged. I think that was the hardest decision a president has had to make, and yet I think it shortened the war.

An interesting thing about the Japanese. In Nagasaki they have observed the anniversary of the atom bomb. But then, they never said what they did to Pearl Harbor. Not a word, and I don't think we did either. We ought to say a little more about it: Yes, we did that, but look at what you did here at Pearl Harbor to cause that. But that's never recognized, for some reason.

V-J DAY

Frank Waldrop, managing editor of the Washington Times Herald:

I remember V-E and V-J Days. All these great events, as far as I'm concerned, were the same—looking at type upside down and backward!

Ted Giddings, city editor of the Berkshire Eagle *in Pittsfield, Massachusetts:*

V-J Day was our last extra. After that, radio and television wiped out the extra edition of newspapers our size.

David Soergal "just happened to be in Times Square on V-J Day".

It was wild; you couldn't walk through the streets—Fortysecond and Broadway was just a mass of humanity.

Simon Greco, a conscientious objector:

When the war ended, I expected some great religious feeling to take over. In other words, I really expected all the wheels to stop, theaters to close, bars to close, trains to stop running. Something irrational. Nothing happened. A bunch of people gathered in Times Square, some gals getting laid. And that was the end of it. The wheels were going, the bars were open, the pool halls were open, the factories were running, almost as if nothing had happened. It was really just kind of a psychological shock.

Lois Raymond in Sedgwick, Maine:

My younger daughter had been spending that summer with a friend of hers. They were coming here for the last two weeks before school. The girls caught the train in Boston, got off at Bangor, and then took the bus. As they went through Orrington, there were people out banging on washtubs and covers and whatnot, and they knew the war was over. A young serviceman on the bus popped up and kissed Rosemary, saying, "I always swore I would kiss the first pretty girl I saw when the war was over."

Mary Studwell in Stamford, Connecticut:

They just stopped everything, including the buses. I lived about three miles outside the main body of town, and a whole bunch of us teenagers walked down into town and formed a big conga line all through the town. It was just a silly thing, letting off steam. They called out the Home Guard, and they just cheered.

Regina Wilk:

I know we were eating dinner at the time when we heard about the war ending, and we all just went hysterical. We didn't finish our meal; the family all seemed to get together, and we just went downtown. Everybody was one family there;

the streets were packed and all. Everybody was so glad. My husband happened to be home at the time, and there was jubilation, because he was slated to go again. He didn't tell me until after that he was on rest-and-recuperation leave and that he was going to go back.

Esther Dudley:

We were working, as usual, and when the news came, they let us off. Everybody went home, and a couple of friends came over, and we sat there and had a couple of good ones.

Mary Dandouveris, working on a weekly newspaper in Lake Geneva, Wisconsin:

Our weekly didn't have a ticker, so when the end of the war came, the story was of how the local folks celebrated—it was a wild celebration. Snake lines all over town, and, because it was a resort town, there were lots of bars and places where you could dance—they were wide open that night. Everybody went in and out. I don't think anybody asked if you had money or not. It was joy and pandemonium in that town. The chap who used to be the head of the composing room was home from the service, and I followed him all around and did the color story. I remember the poor hung-over editor coming in the next day. But we got the paper out on schedule in spite of the celebration.

Because I knew that the Milwaukee and Chicago dailies all came into this town, I wanted a different headline for my paper. So I decided I would do it in French—"La Guerre Est Finis"—but the editor said, "Are you sure that guerre is feminine, or masculine?" He really rattled me, so I decided I had to call around, but I couldn't find anybody. They were all out of town that weekend. I finally decided to go with it and trust my instincts that it was a feminine noun. When I got back to my last year in journalism school, I found that with all the papers the journalism department had put up on the bulletin board as examples of how the dailies had treated the end of the war, mine was there, too, as an example of how a weekly could compete with a daily in covering local color.

Heli Swyter:

On V-J Day we were at Camp Lejeune, and I remember the shouting in the streets when it came. I picked up one of those firecrackers. And also there was shooting, all the guns. I found a bullet in the street, and I put a red ribbon around it; we have it on our Christmas tree always every year since then.

11

Aftermath

What was the impact of the war years on our cities, towns, institutions, the nation, and the people themselves? In these concluding pages a few Americans who were on the home front give their answers.

Carey McWilliams:

It is very difficult to assess the effect of the war on the nation. I have always been about three-quarters pacifist. While I've never been quite able to make the total commitment, I think the war has had some long-term unfortunate effects on American life. I admire those of my friends who were consistently pacifist and who right straight through said, "It's a mistake to fight; violence is violence, and there will be unfortunate circumstances." But I've never been able to convince myself.

At the end of the war we were unquestionably going to be the top military power in the world. And I think this predisposed us to take the position that we were going to police the world, we were going to do this, we were going to do that. And as I see it, the period that extends from 1945, the dropping of the bomb, our withdrawal from Vietnam, Nixon's ouster—

that's all tied together as one. You say: "What effect did World War II have?" Well, World War II set the stage for the Cold War. You can't separate them.

The Reverend Harold Toliver:

Just like the total community, black and white, everybody was anxious for it to be over. When it finally came to a conclusion, I think it set in motion that "Here we are now. What are we going to do about life as we try to reestablish it in our community?" And the first thing we knew, we blacks found ourselves facing some of the very same problems—prejudice, racism, intolerance—which precipitated the war. Some grew very much discouraged and said, "Well, you see, it wasn't worth it." But the majority of the people, I think, just rededicated themselves to the struggle and said, "This has to go on." If the war did nothing else to me as a minister—or just as an ordinary person—it made me more determined to give what little energy I had to bringing people of the world together. I suppose you might describe me as a populist, a person who believes in the people coming together, all races and types, learning to understand one another and to get along. We have the beginnings of that in the United Nations, with all of its weaknesses and faults.

Marquis Childs:

What it did was to start this business of background information given on a confidential basis—and it wasn't just General Marshall and Admiral King; everyone did it. It became a common practice. Later someone invented the phrase *deep backgrounder*.

Melville Grosvenor:

I think that World War II was a great thing for America. It unified us—made a country out of us. Before the war, we were a bunch of vacillating isolationists displaying not much character. But the war and the victory showed us what we could do in the world. Showed us the role we could play. However, it is honest to admit that it did us some harm. The victory caused us to think that we could dominate the world. Ever since the war, in every part of the world, we've been trying to tell individual countries what to do and what not to do, and we still are. I think it's goddamn foolishness, if you don't mind me saying so.

R. W. Danischefsky in Washington:

As a result of the war, the public generally and industry, too, became more aware of the government's influence on our everyday life. It wasn't too long after the war when most big industry began to move offices here. I think today practically all of your larger industries have representatives in Washington because of the influence and the participation by government.

Rep. Ray Madden (D-Ind.):

A war like that changes a lot of things. One of the most ridiculous things that happened was that it gave the military a lot of power. Hell, if we had not had World War II, we probably would not have had Eisenhower in the White House. There was a period of eight years when the country sank more and more in debt. We had three depressions under Ike because he did not know anything about running a government, but you could not blame him. He got elected because he was made to order for the same money changers that ran the government in the 1920s—the DuPonts, Andy Mellon, and that group.

Newton Tolman:

It certainly speeded up all kinds of things like going to the moon, outdoing the Russians. I would say that the national impact was to give the technocrats, or whatever you call them—big-business people—the green light to totally pollute the national government.

World War II got government into business and business into government, and we're still there.

Hezekiah Goodwin:

The war brought about changes that started and more or less mushroomed. Higher taxes. The man who would paint your house used to work for seventy-five cents an hour; now he gets six dollars. The same was true of the carpenter, the plumber. Those are changes, that, if the war didn't bring about, it certainly made possible. They wouldn't have occurred otherwise. We know the war cost us in permanent inflation. It brought about great social changes which were probably needed, but nevertheless had a hell of an impact on us here. These small farms, the success of them is predicated on cheap labor. There was no denying it; there no longer was any cheap labor.

Jack Altshul:

The war was the dividing line between depression and the prosperity that followed. And what it took to get that was the boys that were killed. It was a stiff price to pay. Up to that time, twenty dollars a week was a manageable salary. Many people would have signed away their souls for a hundred-dollar-a-week job for life. They couldn't see beyond that. I certainly couldn't. Then all of a sudden you get the wartime boom, and just as suddenly a few years later the war is over. Luxuries that only millionaires could have, before the war, suddenly became available to everybody on credit—refrigerators, televisions, dishwashers, washing machines.

Richard Lingeman discusses the impact of the war on the nation from the special vantage point of someone who spent five years researching the subject.

I think the war had an obvious economic impact in bringing the country out of the doldrums of the Depression by stimulating industry—making a lot of corporations richer and bigger and starting this relationship between military procurement and big corporations called the military-industrial complex. It moved a lot of people around. They migrated to the cities for war jobs, and I guess some went back home after it was over, but there was a lot of permanent migration.

The war was also a significant turning point for women. They were needed so suddenly and to a great extent temporarily, all kinds of jobs were open to women—not only industry, but driving buses, managing baseball teams, police work. Suddenly all the traditional barriers broke down, with blacks and women in better jobs. After the war, of course, it was the old "last hired, first fired" thing, but it must have implanted something, certain expectations or awareness on the part of blacks and women.

It was a period of great moral upheaval. There were, for example, the Allotment Annies—not a lot of them, but there were enough—who married servicemen just to collect allotments, insurance benefits, and whatever. One woman married I don't know how many flyers, about ten, I think. They'd pick flyers because they had the highest mortality rate.

I think most people have a nostalgia for those days, the time of a good war, a just war. Some guys in the army did have a sense of adventure, going off to faraway places, exotic places. If they could avoid the fighting, there was that excitement, that adventure.

Alison Arnold on the Boston Herald:

I think the war had a great impact on the social scene. It broke down all the social barriers, and now society is sort of a forbidden word. It ironed out all the class distinctions. I don't know what caused it, but I know that when I first went to the [Beacon] Hill, we weren't allowed to use any names in the story that were not in the Social Register. Then, after the war, all that was gone, and we democratized society.

Nelson Poynter:

The GI Bill of Rights, of course, had more to do with thrusting us into a new era than anything else. Millions of people whose parents or grandparents had never dreamed of going to college saw that they could go, and I don't have to tell anyone what a broad effect that has had on so many of the private and public institutions within our society. Essentially I think it made us a far more democratic people, because people could think more nearly in terms of equality.

Helen Wilson, University of Michigan:

I think it loosened up the regulations at the university a great deal. When the veterans returned after the war, they were a much older group of students. They tripled the enrollment, and some of the stuffy old professors had problems dealing with the fellows who had been through the war. They were really a very sheltered group of old fuddy-duddies, and the military returnees were more than they could cope with.

I think the war also elevated women. They had to be accepted as replacing men at home. I applied to law school in the spring of 1945, and I think that's why I got in. It probably was the start of the women's movement.

Lois Raymond:

I was working at the University of Chicago right after the war. I remember talking to various faculty people who said the best students they ever had were the GIs. They had been out long enough to really know what they wanted to do.

Dean Elmer Louis Kayser, George Washington University, Washington, D.C.:

The war tended to magnify everything around here. It seemed to magnify our mission, to magnify our commitments, to magnify our ideas and our efforts and the expression of them in tangible development. It was here, for example, that the first announcement was made about atomic fission—at one of those conferences on theoretical physics that used to be held in cooperation with the Carnegie Institution of Washington. The university was given so many more opportunities to expand in wartime Washington. The times were themselves more spacious and once and for all demonstrated, I think, the fact that the university of the future was to be the great urban university, rather than the cow college and cloisters of the past.

Al Sweeney:

Efforts to desegregate Washington didn't gain impetus until after the war. A lot of the fellows came back, and, on top of it, the GI Bill of Rights gave opportunity to a lot of them to go to college, and they became part of the whole movement. Most of the leaders were ex-GIs in the army, ex-military.

Washington at that time had a caste system within the black community. Some of the older families, light-skinned families, wouldn't accept the darker skinned people. That was the end of the black caste system in Washington. The people came from all over the country to work in government. More blacks came into this town from all over, from the South, the Midwest; and the great majority of blacks that came during the war stayed. It was the only place a black could find a white-collar job. It was pretty rare to find a real Washingtonian.

Bryson Rash, with NBC and ABC during the war:

It was the war that really developed electronic journalism. Prior to World War II there weren't many people on the air doing news. The capability of conveying war via electronic media occurred in the Spanish civil war, where for the first time you got broadcasts from battlegrounds, from areas of conflict and capitals that were at war. I think one of the most famous of these early broadcasts was H. V. Kaltenborn reporting on the Spanish war with the sound of guns heard in the background. Then we had the electronic capability of instant communication via shortwave, and that was something new.

Merlo Pusey, Washington, D.C.:

The war really made Washington, for the first time, a world capital. All the top Allied people came here.

It was a more difficult place to live after the war, I think, because the war brought a tremendous influx of people; it got to be a crowded city. And they didn't go home.

Frank Platt, Louisville, Kentucky:

Prior to the war Louisville was living in the past. But the war changed all that. People could no longer have the closed society they had had. There were just too many Yankees and others that moved in there. General Electric opened up a huge industrial park there with somewhere between 16,000 and 20,000 people. There is big, good industry there, well diversified. Before the war it was primarily tobacco, liquor, and horses.

Esther Dudley, Philadelphia:

Jobs were plentiful in Philadelphia during the war, and money was just flowing to the war workers. It was an arsenal, produced textiles and all sorts of things for the service, and, I think, Philadelphia was the goal of many unskilled Negro families migrating from the South. I think, like any industrial city, that was about it. That was the start of unskilled labor coming up and causing quite a few of our racial problems.

Newton Tolman, Nelson, New Hampshire:

Well, I would say that it was the end of a way of life, an end of a way of thinking, the end of education, and certainly the end of any kind of local autonomous government. I could name you a dozen guys I went to school with—they were working, trying to, selling real estate, or running a tractor, or any number of things; they were just about making it. One was even a magna cum laude graduate of the Yale School of Forestry. They went into the army and stayed. They became army bureaucrats. I meet them even today. Most of them have died from too much drinking and easy living and one thing or another. But they stayed with it. They became our rich; colonels with retirement pay and everything else.

Joseph Skelly, New York City:

The war brought about the establishment of rent control, which is still in existence in New York and many other cities and which has had a big effect on the state of city houses and real estate. It's a very moot question; there are two sides to it certainly. But rent control is by no means an unmixed blessing. It's had a lot of unfortunate results. The war brought the United Nations to New York City, and that, I think, had quite an effect on the general international tone of the city.

Gus Robbins, Hopewell, Virginia:

I think that the war helped develop it [Hopewell]. I really do. We were pretty active in the war effort with our big chemical plants there, and business stayed pretty good after the war. And Camp Lee is still there. It's Fort Lee today—the biggest quartermaster training center in the world. We've got more retired colonels around than you can shake a stick at. You see all the colonels come to the quartermaster a year or two before they retire. They're putting them on the shelf, getting ready to kick them out. They like it in Virginia, so they stay.

Jerome Thirion, Buffalo, New York:

Buffalo before the war had a basically sound economy. Everybody had a good job. The social levels were pretty well established, and you didn't have a seasonal economic situation. The war, of course, inflated everything. Buffalo had a lot of defense plants, and those who worked in the plants made easy, free money during the war. But after the war it was kind of slow.

Paul Kneeland, Medford, Massachusetts:

In Medford the war didn't mean a thing; Medford just slept right through it, except for the availability or unavailability of certain things, such as tires, gasoline, et cetera.

Rudolph Spitzer, Kenmore, New York:

I think the effect of the war on our town was probably no different than on thousands of similar communities throughout the nation—boom times with cost no object for a couple of years and then a gradual settling down to normalcy. Aside from that, I cannot see much change. The world is in a turmoil, and we still have wars.

Coralee Redmond moved from Beach, North Dakota, to Tacoma, Washington, during the war but returned to Beach each summer with her sons.

Beach is a small town, a farming center where lots of wheat was raised. Many farmers in World War II moved into town and left their sons to run the farms as their reason not to be drafted. But the boys and men who lived in town, they all went into the service. We lost some boys who were almost like sons to me—they were my daughters' and sons' ages. We lost our minister too, who we were very fond of. He was a chaplain in the service. The war had its impact in Beach.

The war increased the population in Tacoma, because many people who came out to work in the defense plants stayed. People who were coming out of the service liked the Pacific Northwest and stayed—either here in Tacoma or round about. I would say the town really grew. The war changed my life, and it's hard to figure out for the better or for worse.

Stephen Ailes:

Working in Washington during the war was a real education for me. You know, your attitudes are tremendously affected by your environment, and I'd been practicing law up in Martinsburg [West Virginia] with a Republican lawyer who was quite conservative. Then I came down here, and the legal staff I was working with and the economists were a whole lot of young guys who were far more liberal in their point of view than anybody I'd ever associated with.

Working in the Office of Price Administration was an incredible opportunity. It was my first association with really top-notch economists. I got a look at the whole American business structure and learned a lot about how the government operates, where the levers are, how Congress functions. My God! I wouldn't put the whole country at war just to train someone, but I must say it was an unbelievable experience.

Sid Luckman, Chicago Bears quarterback:

The war, really, to me was one of the most crushing things that could ever happen. You saw your friends go to war, you saw some of them killed, some of them wounded, you also saw one of the finest groups of young men ever assembled in the history of sports—the Chicago Bears of 1940–41–some of the finest men the good Lord has ever put on this earth, so dedicated to each other, so dedicated to George Halas. To see it all dissipated by a horrible catastrophe that was so unnecessary to the world, it was a very disheartening situation.

However, in the final analysis, all of us were very happy to pay the price. Freedom and democracy prevailed, and the world continued being at least a place to be able to live the kind of life you always hoped for and not have to live under dictatorship and fear. So whatever the price was and whatever it cost all of us, it was worth it.

Erwin Hargrove, who was fourteen on V-J Day:

The amazing thing to me is that it had such little effect on me. I wonder if there isn't a generalization you could make here that great public events are only tangential to the lives of ordinary people. I remember seeing a documentary on television about the appeasement during the war years in England. The interviewer asked a working-class woman why people ignored Churchill and if she was conscious of the importance of Hitler and the rise of aggression and so on. And she said, "How was I supposed to know? I was worried about the really important things, like my husband and his job, and the children—that they had enough to eat."

Jack Altshul:

I'd like to think whatever talent I had helped me get ahead at *Newsday*, but there's no question that the war pushed me into the city editorship there. And that was the turning point in my career.

Necei Degen:

The man that I married had come from the Midwest. He would never have come East had it not been for that great war. Many of the people who came East whom I met changed the complexion and character of my life personally. So it affected my life, from that point on until this day.

Kent Chetlain:

I think it made us more conscious of the world about us. It brought to us the names of far-off geographic places that we would have never been exposed to. For example, I can remember Minsk, Oreal, Smolensk, Kharkov, and places like that. These names became familiar to me for the first time, and the different Pacific islands like Guadalcanal, New Britain.

Joseph Skelly:

The war brought my wife and me together. I think we quite likely wouldn't have gotten married if it hadn't been for the war. It was a very definite result of the war, and I'm glad.

Merlo Pusey:

I suppose it was a great stimulus, because it was a wonderful period in the journalistic field. It stimulated me to get more serious in the book area. I wrote this book, *The Way We Go to War*, and since then I've sort of had the disease which I gather you have. I always say it's a disease; when you get it, you don't get over it. The war stimulated me to do this work and, I guess, contributed a great deal to my knowledge about the country and the government and the world.

Paul Kneeland:

If the war had not come about, I don't think I'd have had the nerve to ask for a job on a Boston newspaper. In late 1941 the *Globe* started hiring war replacements. We all signed releases that we were temporary employees—I was one of twenty-four. Twenty-two of the reporters were told that they were no longer needed at the end of the war. They kept two—a graduate of Harvard University, and me, a high school graduate. Today you couldn't get a job there as an office boy unless you had a master's degree. The war opened up an opportunity that might not have come otherwise.

Joseph Clement:

I don't think the war did anything for my career really. I didn't advance myself; there was nothing I learned there that

I could have used for any advantage later on. It was just really a blank four years as far as I was concerned. In fact, I had to start all over again in getting into consumer goods, and at that time you could sell anything you made, so who needed a designer? I finally managed to get back in and became a chief designer for Wurlitzer after the war. I designed jukeboxes, of all things. A far cry from the war, so I felt that any part of my war effort was useless to me personally.

George Garrott:

Looking back on it, it was an exciting time for me. I felt I had bogged down in New York. What I wanted to do was go to Paris and work for the Paris *Herald Tribune* and write novels. But in those days before the war, anybody who had a job held onto it. So when the war came along, it jolted me out of that comfortable chair I had been sitting on in the newsroom of the *New York Times*. I got out of the office and moved around as a live, active reporter, especially after the war, for the USIA. I went on the Truman trip to Wake Island, the secret trip to meet General MacArthur. I got a three-week press trip to Europe and another three-month trip to the Far East. On one trip with Truman I spent eight weeks in Key West, and driving back through Florida, I figured "Gee, this is the part of the country I want to live in."

Don Baldwin:

I think it was good for my life. I got started quicker and was able to do some things that I would not have been able to do if a lot of AP guys hadn't been going out into foreign service to cover the war. It created job openings that I was able to seize on. We were coming out of the Depression, and newspaper jobs were very difficult to get. It would have been much harder to get out of Idaho and into big city operations without the war.

John Lacey:

It changed my career completely. From a patent attorney working in private practice, I became a contract employee and was one for thirty years, not with the government, but with Johns Hopkins.

Marquis Child:

I was under contract with the *St. Louis Post-Dispatch* when Raymond Clapper was killed in February 1944. He was flying off of an aircraft carrier in the Pacific somewhere. The syndicate then asked me to do a column and to take over as many of his clients as I could. That made a terrific change in my life. Joseph Pulitzer was very reluctant to release me—I remember telephone conversations of three or four hours—but finally he did. It dramatically changed my life, and it has never been the same since.

Mary Lacey:

It had so many emotional overtones to it that it really is hard to assess. Because I managed to live through it and survive, I guess it made me a stronger person, more aware of things, more appreciative of happiness in my second marriage, never knowing what's going to happen to somebody the next time you turn. It probably did something to sharpen my awareness of human relations. I hope it had some good effect.

Evelyn Keyes:

I was just then changing from a bigot into a liberal. I was out of the South, from Atlanta, a total bigot, and I was slowly learning. Hitler helped me to understand how dangerous bigotry is. I happened to be in my formative years when the war came along, just becoming an adult. I went to Hollywood at a time when they were making a lot of pictures; that's not so now. The studios were at their zenith, and pinups were fashionable. There's luck in coming along at the right time.

Jane Malach:

It's probably a terrible thing to say, but when I look back on it, it was a beneficent experience. In spite of the emotional impact, it was a very broadening experience, and I would never had had it otherwise. People were picked up from where they had lived all their lives and plunged into something. They had to adjust.

Betty Bryce in Mount Pleasant, Michigan:

I can tell you one thing the town is not as patriotic as it was. On Memorial Day hardly anybody shows up, not even your veterans' organizations. If you get the color guard out, of course, the kids will always get in with bicycles, but people just don't seem to salute the flag. The young children have no respect at the cemetery when you're holding a service. And this is bad. I don't know—when I look at that flag, to me the red's a little redder, the white's a little whiter, and the stars are a little brighter because of all those boys who gave their lives. And at Arlington Cemetery in Washington, D.C., when I was sitting there one Sunday, I thought, "If all those boys in those graves were to rise up, I wonder what they would think about why they had died, and the way conditions are now, if it was worth it." I just wonder.

TRUE ACCOUNTS OF THE HOLOCAUST

═══ THE CIVIL WAR ═══

REFLECTIONS ON THE CIVIL WAR by Bruce Catton
0-425-10495-8/$4.95
The last great work of Bruce Catton, this is his last will and testament to the American people. Edited after his death from many hours of tapes, it paints an intimate portrait of the experience of war. From the larger-than-life figures of Lincoln and Lee to the young Union soldier John B. Geyser, whose sensitive drawings enhance the pages of this book, we know what it was like to be there.

THE UNDERGROUND RAILROAD by Charles L Blockson
0-425-11588-7/$4.95
Dramatic, unforgettable stories of daring escapes to freedom on the Underground Railroad. In these pages are inspirational, first-person accounts of slaves such as Harriet Tubman and Frederick Douglass who escaped bondage in the face of overwhelming odds.

JOHN RANSOM'S ANDERSONVILLE DIARY with an Introduction by Bruce Catton   0-425-10554-7/$4.95
"A great adventure story...extraordinarily observant,
eloquent and moving." —*PUBLISHERS WEEKLY*
John Ransom was a twenty-year-old Union soldier when he was captured in 1863 and became a prisoner of war. Held in the infamous Andersonville prison until he was near death, Ransom never gave up his love of life. His diary is a testament to the indomitable human spirit and provides a unique viewpoint of the most wrenching of America's wars.
